The Wounded Heart

Chicana Matters Series

Deena J. González and Antonia Castañeda, editors

Chicana Matters Series focuses on one of the largest population groups in the United States today, documenting the lives, values, philosophies, and artistry of contemporary Chicanas. Books in this series may be richly diverse, reflecting the experiences of Chicanas themselves, and incorporating a broad spectrum of topics and fields of inquiry. Cumulatively, the books represent the leading knowledge and scholarship in a significant and growing field of research and, along with the literary works, art, and activism of Chicanas, underscore their significance in the history and culture of the United States.

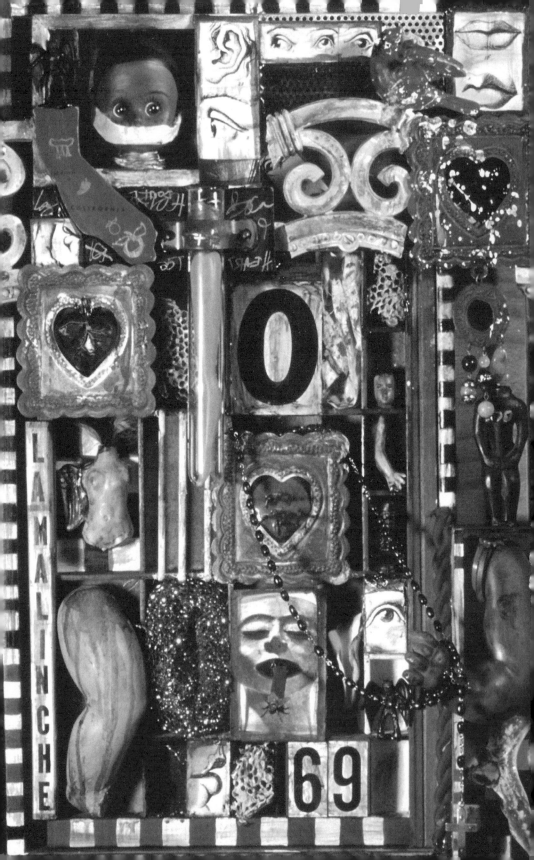

The Wounded Heart
Writing on Cherríe Moraga

Yvonne Yarbro-Bejarano

University of Texas Press   *Austin*

An earlier version of chapter 1 appeared as "Deconstructing the Lesbian Body: Cherríe Moraga's *Loving in the War Years*," in *Chicana Lesbians: The Girls Our Mothers Warned Us About*, ed. Carla Trujillo (Berkeley: Third Woman Press, 1991).

An earlier version of chapter 2 appeared as "Cherríe Moraga's *Giving Up the Ghost*: The Representation of Female Desire," in *Third Woman*, 3: 1 and 2 (1986).

An earlier version of chapter 3 appeared as "Cherríe Moraga's 'Shadow of a Man': Touching the Wound in Order to Heal," in *Acting Out: Feminist Performances*, eds. Lynda Hart and Peggy Phelan (Ann Arbor: University of Michigan Press, 1993).

Illustrations in this book are details from an assemblage by Sheri Tornatore.

First edition, 2001

Requests for permission to reproduce material from this work should be sent to Permissions, University of Texas Press, Box 7819, Austin, TX 78713-7819.

♾ The paper used in this book meets the minimum requirements of ANSI/NISO Z39.48-1992 (R1997) (Permanence of Paper).

Library of Congress Cataloging-in-Publication Data

Yarbro-Bejarano, Yvonne.
The wounded heart : writing on Cherríe Moraga / Yvonne Yarbro-Bejarano.— 1st. ed.
    p.   cm. — (Chicana matters series)
Includes bibliographical references and index.
ISBN 0-292-79607-2 (alk. paper) —
ISBN 0-292-79608-0 (pbk. : alk. paper)
    1. Moraga, Cherríe—Criticism and interpretation.
2. Women and literature—United States—History—20th century.   3. Mexican American women in literature.
4. Mexican Americans in literature.   5. Lesbians in literature.
I. Title.   II. Series.
PS3563.0753 Z96   2001
818'.5409—dc21   2001017139

Dedicated to Eleanor Soto

In Memoriam

Lora Romero
(1960–1997)

Raquel Mendieta
(1951–1999)

Contents

Acknowledgments

Thanks first and foremost to Cherríe Moraga for her work and permission to quote from it. I would also like to acknowledge Theresa May of the University of Texas Press and Deena González, series editor, for their patience, and Deena in particular for her useful comments on the manuscript. I am deeply grateful that Lora Romero took the time to read it and give me her insights. I am indebted to Alicia Schmidt-Camacho for many inspiring conversations and valuable editing suggestions. To the students of my 1995 Stanford seminar on Race, Gender, and Nation for their challenging discussions of *The Last Generation*, and to Estelle Freedman for inviting me to present the chapter on *The Last Generation* in the 1995 Feminist Studies colloquia series: thank you. I am grateful to my colleagues Rudy Busto and Paula Moya for their input on the chapters on *Heroes and Saints* and "Waiting in the Wings," respectively. Undergraduate research assistant Celina Ramírez helped with typing revisions and library work. Special thanks to graduate assistants Karina Hodoyán and Raúl Coronado, Jr., whose participation was crucial in the final stages of completing the manuscript, and for Raúl's careful reading of and astute comments on chapter 5. I am forever thankful to Eleanor Soto, who supported me in many ways throughout this process.

Title Abbreviations

Bridge	*This Bridge Called My Back*
Loving	*Loving in the War Years*
Ghost	*Giving Up the Ghost*
Shadow	*Shadow of a Man*
Heroes	*Heroes and Saints*
TLG	*The Last Generation*
"Wings"	*"Waiting in the Wings"*

Introduction

Chicana Lesbian Writing and the Intersection of Cultural and Critical Practices

The essays collected in this book span a ten-year period and record the development of a critical practice as much as they trace the different facets of Cherríe Moraga's work as poet, essayist, editor, dramatist, and public intellectual. Taken together, the essays offer a kind of periodization of Chicana/o studies that suggests, gratifyingly, that the body of Chicana lesbian writing has radically transformed the terms for conceptualizing identity and community. The articulation "Chicanas/Chicanos" need no longer refer to the male-centered, essentialized subject of cultural nationalism nor the passive, pathologized subject of social science discourse. Thanks in large part to the creative struggle of Chicana feminists and Chicana lesbian feminists in particular, the idea of "difference within" ourselves and within our communities has multiplied, rather than fragmented, sites of social action and critical intervention.[1] Although the position of Chicana lesbians in cultural, political, and academic institutions, and in the U.S. economy, remains precarious, a glance at the array of Chicana texts since the 1981 release of *This Bridge Called My Back* demonstrates a vital shift in the critical terrain for writing identity and community.[2]

With Moraga as creative interlocutor, I have been fortunate to participate in the process of building a field of inquiry, constructing new critical practices by learning from the limitations of earlier ones that neglected the acknowledgment of race or sexuality. My work is located at the junction of Chicana/o studies, feminist studies, and queer theory; I take from each a critique that questions the ingrained lines of inquiry of the others to produce a rich and theoretically stimulating theoretical apparatus. A sign of the enrichment of this continuing dialogue is that I am able to pose these issues, formerly defined as "private" by academia, as legitimate sites of intellectual inquiry.

Moraga's work has been extremely influential in the ways those of us involved in current debates on culture and identity think about the intersections of race, class, gender, and sexuality. Her writing has informed the contemporary understanding of identity as being constructed in an ongoing, open-ended process. The project motivating my analysis is to get beyond the acknowledgment of the multiple categories of difference ("race, class, gender, and sexuality") to an analysis of the relational complexity of the "in-between" spaces where these categories intermingle. Complementing work by Norma Alarcón and Chela Sandoval, who show consciousness to be key in identity formation, my essays focus on the neglected/repressed body and related material zones of sexual practice, desire, and pleasure.[3] I see our work in Chicana/o studies as a collective undertaking to explore and envision the meanings of "Chicano." My essays show how its representation changes over time, for example, in the turn to nationalism in Moraga's more recent texts.

My discussions of the multiple crossings and interweavings of categories of identity in Moraga's writing contribute to the development of a language to talk about sexuality as potentially empowering and important for political work. I couch my analysis of Moraga's strategies of representation within the notion of "a politics of enunciation" (Mercer, 194) attuned to the politics of location in the utterance. The struggle to "give voice" or "make visible" experiences, identities, and subjectivities that have been historically marginalized raises political questions of agency: who is empowered or disempowered to "speak" of difference (Mercer, 194). My work explores the place of desire within politics, and links close textual readings of the intricate workings of racialized desire to Moraga's liberatory project of making desire(s) legible.

Cherríe Moraga's work spans a range of genres and speaks from multiple sites of struggle. In compiling my essays for this collection, I am struck both by the fluidity of Moraga's analysis of difference and by the coherence of her imagery in evoking the contradictory ways in which race, class, gender, and sexuality shape identity. My own engagement in the critical project of investigating the articulation of racialized desire follows a similarly divergent path, responding to the context in which the original essays were written.

Part 1 consists of chapter 1, which centers on Moraga's writing of the body. The first version of this essay, published in the anthology *Chicana Lesbians*, edited by Carla Trujillo in 1991, discussed images of the body in *Loving*, with some discussion of the meanings of the head in *Shadow* and *Heroes* as it relates to the project of (de) and (re)construction of the lesbian mestiza body examined in the essay. This analysis laid the ground for another piece I wrote on the lesbian body and strategies of lesbian representation in Latina writers and visual artists, published in *¿Entiendes? Queer Readings, Hispanic Writings*[4] in 1995. In revising the essay on Moraga's writing of the body, I expanded the textual examples to include discussion of images from *Ghost*, *The Last Generation* (1993), and the essay "Waiting in the Wings: Reflections on a Radical Motherhood," which I read in its next-to-final form in 1994. The revision of this and the other essays collected here has increased my appreciation of the remarkable degree of intertextual coherence in the development of key imagery in Moraga's writing.

Chapter 2 on *Giving Up the Ghost* (1986) was actually written before the analysis of the lesbian body in Moraga's *Loving in the War Years* presented in chapter 1. My original essay on *Ghost*, published in *Third Woman* in 1986, focused on the representation of female desire. I revised the essay around that time for an anthology that never materialized. The revision places *Ghost* in the larger framework of feminist theories of representation, particularly of alternatives to dominant theater, and in the context of national and international debates within feminism going on in the wake of *Bridge* (1981) and the increased awareness of racial issues and differences among women. I offer a reading of Moraga's autobiographical essay "A Long Line of Vendidas" (*Loving*) as the theory and the set of thematic concerns infusing the theatrical practice exemplified in *Ghost*. I have grouped this essay on *Ghost* with the two chapters on *Shadow of a Man* and *Heroes and Saints* to form part 2 of the book, concentrating on Moraga's writing for the theater.

Besides the early analysis of *Ghost*, part 2 includes an introduction to and overview of Moraga's plays. I discuss her dramaturgy in the context of dominant and alternative Western theatrical traditions, including Chicana/o and feminist theater, and outline the principal themes of her plays and their relationship to one another. Chapter 3 on the play *Shadow* captures, I hope, some of the liveliness of the moment of its groundbreaking production at the Eureka Theater in San Francisco in 1990 and of contemporary debates on "difference within" the Chicana/o "community." These debates included a critique of sexuality and the family. Written around the time of the 1990 "Chicano Studies/Cultural Studies" conference at the University of California at Santa Barbara, chapter 3 also reflects some of the cross-fertilization of the two fields going on at the time, and particularly the influence of Stuart Hall. Chapter 3 focuses on an analysis of the characters in *Shadow* to illustrate the potential of theater's performative dimension in highlighting the constructedness of racial, gendered, and sexual identities. Chapter 4, an unpublished essay written in 1994 on *Heroes and Saints*, examines how the theme of pesticide poisoning and the image of the head place *Heroes* explicitly in dialogue with the Chicano theater movement. It also attempts a reading of the play through the lens of a theory of the collective experience of "joy" developed in African American cultural studies.

Part 3 gathers together three previously unpublished essays that look at the discursive production of identities in Moraga's writing. I wrote the first version of chapter 5 on *TLG* in 1993 at Hedgebrook (a women writers' retreat at Whidbey Island in Washington State) as part of an earlier book project comparing Gloria Anzaldúa and Moraga that turned into this collection of essays. I wrote the final chapter over the summer and fall of 1995 after teaching the unpublished version of "Waiting in the Wings" in Spring Quarter at Stanford.

Chapter 5 examines the centrality of sex as both practice and metaphor in Moraga's work, and the thematic blending of the sexual and the spiritual, both Christian and indigenous. It centers on the short story "La Ofrenda" as an example of the textualization of racialized desire and identity. The analysis of racial identities continues in the discussion of *TLG* in chapter 6, which concentrates on the representation of whiteness in the realms of cultural nationalism, the family, and lesbian desire. Moraga's naming of whiteness in this text and my analysis of its representations point to another key item on the new research agendas of ethnic, feminist, and queer studies. As Mercer points out, "for all our rhetoric about 'making ourselves visible,' the real challenge in the new cultural politics of difference is to make whiteness visible for the first time, as a culturally constructed ethnic identity historically contingent upon the violent denial and disavowal of 'difference'" ("Welcome to the Jungle," 215). The collection ends with chapter 7, an analysis of "Waiting in the Wings" focusing on how Moraga privileges writing as the site for the production of the new self: the (butch) lesbian mother.

Moraga's insistence on taking sexuality seriously as a category of analysis has made us aware of the need to reclaim our passion as academics, to interrogate what moves us deeply to do what we do, to identify where and how we experience our pleasure as well as our pain, and to envision the possibility of joy in a cultural context that acknowledges the differences among us, whether in the continuing struggle for social justice or in the understanding of continuity and change in the generational cycle of life and death. These essays reflect my own history over a ten-year period of academic passions, textual pleasures, and hopeful joy in a collective undertaking to envision what "Chicana/o" means.

PART I

The Body

(De)constructing the
Lesbian Body

In her writing, Cherríe Moraga enacts an impossible scenario: to give voice and visibility to that which has been erased and silenced. Constructed as radically other by the tradition that defines literary authority as white, male, privileged, heterosexual, and culturally dominant, Moraga opens up a space in her writing for the representation of Chicana lesbian subjectivity that is shaped across and through a multiplicity of discourses, unlike the unified female subject of much white feminist theory (Alarcón, "Theoretical," 357). As Norma Alarcón points out, many of the positions from which the Chicana subject speaks are occupied in relation to racial, class, and cultural conflicts and divisions, as well as gender ones. As critics renew the emphasis on race, culture, and class as categories of subject formation and oppression, it is crucial to remember that these categories are themselves inflected by constructions of dominant and subordinate sexuality. The mapping of subjectivity and oppression in Moraga's writing is the cartography of lesbian desire, the unspeakable speaking and unrepresentable desire of lesbian subjects *of color*, Chicana *lesbians*.

The sexual specificity of Moraga's concerns is pre-texted in the title of her first book, *Loving in the War Years: Lo que nunca pasó por sus labios*. Chicana lesbians are embattled not only on the streets but also on the field of representation. The attempt to make visible what has always been invisible and to say what has never been said (*lo que nunca pasó por sus labios*) involves the textual construction of the lesbian body and lesbian desire as well as the deconstruction of conventional codes that govern the representation of female desire and the female body (for example, encoding the female body as object of male heterosexual desire).

But heterosexism and homophobia are not just "out there." Chicana lesbians are besieged from within as well as from without. They struggle with the internalization of oppressive attitudes and representational codes in the area of sexuality as well as race, culture, and class. Moraga, as a Chicana lesbian writing subject, cannot inhabit a "pure" place of opposition or rejection from which she can construct or destroy the representation of female desire and the female body. Instead, lesbian desire and the lesbian body themselves become the field of negotiation and (de)construction, Gloria Anzaldúa's "borderlands," the "third space" of flux and translation (Anzaldúa, *Borderlands*).

Cherríe Moraga, born in 1952 to a working-class family in Los Angeles, has fashioned theater, poetry, and essays from poignant reflection on her personal experience. Moraga completed her bachelor of arts in English at Immaculate Heart College in Los Angeles and went on to receive a master of arts in Feminist Literature at California State University in San Francisco. She first made her mark in feminist scholarship with the publication in 1981 of *This Bridge Called My Back*, a collection of writings by women of color compiled jointly with Gloria Anzaldúa. She has long been an activist and teacher in San Francisco, instructing working-class women in writing, and directing students of color in theater projects. Coming into language as a writer and speaker has also been a coming into a complex public identity as a Chicana lesbian artist. The daughter of a Mexican mother and Anglo father, Moraga has had to reckon with the various racialized and gendered assignations given to her light skin and butch identification.

I would like to focus here on the representation of the body as site of the struggle to represent Chicana lesbian desire. In this sense Moraga's writing embodies a "sexual/textual" project that disrupts the dualisms of mind and body, writing and desire. These concerns run through all her writing, beginning in the preface to *Bridge*, in which she develops the title image: "How can we—

this time—not use our bodies to be thrown over a river of tormented history to bridge the gap?" (xv).

This bridge-body is rarely recuperated in its entirety in the poems of *Loving,* but rather in fragments. Virtually every poem in the collection hinges on some part of the body: "the part of the eye / that is not eye at all / but hole" in "Fear, a Love Poem" (33), the "very old wound in me / between my legs" in "Passage" (44). In "Raw Experience," the poetic voice observes as her body fragments into hands, face, and mouth: "I watch myself for clues, / trying to catch up / inhabit my body / again" (49). Moraga's poetry constantly takes apart the entire female body, recognizing how it has been appropriated and attempting to reclaim it. In "The Voices of the Fallers," the representation of the body falling in pieces explores the potentially fatal perils of lesbian existence.

I was born queer with the dream
of falling
the small sack of my body
dropping
off a ledge
suddenly.

One by one, the parts of the body fragment from the whole and fall through space, to reassemble only in sickening impact with the ground:

Listen.
Can you hear my mouth crack
open   the sound
of my lips bending
back against the force
of the fall?

Listen.
Put your ear deep
down
through   the opening
of my throat and
listen [. . .]

her   shoulder first
tumbling

the cliff   the legs

following
over
her head [. . .]

her body's
dead

silent

collision
with the sand. (*Loving,* 1–3)

The pervasive imagery of mouths, lips, and throats plays a key role in re-membering this fragmented lesbian body. In an interview with Moraga, Mirtha Quintanales connects this imagery to the fundamental importance of the task of speaking the unspoken ("trying to make it *be* said, to come out of your mouth" [12]) in Moraga's writing. In Moraga's sexual/textual project, the mouth fuses two taboo activities: female speaking and lesbian sexuality. "Mouth" and "sex" merge, both represented as organs of speech and sex. In this context of speech/sex, the lesbian body is "whole":

Stretching my legs and imagination so open
to feel my whole body cradled
by the movement of her mouth, the mouth
of her thighs rising and falling, her arms
her kiss, all the parts of her open
like lips moving, talking me into loving. (*Loving,* 140)

Moraga develops this connection further at the end of the essay "A Long Line of Vendidas" in *Loving*:

In recent months, I have had a recurring dream that my mouth is too big to close; that is, the *outside* of my mouth, my lips, cannot contain the inside—teeth, tongue, gums, throat. I am coming out of my mouth, so to speak [. . .]
    I say to my friends as I drive down 91 South, "The Mouth is like a cunt."
    [. . .] My mouth cannot be controlled. It will flap in the wind like legs in sex,

not driven by the mind. It's as if la boca[1] were centered on el centro del corazón,[2] not in the head at all. The same place where the cunt beats.

And there is a woman coming out of her mouth.
Hay una mujer que viene de la boca. (142)

This remarkable passage redistributes the anatomy of the lesbian body, de-centering the mind and the head and locating "la boca" (newly defined as "mouth/cunt") in the heart. The process reveals that not only our attitudes about our bodies but our very bodies themselves are constructed. If this is so, Moraga's writing seems to suggest, there's nothing to stop us from re-constructing them from the blueprint of our own desire, however implicated those desires might be in hegemonic discourses of gender and sexuality.

The recuperation of the newly reconstructed lesbian body in its entirety needs to be read in the context of Corky's rape monologue from Moraga's play *Giving Up the Ghost* (see chapter 2). Corky relives for the audience how she was raped. In sexual play with an older cousin, she had experienced her vagina pleasurably, as "wet 'n' forbidden," though still a child's in contrast to the older girl's "wide 'n' deep like a cueva"[3] (*Ghost*, 42). But with the rapist, "there was no hole / he had to make it / 'n' I saw myself down there like a face / with no open-ing / a face with no features / no eyes no nose no mouth / only little lines where they shoulda been" (*Ghost*, 43). With the shout "HE MADE ME A HOLE!" she disappears from the play. The passage from "wide 'n' deep like a cueva" to "a face with no features" charts the itinerary the writing takes to redeem this con-struction of the mestiza, not only her body but her very self-image ("he made me a hole").

The possibility of reconstruction (and in this case, the surgical overtones are appropriate, given the brutal violation of the little girl's body) is glimpsed in her description of "down there" as "a face with no features / no eyes no nose no mouth / only little lines where they shoulda been." The hands play a crucial role in making the "hole" a mouth again that may speak in sex ("I never cried as he shoved the thing / into what was supposed to be a mouth" [*Ghost*, 43]). Sexual practice becomes the battlefield in which the hands are represented as both organs of lesbian sex and the means of victory over the forces that sepa-rate women from their bodies and one another. In the story "La Ofrenda," the hands are represented within a dynamic of betrayal between women ("There was blood on my hands and not from reaching into those women but from Tiny's hide" [*The Last Generation*, 80]) and the healing and possibly redemp-tive potential of sex: "So, I put my hands inside her. I did. I put them all the way inside her and like a fuckin' shaman I am working magic on her, giving her someone to be" (*TLG*, 83). Similarly, in *Ghost*, Marisa recollects how she used her hands to help Amalia survive, representing them not as the tools of the shaman but in the imagery of the battlefield that recalls the high stakes of "loving [women] in the war years":

It makes you feel so good,
like your hands are weapons of war
and as they move up into el corazón de esta mujer[4]
you are making her body remember
it didn't hafta be that hurt, ¿me entiendes?[5]
It was not natural or right
that she got beat down so damn hard. (*Ghost,* 57–58)

As in the earlier passage re-membering the body, the place of possible magic, or victory, is the location of both heart and sex. Marisa also recalls how she struggles to sustain as memory the sight of Amalia's hand inside her as a possible release, or transformation, vis-à-vis the gender roles that hold her sexuality prisoner:

I held the moment.
Strained, that if I looked long and hard enough
at the woman's hand full inside me
if beneath the moon blasting through the window
I could picture and hold pictured in my mind
(*MARISA takes AMALIA's hand*)
how that hand buried in the wool of my hair
her working it, herself, into me
how everything was changing at that moment
in both of us. (*Ghost,* 31–32)

The impermanence of this re-membered body and the ultimate failure of this erotic transformation in *Ghost* dramatize the weight of the representational and discursive traditions against (and within) which Moraga works.

Another such battlefield is the discourse of the lesbian monster. The nature of lesbian monstrosity lies in the mistaken conflation of gender (sense of self as male, female, or ambivalent) and erotic identification (sense of self as erotic subject or object, top or bottom, butch or femme in an erotic encounter). In the classic psychoanalytic formulation of active masculine desire and passive feminine desire, normalcy or deviance is based on the gender of the object choice. In this schema, it is deviant for a woman to desire another woman. Lesbian and gay Chicanas/os must negotiate the often contradictory meanings which Euro-American and Mexican American cultures ascribe to sexuality and sex-object choice. Mexican communities have traditionally assigned meanings to sexual practices organized around sexual roles "articulated along the active/passive axis of sex/gender/power" (Almaguer, 77). Mexican cultural nationalism maps this active/passive binary onto racialized gender roles constructed as the originary icons of *mestizaje*: the active, overvalued male figured as the European conqueror, *el chingón*,[6] and the denigrated female figured as the indigenous "mother" of the Mexican nation, *la chingada*[7] (Paz, 1961). Within the cultural polarities of *chingón/chingada*, active lesbian desire is multiply deviant for its assertion of a female sexual agency apart from the penetrating masculine partner. Moraga's exploration of lesbian desire is thus necessarily linked to an interrogation of the racial construction of the mestiza subject as passive sexual object.

Contemplating the legacy of Octavio Paz's narrativization of the conquest and its impact on mestizas' bodies and sexualities, Moraga writes in *Loving*:

> If the simple act of sex then—the penetration itself—implies the female's filthiness, non-humanness, it is no wonder Chicanas often divorce ourselves from the conscious recognition of our own sexuality. Even if we enjoy having sex, draw pleasure from feeling fingers, tongue, penis inside us, there is a part of us that must disappear in the act, separate ourselves from realizing what it is we are actually doing. Sit, as it were, on the corner bedpost, watching the degradation and violence some "other" woman is willing to subject herself to, not us. And if we have lesbian feelings—want not only to be penetrated, but to penetrate—what perverse kind of monstrosities we must indeed be! (119)

This passage is followed by a dream that can be interpreted as a "potent sexual vision" of the self as transgressive female *chingón*:

> *I am in a hospital bed. I look down upon my newly-developing body. The breasts are large and ample. And below my stomach, I see my own cock, wildly shooting menstrual blood totally out of control. The image of the hermaphrodite.* (119)

The potential empowerment in this reconstruction of the lesbian body that blends male and female creativity is hampered by the sense of sinfulness it evokes in the young dreamer in a context of religious prohibitions: "By giving definition and meaning to my desires, religion became the discipline to control my sexuality. Sexual fantasy and rebellion became 'impure thoughts' and 'sinful acts'" (*Loving*, 119).

In a poem from *The Last Generation*, "I Was Not Supposed to Remember," the notion of monstrosity links "lesbian" and "half-breed" in the image of the "mongrel animal":

Mongrel is the name
that holds all the animal I am.
[. . .]
I, a lesbian monster
she recommends hormones
have you always been this hairy
yes, I say, I remember since I became a woman
with hair lots of it does that make me a woman
or a lesbian
or an animal?, which brings me back to mongrel
and the hybrid sheep-goat I saw
in a magazine once
with pitiful pleading eyes
trying to bust out
of her genetically altered face

and I saw my face in there
no matter how much I am loved
no matter how much woman
I am no matter how many women
hold and suck me
I am mirrored in those pitiful
lonesome
product of mutation
eyes. (100–101)

Here, "hairiness" connotes unnatural deviance from proper gender role, from racial "purity," in contaminating closeness to the natural world (excess). In an attempt to deconstruct the impact of these narratives on the mestiza lesbian body, Moraga's writing focuses mainly on its fragmentation and the partial redefining of its parts, yet with a vision of a new way to be whole that would respond to the "desire for integration" reflected in the dream of the hermaphrodite and the representations of the lesbian body fusing heart, hands, and head in sex (*Loving*, 119).

For Moraga, integrating the self means contending with her ambiguous position as the daughter of a Mexican mother and Anglo father. She seeks to resolve this tension by linking the "half-breed" to the "mestiza," drawing a symbolic analogy between her Anglo father and the Spanish *chingón*, and her Mexican mother and the indigenous *chingada*. This construction remains unstable, however, partly because it fails to interrogate cultural nationalism's reification of the indigenous woman, and partly because it seeks to yoke together two very distinct notions of "race" and colonial histories. (I will return to the limits of this construction, its retention of the very binarisms it seeks to explode, in my discussion of Moraga's queering of cultural nationalism in chapter 6.) For Moraga, *mestizaje* signifies a liberatory project of crossing boundaries, while the notion of "half-breed" relies heavily on a biologized, genetic discourse of race and racial purity. Here, the "half-breed" speaks for that aspect of herself which cannot find resolution, which is denied wholeness by the racial and sexual discourses operating on her.

In "Anatomy Lesson," the heart is associated with the dangers of "loving in the war years," as expressed in the title poem: "maintaining / this war time morality / where being queer / and female is as rude / as we can get" (*Loving*, 30). The heart in "Anatomy Lesson" is a detachable piece of the anatomy that must be placed in the back pocket "when entering a room full of soldiers who fear hearts" (*Loving*, 68). The power of the absent heart makes the soldiers beg to see "what it is they fear they fear." But the poetic voice warns against seduction, arguing for a strategy of self-protection as long as those who fear have the power:

Hang onto your heart.
Ask them first what they'll give up to see it.
Tell them that they can begin with their arms.

Only then will *you* begin to negotiate. (68)

The displacing of the head in favor of the heart as center and throne of speech/sexuality operates within and against the mind/body duality that permeates Western culture.

In the project of reconstruction and recuperation of the female body in Moraga's writing, the representation of the body in pieces also comments on the ways women are trained to separate from their bodies, sites of base impulses and decay in patriarchal discourses. The opening image of Moraga's second play, *Shadow of a Man*, is the young girl Lupe's disembodied head illuminated by a candle in the shadow of the cross:

> *At rise, spot on LUPE, staring with deep intensity into the bathroom mirror. She wears a Catholic school uniform. She holds a lit votive candle under her chin and a rosary with crucifix in her hand. Her face is a circle of light in the darkness. The shadow of the crucifix looms over the back wall.* (42)

Lupe speaks of her "ex-ray eyes" as she imagines Sister Genevieve naked under her habit. Her curiosity about sex makes her feel different from the other children, who "seem to be seeing things purty much like they are. Not ex-ray or nuthin'" (42). In her monologue she speaks of her sin: "keeping secrets."

To the "shadow" in the title, this scene adds the meaning of the man on the cross, symbolizing the patriarchal collusion between the structures of the church and the family.[8] Catholicism in its institutionalized form not only indoctrinates women to accept suffering and sacrifice as their lot but also inculcates in them the need to sublimate the body and its desires, as captured in the image of Lupe's disembodied head illuminated by a candle in the shadow of the cross. In an interview (Noyes, "The Dream Images," 18), Moraga acknowledges the link between Lupe's guilt over her "ex-ray eyes" and the dream of the hermaphrodite in *Loving* quoted above: "The more potent my dreams and fantasies became and the more I sensed my own exploding sexual power, the more I retreated from my body's messages and into the region of religion."

In the second to the last scene in *Shadow*, Lupe stands once again "*in front of the bathroom mirror, a rosary with crucifix in her hand.*" She lights a candle as at the beginning of the play, but what she does next offers the spectator the hope that she will reclaim her body and move out from under the "shadow of a man":

> *[She] takes out the photo of Conrado her father had left. She studies the image for a moment, measuring it against her own reflection in the mirror. Then she tears the small photo into pieces and drops it into the mouth of the burning candle. The shadow of the crucifix goes up in flames. Fade out.* (82)

The traumatic events of the play (see chapter 3) have brought at least one secret to light: Lupe is Conrado's daughter. Her ability to let go of this damaging truth bodes well for her working through the equally damaging equation of sinfulness with her "secret" sexuality. This particular constellation of images — the girl refusing to be only a head, the purifying role of fire in symbolically destroying "the man," and the crucial involvement of the "mouth" in this liberation ("the mouth of the burning candle")—anticipates the action of Moraga's third play, *Heroes and Saints*, and its main character Cere, who is only a head (see chapter 4), revealing both intertextual coherence as well as remarkable flexibility in Moraga's (de)construction of the mestiza body.

With the character of Cere, Moraga works within and against the mythic bodies of the Chicano theater tradition: the stock characters and allegorical figures of its *actos* and *mitos*, such as the *pachuco, la muerte*, Quetzalcoatl,[9] the sun, moon, and earth, as well as the head of Pancho Villa from Luis Valdez' play *The Shrunken Head of Pancho Villa*. Moraga recognizes her indebtedness to the political and esthetic dimensions of Valdez' play, while at the same time appropriating and transforming the image of the head within a feminist concern with the body and sexuality. Moraga rewrites the mythic head of Valdez' play as female to visually engage the idea that Cere is deprived of her body by environmental racism *and* through the teaching of Mexican Catholicism, reproduced by her mother, that women should repress their bodies as weak and sinful and that they should live only in their "head."

In a reversal of the usual scenario in which women desperately try to rid themselves of the body, Cere is only a head that desperately seeks a body. She delights in her tongue and its multiple possibilities, linguistic, sexual, and visionary: "The power of communication through speech," "the charismatic gift of ecstatic speech," "to give tongue" (108). Frustrated in her attempt to construct herself a body through her sexuality, Cere renounces her mouth as sexual organ and sublimates her sexual energy into a visionary "speaking in tongues" to become the saint of the title at the end of the play, leading the people to ignite the vineyards in an apocalyptic conflagration. The powerful irony and great beauty of the play stem from this central image of the bodiless mestiza head. Despite her lack of a body, Cere still acts as desiring subject, striving in both erotic and political registers for collective justice and communion.

Heroes stages image after image of women's bodies: Cere, her body's absence and presence evoked through her *desire* for a body; her sister Yolanda's milk-filled breasts and the reference to Cere's nursing at her mother's contaminated breasts; Cere's insistence on the physicality of her hair, mouth, and tongue; the broken body and unbroken spirit of Amparo, beaten by the police after her speech at a demonstration. The sisters' love and support for each other is figured through the female body as well: Yolanda dresses and cares for Cere's skin and hair, and at the end Cere relieves the emotional and physical agony of Yolanda's bereft motherhood by sucking her painful breasts. By peopling the stage with women's bodies, *Heroes* reclaims mestiza corporality and testifies to the refusal of this body to disappear in the face of environmental racism or Mexican Catholic repression.

The poem "For the Color of My Mother" represents another disembodied head.

as it should be,
dark women come to me
              sitting in circles
I pass thru their hands
the head of my mother
painted in clay colors

              touching each carved feature swollen eyes and mouth

they understand the explosion, the splitting
open   contained within the fixed expression

they cradle her silence

              nodding to me (*Loving*, 61)

The materiality of the mother's head works against the association with mind and sublimated sexual energy. In its marked mestiza physiognomy ("*the un-named part of the mouth / the wide-arched muzzle of brown women*" [*Loving*, 60]), the head (the mother's legacy) signifies a possible "bridge" among women of color. It is also exemplary of the symbolic chain in Moraga's work which links "brownness" and the indigenous to the idea of home, a female space of safety and eroticism. Moraga's *indigenismo*, which often adopts the codes of Mexican cultural nationalism, originates in this complex desire for both sexual and political union among women. For Moraga, writing as a fair-skinned "half-breed," the identification with the brown women of the poem is figured as a desire for rebirth into a symbolic system valorizing color and femaleness.

Like the shifting meanings of the head, the images of amputation in Moraga's writing do not always signify only loss. In *Heroes*, the priest enters his mind to escape his body, and the bodiless Cere possesses a body through the force of her dreams and her desire. In an earlier draft, a scene between Father Juan and Cere culminates in the ritual of communion, which the priest calls the commingling of their amputated parts, since both are cut off in different ways from their bodies. In the poem "You Call It, *Amputation*" the body registers the loss yet continues to sense the absent part:

You call it
am pu tation

but even after the cut
they say the toes still itch
the body remembers the knee,
        gracefully bending

she reaches down to find her leg gone
the shape under the blanket dropping off
suddenly, irregularly
[. . .]
still, I feel
the mutilated body
swimming in side stroke
pumping twice as hard
for the lack
of body, pushing
through your words
which hold no water
for me. (*Loving,* 82)

The body with its amputated parts is there and not there at the same time, much in the same way women's bodies are theirs and not theirs, constructed as they are in the image of phallocentric desire.[10] The poem captures both the struggle to compensate for this "lack" ("pumping twice as hard") and the barriers to communication erected by these traces of loss written on the body ("your words / which hold no water / for me").

 In other texts in *Loving*, the pain of the body in pieces is associated with the conflicted relationship between the writing subject and her culture, particularly with the faith of Mexican women. While her grandmother is on her deathbed, she appears to the writer in a dream that associates her faith (*la iglesia, la misa*) with a horrible lesion on her body:

 My grandmother appears outside la iglesia.[11] Standing in front as she used to do after la misa.[12] I am so surprised that she is well enough to go out again, be dressed, be in the world. I am elated to see her—to know I get to have the feel of her again in my life.

She is, however, in great pain. She shows me her leg which has been operated on. The wound is like a huge crater in her calf—crusted, open, a gaping wound. I feel her pain so critically. (iii–iv)

Even as her faith is associated with a terrible wound, it provides the space for expressing both loss and continuity ("I feel her pain so critically").

The grandmother's injured leg recalls the battered hips of the women who refuse to allow the moving sidewalk to shuttle them efficiently past the object of their veneration in the Basilica of the Virgin of Guadalupe in Mexico. As in the dream, the writer sees both her alienation and her connection to her culture in these fragments of bodies, willingly wounded for their faith:

the most devout of the Mexican women—las pobres,[13] few much older than me—clung to the ends of the handrailing of the moving floor, crossing themselves, gesturing besos al retrato, their hips banging up against the railing over and over again as it tried to force them off and away. They stayed. In spite of the machine. They had come to spend their time with La Virgen.

I left the church in tears, knowing how for so many years I had closed my heart to the passionate pull of such faith that promised no end to the pain. I grew white. Fought to free myself from my culture's claim on me. (ii)

Moraga's work is steeped in Catholicism, but as she says in the preface to *Bridge*, she does not embrace the resigned faith of institutionalized religion, but the "faith of activists" that "we have the power to [. . .] change our lives" (xviii). In one of her most recent essays, "Waiting in the Wings" (see chapter 7), she distinguishes between the kind of faith "derived from some hard-living," exemplified by certain members of her family, and others' faith as "the insurance policy [. . .] their lives never gave them a reason to cancel" (82). This opposition is defined generationally (she being an exception to her generation). She turns to the syncretic faith of her mother and grandmother to reconstruct it as activism and as a counterbalance to the fear of betrayal by women. In this sense, faith can also mean the belief in the possibility of faithfulness to one another as women, as Chicanas. In "The Pilgrimage," the poetic voice associates the mother's Catholic faith and the daughter's faith in women bonding.

She saw women
maybe the first time
when they had streamed in long broken
single file
out from her mother's tongue—

> "En México, las mujeres crawl
> on their hands and knees
> to the basilica door.
> This proves their faith."

The brown knotted knees were hers
in her dreaming, she wondered
where in the journey
would the dusty knees begin
to crack,
> would the red blood of the women
> stain the grey bone of the road. (*Loving,* 18)

This translation of the concept of faith from one context to another is accomplished through the body in pieces: the bleeding and "brown knotted knees" that construct this faith as racial/cultural affirmation ("En México"), but at the price of the tortured flesh, associated with the mother('s) tongue. Echoing the image of a woman coming out of her own mouth/sex ("hay una mujer que viene de la boca"), the women streaming from her mother's tongue present the oral tradition as the site of the writer's first connection with women.

In the description of the Mexican women whose hips bang against the railing at the Basilica, what separates Moraga from them and from her own body is her "whiteness." As "half-breed," Moraga reconnects with "brownness"—her own, her mother's, that of mestizas and other women of color. As is characteristic of the handling of other body parts, the meaning of "skin" is not fixed, but slides between that of badge of difference and that of porous boundary through which connections can be made. In "It Got Her Over," her skin

had turned on her
[. . .]
In the light of Black
women and children

beaten/hanged/raped/
[. . .]
Her skin had turned
in the light of these things.
Stuck to her now
like a flat immovable paste
spread grey over a life.

Still,
    it got her over (*Loving,* 69–70)

Even though white-skin privilege has helped her survive "in the war years," it cannot help her "get over" her shame at "guilt by association/complicity to the crime":

recently taken to blushing
as if the blood wanted
to swallow
      the flesh.
[. . .]
See this face?
      Wearing it like an accident
of birth.
      It was
a scar sealing up
a woman, now darkened
by desire. (*Loving,* 70–71)

The positioning of "woman" between "a scar sealing up" and "darkened by desire" captures the trajectory from white identification to mestiza desire traced in the essay "La Güera," where "looking white" both afforded privilege and separated her from her mother, until the oppression she experienced by acknowledging her lesbianism connected her with her mother's own silence and oppression (*Bridge,* 52).

    By representing skin color as something she has or becomes rather than as an essence, by detaching "skin" and "face" from the body or calling it a "scar" or an "accident," Moraga displays the constructedness of "race" in much the same way as her representation of the body undermines an essentialist reading. This awareness of race as an empty signifier whose meaning is constructed relationally, rather than as a fixed, biological property, is what allows her to write "my brother's sex was white. Mine, brown" (*Loving*, 90). In Moraga's understanding of the way gender is racialized, her brother's masculinity compensates for his difference from white men, while Moraga's gender and sexual identity remain "brown," the color she assigns to both marginalized and oppositional subjectivities. In her use of color as a sign for the marginal, she recognizes the intricately interrelated categories of race, sex, gender, and culture in her experience of the devaluation of females. Her particular liminal position as a light-skinned daughter of an Anglo father leads her to represent the identification with color as a "choice," a choice which necessarily rests on the symbolic construction of the brown woman as home, origin, and other. If she "grew white" she can also "go brown," as in "For the Color of My Mother": "*I am a white girl gone brown to the blood color of my mother / speaking to her*" (*Loving*, 60). Still, in *Loving*, "going brown" is never a matter of individual will, but rather a negotiation with hidden histories. Skin can establish boundaries and separation:

I want to feel
your touch *outside*
my body, on the *surface*
of my skin.

I want to know, *for sure,*
where you leave off
and I begin. (35)

But it is also a "boundary" in Anzaldúa's sense of a place where two edges meet and mingle (*Borderlands*, 3):

seeing yourself
for the first time
in the body of this sister
[. . .]
like you whom
you've taken in
under your bruised wing
[. . .]
seeing yourself
for the *first* time
in the body of her boyhood

her passion to survive
female and *un*compromising

taking all this under your wing
letting it wrestle there
into your skin
        changing you (*Loving*, 27–28)

In "Winter of Oppression, 1982," the *whiteness* of the bodies of the Jewish victims of the Holocaust provides the shock that loosens the moorage of the concepts "dark" and "white" and permits the perception of "a colored kind of white
people" (*Loving*, 74). The writing subject realizes the impossibility of either
choosing or forgetting aspects of identity, of simply falling back "upon rehearsed
racial memory" (*Loving*, 75). While retaining a sense of the specificity of her
own oppression as a Chicana lesbian, she struggles to make connections with
other kinds of oppression:

I work to remember
what I never dreamed possible
what my consciousness could never
contrive.

Whoever I am

I must believe
I am not
and will never be
the only
one
who suffers. (75–76) [14]

    The dismantling and recomposition of the lesbian body in Moraga's writ-
ing is part of a process of making sense out of the rifts and splits of our shifting
and multiple identity. I stress the "process of making sense" rather than the production of a fixed meaning, for it is the multiplicity of meanings that attach to
the parts and the whole of the lesbian body/text that allows for diverse discon-
nections and connections to be made, from "a colored kind of white people"
to the cluster of alliances particularly significant to this process:

la lengua que necesito
para hablar
es la misma que uso
para acariciar

tú sabes.[15]
you know the feel of woman
lost en su boca
    amordazada[16]

it has always been like this.

profundo y sencillo
lo que nunca
pasó
por sus labios[17]

but was
    utterly
    utterly
    heard. (*Loving,* 149)

The tongue that both speaks and caresses connotes the mother('s) tongue, the Spanish of the text recalling Moraga's journey to her mestiza desire as well as the women she first heard coming out of her mother's mouth. The insistent repetition ("utterly / utterly") calls attention to the multivalence of *Loving in the War Years'* subtitle ("Lo que nunca pasó por sus labios"): from the impossible utterance of (mestiza) lesbian sexuality within the realm of representation, to the writing of a lesbian desire that need not be spoken to be heard, just as the mouth muzzled in sex still speaks.

PART II

The Plays

A search through hundreds of years of Western dramatic literature, including alternative theater traditions, would yield few plays with the racially and
sexually subordinated voices heard in Cherríe Moraga's
plays. The privileged male subject and author of the
Western drama have enjoyed a monopoly on whose
stories get to be told, whose quests and conflicts
represented. In the Aristotelian tradition, it is the
male subject's life, carried to the stage through a particular structure of imitation ("mimesis") involving
appropriate forms (tragedy, narrative), and prescrib-
ing an appropriate reception (empathy, catharsis),
that is offered for supposedly universal identification
to an ideal audience of equally privileged spectators.
The traditional representation of woman on stage has
been as the "other" of this privileged male subject,
usually the object of his desire, a position also am-
biguously occupied by the racial other, male or female.
The action most female characters grapple with is the
dilemma embedded in a relationship with a man.

Chicano theater (*teatro*) challenges some of these
hierarchies hidden in "universal" Western theater, par-

ticularly those of race and class. Chicano theater emerged from the oral and performative traditions of Mexican and Mexican American campesinos who came to work in U.S. agriculture as a migratory, exploited labor force. Out of the civil rights and farmworker movements of the 1960s and 1970s, Chicano theater crystallized as a recognizable form of interventionist drama. Perhaps the most famous example of this tradition is El Teatro Campesino, a collective ensemble theater founded by Luis Valdez in 1965. The *carpa,* the popular tent show of campesino theater, became a tool for political organizing and consciousness-raising in the fields of California as an accompaniment to the mobilization of the United Farm Workers' struggle. Chicano theater draws on folk and vernacular forms, as well as a range of "high" cultural genres, to create a performative tradition which defies easy categorization while it seeks to dramatize those histories otherwise absent from the stage. It can alter the axes of reception by seeking out and developing Chicano audiences. It has excelled in creating working-class characters of color for diverse Chicano audiences in non-traditional venues, protesting the social injustice that has characterized Chicano experience in the U.S. and affirming cultural identity. Chicano theater has provided the opportunity for Chicano audiences, traditionally excluded as subjects of the drama, to identify with representations of their lives.

Like most political theater traditions, the Chicano theater movement as a whole has been issue-oriented, placing greater value on the dramatization of social conditions than on the subjective experience of them, and working with a particular definition of the political that does not see issues of gender and sexuality as part of the struggle. For the most part, Chicano theater does not provide many opportunities for women (especially lesbians) or gay men to be the *subjects* of the drama.[1] The plays that form the canonical Chicano theater repertory tend to perpetuate the hierarchy based on gender, confining the representation of women within the polarized gender structure that theater reflects and reproduces. In relationship to the male subject, Chicanas continue to be represented as "other" (that which is not male), and as objects of desire or derision (Broyles-González, *Teatro Campesino,* 135).

Feminist theater, in its commitment to "centering" women characters, staging their stories, and representing issues of gender and sexuality, makes female viewers, for once, the ideal spectators. The female subject of the drama can redirect Western theater's obsessive focus on prescribed gender roles within the heterosexual couple, particularly when the drama is about *her* desire, and even more so when the object of the female character's active desire is another woman. However, the scarce representations of lesbian or female homoerotic desire in Western dramatic literature still partake for the most part of the privileges of class, white skin, and membership in the dominant culture. The perspectives of playwrights who are lesbians of color and lesbian-of-color characters are practically nonexistent. Thanks to Chicano and feminist theater, Chicanos and some women now have the opportunity to interact with staged representations of themselves as subjects, accepting or rejecting identification with them. But lesbians of color continue to be radically de-centered in relation to the ideal spectator position of the drama.

The continuing underrepresentation of women of color in general and lesbians of color in particular, in both Chicano and feminist alternative theater traditions, calls forth a critique of the political or theoretical paradigms that engage single categories of oppression or experience (gender and sexuality *or* race/ethnicity and class). Moraga's work for the theater embodies a model of interwoven structures of domination, mobilizing the categories of race, culture, class, sexuality, and gender in complex interactions. In each play, the characters' sense of self—of their gender, race, sex, and class positioning within a hierarchical social structure—is played out on the cultural ground of the working-class Chicano family. The poetic bilingual force of these characters places Moraga's plays within *teatro's* working-class linguistic tradition, drawing on and transforming the rhythms, beauty, whimsy, and passion of everyday Chicano speech.

By insisting on Chicano lives and Chicano language as appropriate matter for the theater, and by creating Chicanas as desiring subjects, Moraga's published trilogy of plays (*Giving Up the Ghost, Shadow of a Man,* and *Heroes and Saints*) invites Chicanos, including Chicanas and Chicana lesbians, to take up the ideal spectator position monopolized for so long by white, heterosexual, and economically privileged viewers. Yet, in her commitment to examine Chicana/o lives in all their complexity and contradictions, she eschews the mandate to produce "positive images," and thus she also problematizes the traditional structures of identification in the theater. Even those "ideal" spectators most directly aligned with the subjects of her dramas are often alienated by these representations. Within Brechtian and other political theater traditions, the playwright challenges the comfort level of the spectators to place them in a potentially more productive position for critical reflection and change than straightforward identification would. For Isaac Julien, although the strategy of positive images may stem from the best intentions of redressing imbalances in the field of representation—as in the Chicano theater movement's creation of working-class male subjects of color—it is bound to fail as it will never be able to address questions of ambivalence or transgression (261).

Moraga goes against the grain by impeding a complacent spectator position for non-Latino and Latino viewers alike, as evidenced by Ramón Saldívar's comment that for many, Moraga is "too blunt": "There are those who think you should keep the criticism within the family, so to speak" (Jamison).[2] Moraga's theater is never a matter of providing easy identifications, yet Chicana/o spectators of all

ages and kinds, including nuns and priests in the case of *Heroes,* recognize themselves in these representations of Chicano life. It is this contradictory movement
of attraction and rejection that creates the space for both affirmation and critique
in her plays.

Moraga's exciting trilogy of plays also makes a significant contribution to the
formation of a body of work for the theater by lesbians of color. Given the historical silence and invisibility imposed on Chicana lesbians, it is not surprising
that Moraga's first play places the Chicana lesbian and her desire center stage.
Giving Up the Ghost initiates Moraga's theatrical investigation of the erotic sense
of self and other, which is conditioned in both negative and positive ways by Mexi-
can/Chicano beliefs and attitudes about masculinity and femininity. In all three of
these provocative plays, the perceptive exploration of the characters' sexuality is
undertaken from a uniquely Chicana lesbian sensibility regardless of whether a Chicana lesbian character is on stage. Moraga's keen interrogation of lesbian desire, in
dynamic interplay with cultural constructions of heterosexuality and gender, positions her to see the entire spectrum of Chicana/o sexuality in new and insightful
ways. In the title essay of *The Last Generation,* Moraga writes:

As a lesbian, I don't pretend to understand the intricacies or intimacies of Chicano gay desire, but we do share the fact that our "homosexuality"—our feelings about sex, sexual power and domination, femininity and masculinity, family, loyalty, and morality—has been shaped by heterosexist culture and society.
As such, we have plenty to tell heterosexuals about themselves. (159–160)

Moraga's characters, as erotic or desiring subjects, struggle within and against the
imprisoning constructions of gender (particularly feminine passivity versus active
masculinity). The sexuality of figures like Amalia in *Ghost,* Manuel in *Shadow of a
Man,* and Cere in *Heroes and Saints* moves along a continuum that resists the binary formulation of "heterosexual" or "homosexual," inviting a Chicana/o audience
to imagine a more protean sense of sexuality.

The plays stage intense conflicts involving the cultural value placed on men
and Chicanas' betrayal of themselves and other women due to their internalization of men's supposed superiority. Throughout the trilogy, "man" represents this
patriarchal vision of the male subject's superior power, value, and desirability. The
deconstruction of "man" and the transformation of mestiza betrayal in her writing are necessary for Moraga's liberation as a Chicana lesbian. While Chicana lesbians may have blazed the path in this critique, Moraga's vision is one in which
all members of our far-from-homogeneous "community," particularly Chicano gay
men, analyze their relationship to "man."[3]

Until the 1990s, Moraga was better known as a poet, essayist, and editor than as a playwright. She started writing for the theater after the publication of the intensely autobiographical *Loving in the War Years* (1983), when the poems she was working on "started turning into monologues" (Yarbro-Bejarano, "Cherríe," 173). The result was *Giving Up the Ghost,* a two-act play in verse first published in 1986, which juxtaposes the poetic monologues of three female characters: Marisa, Corky, and Amalia. Moraga regards *Ghost* as a transitional piece between her poetry and her work for the theater, in the tradition of *teatropoesía*.[4] The spontaneous and independent emergence of the characters' voices in *Ghost* represented a significant departure from her essays. The essay and the theater perform different functions in Moraga's writing: the essays attempt to make sense of the contradictory aspects of her identity, especially the intersections of race and sexuality; her theatrical characters embody these contradictions.[5] Since they "live" in the flesh, so to speak, they voice truths the analytical mind rejects, represses, or censors. The essays clarify points, but the voices of *Ghost* begin to manifest, from a more unconscious level, the "wounds" the essays analyze (Moraga, lecture at the University of Washington, 1990).

Theater is a perfect medium for addressing the underlying concerns with identity as constructed and open-ended in Moraga's writing as a whole. Discussing the social protest theater of the 1960s and 1970s, Harry Elam relates the "inherently ephemeral" property of performance to current debates on identity:

Each performance is different. As performed identities, the characters and figures on stage must be constructed with each new performance before an audience and are not, therefore, fixed. Thus, even with their supposedly absolute racial politics, El Teatro [Campesino]'s and B[lack] R[evolutionary] T[heater]'s social protest performances of the 1960s and 1970s strategically constructed identities and used the "transformative power" of the theatrical event to advocate change. (14)

Besides providing access for a large audience different from the readers of books, the theater—in its construction of characters and its unique performative dimension in bringing roles to life—parallels and illuminates the constructed nature of race, gender, sexuality, and identity in general. This may be easier to perceive in performances that feature cross-dressing or cross-racial character construction, as in Anna Deavere Smith's work (*Fires in the Mirror*) or in Brechtian styles of acting in which actors cultivate a space between themselves and their character. But all forms of theater, with its contradictory movement between illusionary character and the actor's material body, possess the potential to undermine a fixed or absolute notion of the categories of identity.[6] Moraga's sensitivity to the *unfixity* of identity is valuable not because identity is thus rendered a field of play or subversion, but because it demonstrates that identity is constructed by relationships of power which may be answered and acted upon.

With the script of *Ghost,* Moraga gained entry to the INTAR Hispanic Playwrights-in-Residence Laboratory in New York City, directed by María Irene Fornés, a highly acclaimed Cuban-American playwright and director. Moraga attributes her ongoing fascination with the theater in part to Fornés' iconoclastic exercises that stressed the visualization of character rather than linear plot development. During her residency at INTAR in 1985, Moraga wrote the initial draft of her second play, *Shadow of a Man,* which premiered in 1990.

Since the premiere in 1992 of her third play, *Heroes and Saints,* published in her 1994 collection, Moraga has continued to concentrate her energies on the theater. She adapted the Quiché Maya creation myth in *Heart of the Earth: A Popol Vuh Story* for the 1994 International Festival of Puppet Theatre in New York (premiere at INTAR Theatre in January 1995). In its multilingual blend of English and Spanish (including Chicano and urban speech) and indigenous American tongues, *Heart of the Earth* evokes a pan-American identity. Other recent and ongoing theater projects feature innovative community involvement and activism. DramaDIVAS, a writing and performance workshop for lesbian/gay/bisexual young people of color at Brava! for Women in the Arts in San Francisco, provides job training in theater production to those seventeen and younger. *Circle in the Dirt: El Pueblo de East Palo Alto* (1995) was commissioned by Stanford's Committee for the Black Performing Arts as part of a collaborative project bridging the Stanford and East Palo Alto communities. It dramatizes the multiracial history of East Palo Alto, drawing extensively on the project's interviews with the people who live there.

Watsonville: Some Place Not Here received the Fund for New American Plays Award in 1995 (as did *Shadow* in 1991). It combines three cataclysmic events in the life of this small, Mexican American coastal town: the cannery workers' strike against Green Giant in the mid-1980s, the earthquake of 1989, and the appearance of the Virgin of Guadalupe on an oak tree in 1992. The play centers on the public voice of female leadership in labor and immigration issues—the picket lines, the streets, the speakers' circuits, the radio stations, and the bargaining table—and the crossing of the spiritual and the political in the miraculous shrine. As in *Circle in the Dirt,* the characters are composites of the women interviewed for the project, including *mexicana* and Chicana activists, community organizers, cannery workers, and "Guadalupanas" (devotees of the Virgin of Guadalupe) who maintain the tree shrine. Commissioned by Brava, *Watsonville* premiered in May 1996 at the New Brava Theater Center of San Francisco.

Moraga has also written a dramatic retelling of the myths of child-killers La Llorona and Medea, setting *The Hungry Woman: A Mexican Medea* in the aftermath of a U.S. equivalent of the ethnic wars of Eastern Europe. Medea's drama of motherhood plays out in a prison psychiatric ward in an arid border region between newly constituted racial territories to which queer *raza* have been banished. *Medea* was commissioned by Berkeley Repertory Theatre and had one staged reading there and another at the Mark Taper Forum's New Works Festival in Los Angeles in 1995.

The plays published in *Heroes and Saints and Other Plays* are like concentric circles that ripple outward from *Ghost*'s intense focus on Chicana subjectivity and sexuality, through the larger context of the Chicano family in *Shadow,* to the epic sweep of *Heroes'* representation of collective oppression and resistance. *Ghost* and *Shadow* put on stage the feminist project of the "personal is political": how women's daily experience *as women* is not just individual but part of a whole system of interactive oppressions. The third play in the trilogy, *Heroes,* marks a shift to the "political is personal": how environmental racism is experienced on the subjective level, including the sexual and the erotic. It was this shift, I believe, from the "personal is political" to the "political is personal" that facilitated the inclusion of *Heroes* within the 1992 TENAZ festival in San Antonio. Until that time, Moraga had seen only one of her plays produced by a Latino theater company.[7]

Shadow and *Heroes* seem more conventional in structure and form than Moraga's first play, *Ghost,* yet they also reveal the innovative nature of all of Moraga's writing for the theater, drawing on both Euro-American and Chicano/Mexican performance traditions. *Shadow*'s melodrama plays against its humor, intimacy, and fantasy, while *Heroes'* epic dimension leaves room for a series of emotional climaxes in the second act that bring the important personal relationships in the play to a head. Moraga's hybrid dramaturgy extends to her use of music: a multilayered mix of indigenous American, Mexican, and urban Chicano rock, Motown, Soul, and Tex-Mex.

Moraga's unique dramatic forms suit her project of bringing new possibilities to the experience of the theater. Through these forms—in the writing, staging, language, music, and blend of different genres—Moraga's playwriting changes our relationship to the theater by showing what it is like, from the perspective of Chicana and Chicano subjects, to feel trapped in gender roles or the family, or to experience environmental racism in the flesh. The trilogy lays bare the impact of these experiences on primary relationships, as well as the empowerment, both erotic and political, that lies in identification with a larger community.

In spite of the differences among the plays of the trilogy, they all share in the tension between the recuperation and the loss of self. Whether within an intimate relationship, the family, or the community, the characters of Moraga's plays strive for autonomy and self-definition but also desire dissolution of personal identity in something larger or other than the self. The loss of the individual self is also the fulfillment of desire (to be one with another), which is what these three plays are fundamentally about. The object of desire may range from the lover in an erotic encounter to the revolution itself, but the propelling force is the need to transform personal and cultural betrayal into more inclusive forms of community.

Writing out of a Chicana lesbian sensibility, Moraga offers a collective space where we can gather and share in these stories of the material realities of our communities. In this sense, Moraga's dramatic writing is both indispensable and far-reaching in its influence, opening up the experience of theater to a whole new group of people: actors, spectators, and critics alike. These three plays are a testimony to the possibilities of theater for exploring our identities and our differences while healing wounds and drawing people together to imagine new forms of communal life.

Giving Up the Ghost
Feminist Theory and the
Staging of Mestiza Desire

The late seventies and early eighties provide the social history for Moraga's first play, *Giving Up the
Ghost*. This was a time of considerable discussion
concerning the exclusionary politics of the white
women's movement, in the wake of *This Bridge
Called My Back*, co-edited by Moraga and Gloria
Anzaldúa. Critiques such as "The Costs of Exclusionary Practices in Women's Studies" (Zinn et al.)
of the racist and classist bias of much feminist theory
led many white feminists to acknowledge the important differences among women and the danger
of privileging the perspective of Western, bourgeois,
heterosexual white women.[1] At times, the challenge
to the white, privileged "woman's voice" of feminist theory was undertaken collaboratively by white
women and women of color.[2] Bell hooks, among
others, stressed the need to expand feminist movements to eliminate all forms of oppression in coalition with Third World men on the basis of shared
racial and class oppression.[3] Hooks' tendency to perpetuate the invisibility of lesbian women of color is
corrected by Gloria Joseph and Jill Lewis in *Com-*

mon Differences, Audre Lorde's important book *Sister Outsider*, and Cherríe Moraga's own essay, "A Long Line of Vendidas" (*Loving*).

The work of women of color who were engaged in the critique and elaboration of feminism operated on a variety of fronts. From a position of solidarity, they opened up dialogue within their communities on sexism and, especially in the case of lesbians, homophobia. While recognizing shared oppression with all women based on gender, they developed a feminist analysis stressing the differences among women and the dangers of theorizing from a privileged position, whether that privilege was based on race, class, or sexuality.

In this chapter I propose a contextualized reading of Moraga's play *Giving Up the Ghost*,[4] within the concerns articulated by feminists of color at the time it was published (1986), with special attention to Moraga's autobiographical essay "A Long Line of Vendidas" (1983). In my analysis of how *Ghost* disrupts both dominant and Chicano theatrical canons, I look at how Moraga's work engages and expands certain categories of white (lesbian) feminist theory as they intersect with the race, class, and cultural specificity of her project.

"A Long Line of Vendidas"

The textual community of "Vendidas" includes writing on interlocking oppressions by such feminist thinkers as Norma Alarcón, Gloria Anzaldúa, the Combahee River Collective, Adelaida del Castillo, Audre Lorde, and Mirtha Quintanales. Addressing "psycho-sexual" concerns from a materialist perspective, "Vendidas" draws on Lorde's "Uses of the Erotic: The Erotic As Power" to analyze the articulation of the sexual and the cultural, suggesting that the empowering potential of cultural constructs of sexuality and identity is in direct relationship to the damage they have inflicted (Lorde, 136–137).[5]

"Vendidas" does not idealize lesbian sexuality or practice a politically correct sexual style. It explores the "raggedy edges and oozing wounds" that haunt "colored female sexuality" (138), wounded by history: "each time I choose to touch another woman . . . I feel I risk opening up that secret, harbored, vulnerable place" (Moraga and Hollibaugh, "Rollin," 403). The power struggles in the intertwining realms of sexual pleasure and other social relationships play out in Moraga's psyche with a uniquely "Mexican twist" (*Loving*, 126): "Should she forget and not use what she knows sexually to untie the knot of her own desire, she may lose any chance of ever discovering her own sexual potential" (130).

In "Vendidas," Moraga analyzes her sense of self as sexual through the gender lens of the myth of La Malinche[6] in ways that resonate with *Ghost*. "Vendidas" critiques the narrative, crystallized in Octavio Paz's influential telling, of how Cortés' mistress, translator, and tactical advisor—Malintzín Tenepal, Doña Marina, "La Malinche"—made possible the defeat of a people and the destruction of their culture through sexual union with the "white" European conqueror. In "La Malinche," signifier of betrayal, the historical experience of colonization is spoken in the language of a racialized and gendered sexuality that produces the "half-breed" or mestizo race. La Malinche is "La vendida," (slang for "sell-out"), as well as "La chingada" (the fucked), constructing woman as soft, passive object, open to penetration. The active subject role is reserved for the *chingón* (*Loving*, 118–119).

For Norma Alarcón, Malinche's equation of woman with sexual slave, open at all times to use by men, is translated through its binary opposite of "La Virgen" into the equally enslaving values of love/devotion that reinforce woman's place of servitude and obedience in a hierarchical, heterosexual familial structure.[7] In this conflation of brown female sexuality with betrayal, Chicanas must "prove" their faithfulness by "putting the male first" in the family and the culture (*Loving*, 105). "Vendidas" examines how the gender polarity of *chingón/chingada* and the representation of femininity as virgin or whore infuse Chicanas' sexuality, especially that of Chicana lesbians. Moraga's writing suggests that these are the scenarios of a wounding but also a place of "passion expressed in our own cultural tongue" (*Loving*, 136).

In "Vendidas," Moraga recalls her first understanding of what it means to be Chicana as a sense of grievance and resentment stemming from the privileged treatment of males and the servitude of females within the family (90–91). The essay focuses on how the cultural mandate of "putting the males first" affects the relationship between Chicana mothers and daughters.[8] The mother is the first woman who betrays the daughter by loving the males in the family more than the females, setting a pattern for all future relationships with women and locking the daughter into a script of saving the mother *as heterosexual*. At the same time, Moraga sees this first experience of loving a Chicana (the mother) as the source of Chicana feminism and her lesbianism.

Moraga personalizes the concept of the essay's title, "Vendidas," in her specific racial, cultural, and sexual identities and histories:

My mother then is the modern-day Chicana, Malinche marrying a white man, my father, to produce the bastards my sister, my brother and I are. Finally, I—a half-breed Chicana—further betray my race by *choosing* my sexuality which excludes all men, and therefore most dangerously, Chicano men.

I come from a long line of Vendidas. (117)

Moraga conflates her mother's story with that of Malinche to dramatize the penalties exacted on women who marry outside the boundaries of the Chicano community. While Mexican identity is already a product of multiple racial crossings, Moraga adopts the term "half-breed" to refer to herself and her siblings in order to denote the racialization of Mexican ethnicity within the U.S. racial structure. The sword over Chicanas' heads has two edges: fear of being "sold out" by other women who put men first, and fear of being labeled a "sell-out" for questioning traditional gender roles and sexuality, for organizing desire independently, either heterosexual or lesbian.[9] Breaking the long line of *vendidas* means re-visioning the family structure:

> Family is *not* by definition the man in the dominant position over women and children. Familia is cross-generational bonding, deep emotional ties between opposite sexes, and within our sex. It is sexuality, which [. . .] springs forth from touch, constant and daily. (111)

The position the text outlines is not separatist, but woman-centered. Chicana feminism means putting women first, "making bold and political the love of the women of our race" (139). This can only be accomplished if Chicanas first learn to love themselves as female and mestiza (136). Finally, Chicana feminism as envisioned in "Vendidas" must include lesbians:

> To refuse to allow the Chicana lesbian the right to the free expression of her own sexuality, and her politicization of it, is in the deepest sense to deny one's self the right to the same [. . .] there will be no change [. . .] in heterosexual relations, as long as the Chicano community keeps us lesbians and gay men political prisoners among our own people. Any movement built on the fear and loathing of anyone is a failed movement. (139–140)

"Vendidas" creates that space of enunciation (Mercer, 204) for the voicing of desire in a political project by retelling the story of La Malinche so that it makes visible the presence of Chicana lesbians within the projects of Chicana/o liberation.

Giving Up the Ghost: An Alternative System of Representation

In *Giving Up the Ghost*, the radical critique articulated in "Vendidas" is translated into a theatrical language that de-centers dominant theater practices.

Ghost breaks with the dominant system of representation in ways that include but go beyond the racial/cultural and class composition of the subject and spectators of the drama. The play constructs a female subject, not merely replacing the male subject of traditional mimesis with a female one, but introducing new structures for its representation: the subject position is "shared" by the two characters Marisa and Amalia, and Marisa is "split" between her present self and her younger self (Corky). The play begins and ends with Marisa's solitary memories of Amalia. Although the lesbian subject, Marisa, appears onstage first and defines the other characters who will appear as her ghosts, she does not monopolize the subject position in the classical manner of the unitary, phallic "protagonist," but rather shares it with Amalia and Corky.

This multiple female subject invites spectators to conceive of Chicana identity as encompassing many different subjectivities and experiences. The simultaneous presence of Marisa and Corky on stage dramatizes the sexual self in process, rather than a unified identity, while Amalia's shifting object choice (men and women), her erotic positionality, and Marisa's motion between active and passive in their erotic encounters put into question the static categories of "lesbian" and "lesbian sex." Besides examining the mestiza subject, the following discussion of *Ghost* as alternative theatrical practice addresses the text's deconstruction of traditional gender representation on stage, the non-narrative form of the play, and audience reception.

Female Desiring Subjects

The multiple mestiza subject/s of *Ghost* carry out an action of desire, departing from dominant theater's heterosexist objectification of woman by representing sexual pleasure among women. Marisa's and Amalia's sexuality moves along a spectrum from lesbianism to heterosexuality, subject and object. The homoerotic desire of these mestiza subjects disrupts the relentless focus of Western theater on sexual difference represented as male/masculine and female/feminine within a universalizing heterosexual polarity. The staging of mestiza desire in a "lesbian" context forces the deconstruction of gendered identity as heterosexual and opens the door to imagining other forms and subjects/objects of desire.

The text is composed of poetic monologues, circling around desire and memory, whose only action is to trace their intricate itineraries. These memories of desire are the ghosts: Amalia and Corky for Marisa; her male lover, Alejandro, for Amalia. Marisa also feels the weight of "man," especially through

Amalia's memories. Exhuming these ghosts of desire is at once a liberating exorcism and a means of understanding their own sexuality. Through their memories, Marisa and Amalia explore the ways in which their cultural experience as Chicanas has shaped their sexuality, for better or for worse. Their monologues are most often directed to the audience, marking the isolation and separation of the women from each other. The rare times they interact on stage signal possible bridges. They tell different stories of their desire but feel "damaged" by the rigid assignment of gender roles. In this sense, *Ghost* carries to the stage the discussion in "Vendidas" of the definition of masculinity as the active *chingón* and of femininity as the passive *chingada*. Both Marisa and Amalia express in contradictory ways their struggle to overcome the cultural polarity of "man" and "woman" in the organization of their sexuality.

Corky's past experiences are the bars of Marisa's prison, which determine her sexual choices and limitations in the present of the dramatic world. Marisa's relationship with her past is brought out theatrically in the first scene of the play. When the lights come up slowly, Marisa is sitting back-to-back with Corky, who is not yet visible to the audience. After her first short speech defining the other characters who will appear as her ghosts, Marisa exits and Corky delivers her first monologue. The structural device of staging the split subject creates the distance between Marisa and her formative sexual experiences necessary for analysis and reflection.

Rejecting socialization in the passive gender roles assigned to her sex, Corky has few alternatives open to her. Feeling herself a free agent and rejecting the restrictions imposed on girls, she considers herself a "dude," packs a blade, and hangs out with the boy Tudy. In this role she indulges in the freedom of action (hopping backyard to backyard and down alleys) denied young girls. Her appropriation of the active role brings with it the associated attributes of the *chingón*, as she inscribes her erotic fantasies of women in contexts of violence and dominance. She is excited by the fights among men that erupt at social gatherings, especially by watching the women trying to pull the men apart:

always envy those batos[10] *who get all cut up at the weddings*
getting their rented tuxes all bloody
that red 'n' clean color against the white
starched collars   I love that shit!

the best part is the chicks
all climbing into the ball of the fight

Chuey déjalo! leave him go, Güero!
tú sabes   you know how the chicks get
all excited 'n' upset 'n' stuff
[. . .] their dresses ripped here 'n' there . . . like a movie (4)

By relating her excitement at these fights to the movies, the text calls attention to the powerful role of popular culture in producing and reproducing gender. Corky and her friend Tudy spend hours acting out fantasies derived from movies of capturing, binding, and stripping women. She identifies her own desire for freedom with the subjugating male who sees woman as "other": "kinda the way you see / an animal you know" (5). Yet she confesses that "deep down inside" she knew she was a girl, realizing that her toughness stems from the wound inflicted on her as other, as female: "I knew / always knew / I was an animal that kicked back / cuz it hurt" (6).

Corky is forced to confront the internal split between her identification with the *chingón* and her repressed self-knowledge as female. Her first confrontation with her female body is played out in a scenario of cultural difference. Corky interrupts the violation of a little white girl whom Tudy has selected to act out in reality what she calls their "sick little fantasies" of predatory domination (10–11). Unsettled by this experience ("after that I was like a maniac all summer" [12]), she rejects the little girl and her family on racial and cultural grounds, resenting their air of superiority. The cultural differences between the two families are incarnated in their different religions. At this point, Corky still finds solace in her culture, symbolized by her mother, who in turn is conflated with "being cath-lic": "'n' it was so nice to hear her voice / so warm like she loved us a lot / 'n' that night / being cath-lic felt like my mom / real warm 'n' dark 'n' kind" (13). Here Moraga again demonstrates the racialization of her desire, the association of darkness with the private, inviolate spaces of belonging and nurturance.

But Corky's feelings of pride, security, and comfort in her culture are undermined when her mother forces her to apologize to the white Protestant family following an altercation. Corky's humiliation is linked to her perception of her mother's capitulation in the face of the dominant culture's intolerance of their difference. This experience teaches her to cultivate a mask of resistance and restraint: "'n' as the door shuts in front of my face / I vow I'll never make a mistake like that again . . . / I'll never show anybody how mad I can get" (19). Corky's sense of the powerlessness of her sex, which led to her identification with the masculine gender role, is exacerbated by this experience of the subjugation and powerlessness of her race and culture as a whole vis-à-vis the dominant culture. The only space for her to be is in the tough stance of the *cholo*.

In a long, painful monologue, Corky describes how she was raped at school by a "Mexican" hired to work on the grounds.[11] Up to this point, Corky had allowed herself to believe it could never happen to her because she denied her femaleness. The rape brings the contradiction between her female body, which is vulnerable to penetration and violation, and her assumption of the gender role of penetrator and violator to an unbearable head, forcing her to confront her sex as an inescapable fact. She does what the man tells her, because, as she says, "I'm not useta fighting / what feels / like resignation / what feels / like the most natural thing in the world / to give in" (42).

Listening to Corky's moving story, Marisa comments bitterly: "He only convinced me of my own name" (43). Corky's experience of rape confirms for Marisa her culture's definition of female as "taken" (*chingada*). In order to widen her sexual choices, not to be limited to either "taker" or "taken," Marisa needs to "give up" this ghost without giving up Corky's fighting spirit. This spirit is expressed in the *cholo*/pachuco stance of rebelliousness toward the *mexicano* values of the older generation as well as resistance to assimilation and discrimination. Corky exhibits this self-styling in the "war zone" of the streets (36) and in her determination to show the world only the "¿Y qué?"[12] mask of indifference carefully placed over the cultural humiliation she experiences when her mother betrays her by forcing her to apologize to the white Protestant family.

Marisa pays for her unexpressed anger through the pain in her legs ("I'm fighting in my legs what I know" [7]). When Amalia calls her a little bird, Marisa comments sardonically, "that's me, the pajarita with legs like steel planks in my bed" (15). This anger, the primary obstacle to her liberating flight of release, is associated with her feelings that women have sexually betrayed her by loving men more: "I never wanted to be a man / I only wanted a woman to want me that bad. / [. . .] The women I have loved the most / have always loved the man more than me, / even in their hatred of them" (14–15). Defining her prison as her passion to compete with "the man" for women's love (8), Marisa is unable to believe that "a woman capable of loving a man / was capable of loving a woman / me" (22). Internalizing her hurt, she blames women and leaves relationship after relationship before she is moved to act on her anger (20). The two parts of the split subject Marisa/Corky interact on stage only twice, first to recite a litany of betrayals, the long line of *vendidas*: "(*CORKY approaches MARISA. THEY count off in unison*) My sister was in love with my brother. / My mother loved her father. / My first woman, the man who put her away" (16).

If Marisa's desire is defined by the poles of imprisonment and longing for liberation from the prison of sex, Amalia's is figured through images of listlessness and death. Amalia's desire has been stifled by her experience of sex with men who use her for their own pleasure (24), or to "dream" (48). She envisions the men who have exploited her sexually in this way as a river of dead bodies, and she herself is associated with images of drowning (26, 51). Amalia comments on her failure to become a wife and mother in line with the culture's definition of woman's role (14).

Amalia is older, uses more Spanish, and is more Mexican-identified than Marisa. Born in Mexico, she clings to the possibility of regeneration through cultural identification with Mexico, a possibility that leaves Marisa "unmoved" (21–22). In one scene she embraces Marisa, urging her to sing her roots and comparing her beauty to the twilight Mexican desert. On a trip to Mexico she "sees" Marisa in the face of a young Yaqui girl: "Same chata[13] face" (21). Amalia feels that if she and Marisa could have lived there in the desert, things would have been different between them. Yet when she dreams that she and Marisa are Indians in a Mexican village, the scenario takes on a nightmare configuration as it becomes clear that Marisa has broken a sacred taboo. Amalia does not fear punishment, only the knowledge that it "*could* be broken" (52). This contradictory connection with Mexico is what she loves in Alejandro, "not so much him / [. . .] I loved the part of México that was my home with him" (25). Returning to Mexico looking for a "cure" for the "American influence / that causes the blood to be sucked dry from you / so early" (49), Amalia hopes her memories will revive and avenge her:

like this ground that weeps
beneath these buildings
[. . .]
con memoria tan violente que
podría destruir todos de estos edificios.[14]
U.S. Embassy. Banco Serfin [. . .]
Nothing remains buried forever.
Not even memory.
Especially, not even memory. (46)

The Mexican desert is a feminized place which promises replenishment in the face of Amalia's alienation in the U.S. Here "Mexico" does not simply refer to nationhood or even ethnicity; rather, its identification with the generic "Indian" transforms Mexico into a mythic place of origins, authenticity, wholeness.

The inclusion of a desiring female subject such as Amalia in *Ghost* echoes the concern for a broad continuum of Chicana feminism expressed in "Vendidas":

We must be the ones to define the parameters of what it means to be female and mestiza.

A political commitment to women does not equate with lesbianism. As a Chicana lesbian, I write of the connection my own feminism has had with my sexual desire for women. This is my own story. I can tell no other one than the one I understand. I eagerly await the writings by heterosexual Chicana feminists that can speak of their sexual desire for men and the ways in which their feminism informs that desire. (*Loving*, 139)

Ghost shows how the sexuality of both Amalia and Marisa/Corky emerges from this same cultural source. Amalia's sexual relationship with Marisa demonstrates her freedom to express her sexuality and choose her sexual partners as she sees fit. To the extent that she organizes her desire independently, Amalia too is defined as "queer" and "outsider." "Vendidas" posits the Chicana lesbian as "the most visible manifestation of a woman taking control of her own sexual identity and destiny" (112). But any Chicana

who defies her role as subservient to her husband, father, brother or son [. . .] is purported to be a "traitor to her race" by contributing to the "genocide" of her people [. . .] In short, even if the defiant woman is *not* a lesbian, she is purported to be one; for, like the lesbian in the Chicano imagination, she is una *Malinchista*. (*Loving*, 113)

The play is ultimately about Chicanas' "right to passion" (*Loving*, 136), the freedom to feel and act according to the dictates of their own desire. Paradoxically, it is the characters' failure in this undertaking that opens the doors to the possibilities beyond the moment of the performance. The realization of shared oppression that reaches into the most intimate precincts of desire and pleasure holds the promise of community.

Amalia's position in the text as both "feminine" and "active," especially in her desire for Marisa, is key to the possibility that Marisa and Amalia can give up their ghosts. Both struggle to define their sexuality against the gender polarity of "man" as hard, active, and closed, and "woman" as soft, passive, and open. At one point Marisa declares: "It's odd being queer. / It's not that you don't want a man, / you just don't want a man in a man. / You want a man in a woman" (29). Marisa also says she sees a man in the feminine Amalia (39). In the sexual relationship between Amalia and Alejandro, the borders between masculinity and femininity are also blurred. When Amalia learns of Alejandro's death, she says, "I just started bleeding and the blood wouldn't stop, / not until his ghost had passed through me / or was born in me / I don't know which" (27). She feels her "womanhood" leave her and Alejandro being born in her; it is in his voice that she expresses her desire for Marisa (28). The textual ambiguity on this point is similar to Marisa's simultaneous distancing and affirmation of Corky, who represents the "origins" of her hard, closed self. Amalia needs to "give up" the negative resonances of "man" in the practice of her sexuality.

Marisa's and Amalia's words in these sexual scenarios, problematic for many readers and spectators who identify themselves as either lesbian or heterosexual, become clearer by teasing apart the intricate relationship between the gender roles they contend with and how they identify and relate erotically. The play captures the erotic exchanges of the two characters within and against "woman" as passive object of male desire and "man" as active subject of desire. Amalia's ability to feel alive again has less to do with the gender of her object choice than with her move from passive sex object to active subject of her desire, while the "man" Marisa wants in a woman is this active female desire for a woman (for her) that she both needs and fears.[15]

Ghost's subversive appropriation of sexual pleasure and erotic positions from heterosexual gender roles resonates with "Vendida"'s empowering statement that Chicanas must "untie the knot of their own desire" in the context of their cultural identity. The second of the two interactions between Marisa and Corky onstage occurs when Corky relives an erotic memory of their mother and father:

kinda like she's sorta hassled 'n' being poquita fría [16]
tú sabes [17] *but she's really digging my dad to no end*
[. . .] he grabs her
between her step 'n' slides his hand up the inside of her thigh (29)

After recounting this memory of desire, "CORKY *throws chin out to MARISA bato-style. MARISA, amused, returns it*" (30). *Ghost*'s representations of Chicano/*mexicano* culture as the source of erotic power and identification anticipate the in-depth exploration of the family as "the place where / for better or worse / we first learn to love" in her second play *Shadow of a Man* (*Heroes and Saints and Other Plays*, 39).

Gender Deconstruction

In the dominant system of representation, women are assigned certain attributes in conformity with the gender of woman, most often as the object of male desire. Certain practices in feminist theater attempt to deconstruct this image of woman, for example, cross-gender casting or drag roles which call attention to the social construction of gender. If all women are implicated in this gender construction process, lesbians have a special stake in the deconstruction and transforming of the theater's representation of gender. For Jill Dolan, "lesbians, in particular, have to debunk the myth that woman even exists, to reveal instead that she has been created to serve a particular ideological order" (10). And in her article "The Actor as Activator," Sande Zeig asserts:

If we as lesbians are fighting oppression, we cannot reproduce the gestures assigned to the class of women, because [they] are the gestures of slaves. To reproduce these gestures in life or on stage is to support and maintain the institution of oppression. (13)

Following Wittig's idea that there is actually only one gender, the feminine, since the masculine is constructed less as "the masculine" than as "the general" (64), Zeig concludes:

So when we as lesbians are accused of looking (in fact, moving) like men, we object. We consciously refuse to give the class of men a monopoly over gestures. Lesbians are reappropriating the gestures that do not carry the stamp of oppression. (15)

Corky and Marisa do not conform to the visual image of "woman" onstage. Their appearance and body language break with theatrical conventions that sexualize women onstage for heterosexual men. They do not "look like men," but do appropriate "the general" (not-woman) in their aspect, gestures, and movements. This is particularly clear in the young Corky, who makes the gestural language of the tough *cholo* her own. She is described as

"una chaparrita"[18] *who acts tough, but has a wide open sincerity in her face which betrays the toughness. She dresses in the "cholo style" of her period (the '60s): khakis*

with razor-sharp creases; pressed white undershirt; hair short and slicked back.
(*Ghost*, 1)

Marisa "*wears her toughness less self-consciously, a little closer to the bone. The sincerity is more guarded. She appears in levis, tennis shoes, and a dark shirt. Her hair is short.*"

Amalia's image and gestures seem to reproduce those "assigned to the class of women." She is described as

"soft" in just the ways that MARISA is "hard." Her clothes give the impression of being draped, as opposed to worn. Shawl-over-blouse-over-skirt—all of Mexican Indian design. Her hair is long and worn down or loosely braided. There is nothing frivolous about this woman. (1)

But Amalia's visual image, which seems to provide an object for the "male gaze," is subjected to a dual process of subversion in that she is the subject of her own desire and the object of a racialized lesbian desire. Her desire for Marisa reorients femininity to the (butch) lesbian's gaze. Amalia's actions on stage relate her visually to Marisa; for example, when she approaches Marisa from behind and embraces her. In Marisa's memory, Amalia's femininity and active role combine: she is all "slips and lace and stockings / and yet it is *she* who's taking *me*" (30). Amalia's racialization speaks to Moraga's strategy for recuperating the mestiza as desiring, rather than passive subject. However, Moraga's *indigenismo*, her generic references to the "Mexican Indian," run the risk of reifying the very subject she seeks to recuperate, as Indianness functions as an affective category, rather than as a historically, materially situated social location. Rather than correct the appropriation of the indigenous within Mexican cultural nationalism, Moraga paradoxically retains the binary of the *chingón/chingada* in its construction of the feminized native subject as outside history.

Non-Narrative Form and the Possibility of Resolution

Feminist critics have examined the complicity of narrative in the representation of "woman." According to Teresa De Lauretis, the Western quest narrative excludes women from the subject position and subordinates them as an object to be attained, an obstacle to be removed, or a space to be conquered by the active male subject (*Alice Doesn't*, 121). Elin Diamond builds on recent theoretical connections between history and the beginning, middle, and end of narrative form in her exploration of the devices employed by women playwrights to disrupt the subordination of women by the "historicizing narrative" (276).

The dominance of narrative form in Chicano theater has buttressed the male subject and imposed an "order of meaning" on history conceived from a male perspective. Chicano cultural nationalism has alternately cast the mythic origins of *mestizaje*, the dominant metaphor of ethnic affiliation and belonging, in the heroic mode, as derived from José Vasconcelos' *La raza cósmica* (The Cosmic Race), or in the tragic mode iterated in Octavio Paz' *El laberinto de la soledad* (The Labyrinth of Solitude). Both narratives retain a biologistic notion of race, and cast women in a servile role of bringing the new mestizo subject into history. Plays plotting the beginning, middle, and end of Preconquest-Conquest-Mestizo reality inscribe, in theatrical forms, the myth of "La Malinche," responsible for the defeat of pre-Columbian peoples and their "fall" into history. Many Chicanas working in theater have used the non-narrative form of *teatropoesía* to interrupt the monopoly of the male as agent of history, although at times they have maintained the same historicizing narrative.[19]

Ghost rejects a historicizing narrative that would provide any order of meaning for the events onstage with a clear beginning, middle, and end. "The" story is replaced by many stories that coexist and at times conflict with each other. Forsaking the inexorable linear movement toward resolution that supports the representation of the unitary male protagonist, Moraga leaves the contradictions and conflicts of the three characters' monologues unresolved. Cutting across each other in time, the monologues impose no chronological ordering of the memories they articulate. They arise as memories arise, through association. At times, these memories are disembodied voices from the dark, voices of desire and repentance. The effect is a multilayered mosaic of desire, remembered and partially recuperated from the restraints of repression. The beginning-middle-end structure of narrative is retained in some of the individual stories but is subverted by the zigzag relationship among the monologues that negates chronology. This technique creates a collage-like field of subjectivity akin to memory, across which various aspects of female desire are expressed. The rupture of linear development supports the sense that the conflicts and contradictions surrounding Chicana sexuality are not easily resolved.

However, as De Lauretis has pointed out, "all images are implicated with narrativity whether they appear in a narrative, non-narrative, or anti-narrative film," due to the hegemony of narrativity as a cultural mode ("Oedipus Interruptus," 36). Keir Elam has also commented on the spectator's tendency to narrativize the "present" events of the dramatic action, reinscribing the coercive structure of narrative in a search for origins, *telos*, and causal relationships between the events (120). While it seems that no dramatic representation can completely escape being narrativized by the spectator, *Ghost* makes this process explicit. The juxtaposition of past (Corky) and present (Marisa) encourages the spectator to understand how Marisa's identity as desiring subject in the present is the result of specific historical and cultural experiences.

While the play offers the vision of liberation through mestizas' love for each other (including sexual love), the structure of the play does not move us neatly from pain to promise. At the end of the play, Marisa is still massaging her anger and her rock-hard legs. At the end, there are only memories, memories that wound but also sustain. The memory of a woman who loved her informs Marisa's redefinition of "familia" in a way that captures the unresolved contradictions involved in deeply ingrained gender and sexual constructions. Marisa still finds hope in a community of women: "It's like making familia from scratch / each time all over again . . . with strangers / if I must. / If I must, I will" (58). This promise of community, of Chicana feminism based on the love of mestizas for themselves and one another, is enunciated at the same moment that Marisa prepares herself for a future that may be worse than the present (58). The possibility is only a possibility, one beleaguered on many fronts, and ultimately not realized in the play.[20] Perhaps one reason for the lack of resolution is that *Ghost* does not produce an account of *mestizaje*, and thus mestiza identity, apart from the indigenist narratives of cultural nationalism. The reification of the indigenous expressed in Moraga's references to shawls of "Mexican Indian design" points to the contradictions arising in articulating the liberatory force of racialized desire. How does the brown woman of Moraga's writing signify as an emancipatory agent?

Spectator Position/Audience Reception

The dominant system of representation posits an "ideal" spectator whose gender, race/ethnicity, and class align him or her in relation to the male subject of the drama, facilitating empathy and catharsis. That this ideal spectator position is far from being "universal" is revealed by a change in any one or all of the categories of spectatorship. The African American man or the working-class white man receives the representation of the white male privileged subject of the drama in a way that foregrounds the different racial or class identities of subject and spectator. In other words, the occupation of the "ideal" spectator position is accomplished by assuming the white privileged perspective.

Feminist criticism, especially psycho-semiotic film criticism, has concentrated on the concept of the spectator as a gendered subject to analyze systems of representation with female spectators in mind. Female spectators simultaneously identify with the woman-as-object (usually of male desire), adopting a passive position, and with the male subject of the action. Laura Mulvey refers to the latter as the "masculinisation" of the spectator position:

As desire is given cultural materiality in a text, for women (from childhood onwards) trans-sex identification is a *habit* that very easily becomes *second Nature*. However, this Nature does not sit easily and shifts restlessly in its transvestite clothes.[21]

This dis-ease is augmented if the female spectator is not of the dominant class, sexuality, race/ethnicity, or culture. While male spectators of color may have to don the white privileged man's "clothes" to occupy this position, they are still men's clothes.

Ghost inverts the dominant hierarchy of spectator position by privileging the individual least likely to encounter her representation on the stage: the lesbian Chicana. The text offers multiple female spectator positions in which race, class, and culture remain the same but sexuality shifts. As was the case with the construction of the subject, *Ghost* alters the structures of identification of dominant theater: these are uncomfortable positions, due to the sexual component of Amalia's relationship with Marisa and Marisa's own non-idealized lesbian sexuality. Empathy and catharsis are further deferred by *Ghost's* non-narrative structure, which obliges even the ideal spectator to participate actively in the construction of her particular narrative.

Most of the monologues are directed not to the other characters but to the audience, which is included as "The People" in the cast of characters, a direct reference to the spectators' active participation in the construction of a narrative, or many narratives, from the possibilities sketched onstage. But the task of sorting out the "story" of Chicana sexuality is only part of the co-production of meaning engaged in by the audience. The performance participates in the process of building communities while stressing internal differences. The staging of identity and sexuality as fluid, contradictory, and multiple offers different audiences (Chicana/o, feminist, gay/lesbian) different points of entry.

The participation of "The People" in the co-production of the play's meaning is affected by what Annette Kuhn calls the "social audience," in distinction to the individual subject/spectator (23). The notion of "social audience" brings into play social, gender, cultural, and economic factors that also determine the reception of the text, shifting the emphasis from the individual, gendered spectator of a particular race, culture, and class to an audience composed of people who share one or more of those characteristics. *Ghost* has played before a variety of social audiences. In 1984, a white feminist theater group based in Minneapolis called At the Foot of the Mountain performed the play as a staged reading. It was also produced by the lesbian Front Room Theater in Seattle in March 1987. Both At the Foot of the Mountain and Front Room are predominantly white companies presenting the work of women of color, a relationship born out of necessity, given the absence of economically viable venues for theater run by women of color. When "The People" to whom Corky, Marisa, and Amalia address their monologues are all women, the possibility of women's community hinted at in the play is reinforced by the interaction among women of different racial, cultural, and socioeconomic backgrounds in the audience. These productions of *Ghost* seek to form alliances among women across class, race, and culture, drawing women of color to see the play and exposing the theater company's usual constituency to the differences among women.

Moraga has also staged readings of *Ghost* for Chicano audiences made up of both men and women. In this context, the text opens up intracultural dialogue on the topics of gender and sexuality. Enacting theatrically the prescription for Chicana feminism suggested in "Vendidas," *Ghost* puts women first, excluding men from the stage and representing mestizas as desiring subjects. In the Chicano context, this involves a critique of entrenched cultural practices that are damaging for women, while the representation of lesbian desire counters the invisibility of Chicana lesbians in the community.

The subject matter of *Ghost* is introduced as "political" in the dedication to act 1: "the question of prisons / politics / sex" (1). The play is political not just for *what* it chooses to represent, but *how* it chooses to represent it, as well as for the reception of that representation by specific and diverse social audiences. The play literally stages the radical concerns expressed by lesbians of color and other women of color involved in the production of a feminism that addresses the interlocking systems of racial, sexual, heterosexist, and class oppression.

Shadow of a Man
Touching the Wound in Order to Heal

Moraga's second play, *Shadow of a Man*, premiered in November 1990 at San Francisco's Eureka Theater and was co-produced by Brava! for Women in the Arts.[1] This unusual production, generated almost solely by women, brought together Brava and two Latinas from different generations, Moraga and director Irene Fornés, who also designed the set. *Shadow* is dedicated to "las Chicanas, that we may come downstage center and speak for ourselves" (Moraga, "Who's Who," 6). My interest here lies in how *Shadow* stages this "speaking for ourselves" *inside* the concept of "Chicano" rather than in opposition to the dominant culture. In Chicano theater history, plays like *Shadow* signaled the "end of the innocent notion" (Hall, "New Ethnicities," 443) of a unified Chicano identity. The action of the play turns around a family's secrets of sexuality and desire, represented through a high-powered melodramatic form; expressive, memorable bilingual characters; and an intense emotional register also capable of lyrical interiority. *Shadow* brings a new politics of representation to the tradition of family drama in Chicano theater (e.g., El Teatro de la Esperanza, *Los Hijos: Once a Family*; Luis Valdez, *The Shrunken Head of Pancho Villa*), displaying a range of subjects, experiences, and identities that represent "Chicano" in the public space of the theater.

The 1980s saw certain conceptions of masculinity and femininity put into question in an attempt to relate issues of gender and sexuality to race and ethnicity. Writers like Moraga, Anzaldúa, and other contributors to *This Bridge Called My Back* theorized multiple subjectivity and refused to choose among aspects of their identity to "belong" in any one community, thus challenging the unifying concept of certain cultural nationalist strands of 1960s social movements.[2]

Moraga's remarks at the OutWrite '91: National Lesbian and Gay Writers Conference in San Francisco illustrated this new location of difference "inside the notion of ethnicity itself" (Hall, "New Ethnicities," 447), concentrating on the potential coalition among Chicana lesbians and Chicano gay men. Anticipating the notion of "Queer Aztlán" elaborated in an essay with that title in *The Last Generation* (1993), Moraga revisited some of the tenets of Chicano nationalism in her speech, such as the connection with the indigenous and the land, to envision new political subjects and a new movement crossing Chicano nationalism with Queer Nation.[3] The interrogation of "nation" as a possible space of nonhierarchical heterogeneity places the family under scrutiny, as well as the misogyny and male privilege of Chicano gay men. In a "queered" notion of extended family/nation, lesbians and gays could play a special role as "two-spirited" people.[4]

In the field of Chicana/o cultural production, gay men have recently begun creating a public voice and presence. Their perspective enriches the cultural project of addressing the material conditions of psychosexual experience, adding to the analysis of mestiza/o desire a series of reflections on men's love for brown men and the racialization of their desire. As Leo Bersani asserts, "sexual desire for men can't be merely a culturally neutral attraction to a Platonic Idea of the male body; the object of that desire necessarily includes a socially determined and socially pervasive definition of what it means to be a man" (208–209). Writing the kind of "familia" that embraces both men and women without privileging one over the other depends on an interrogation of this social construct of "man."[5]

Building a "familia" which operates simultaneously as the private space of personal relations and as a basis for membership in the public sphere entails a compassionate yet unflinching analysis, as in *Shadow*'s exploration of the destructive privileging of "man" in the bosom of the unreconstructed family. The epigraph of *Shadow* states:

Family is the place where
for better or worse
we first learn to love.[6]

The play represents, with particular insight, the fate of the two Rodríguez daughters, Leticia and Lupe, still in the process of being shaped by these family dynamics.[7]

The exclusive focus on the lives of the members of a working-class Chicano family de-centered, and at times disconcerted, non-Latino spectators. The bilingual voice of the play was a source of particular discomfort for some. Certain white critics criticized the bilingual dialogue as a "drawback" (Wright) or referred to the play's "frequent excursions into Spanish" (Winn). The interviewer in the *Open Window* program (a November 6, 1990, televised program out of the University of California, Berkeley) mentioned the "novelty" of the script's mixing of Spanish and English (a novelty with a twenty-five-year history in Chicano theater). In the program of the Eureka/Brava production Moraga writes: "The blending of Spanish and English found in this work is very common among first-generation Chicanos/Latinos and those living in the barrios of the U.S. This is the 'natural voice' of the play and its characters" (5). Writers such as Moraga and Anzaldúa claim Chicano language as a legitimate medium for discursive self-production as mestizas, who are constituted by racial, cultural, and linguistic hybridity. As Minh-ha Trinh comments, "woman as subject can only redefine while being defined by language" (44).

Shadow is equally challenging to some Latino spectators because of its treatment of gender roles and sexuality. While her language draws on important Chicano *teatro* traditions, Moraga is critical of its silences.[8] *Shadow* carries the intimate family dynamics of gender to the stage from a perspective of solidarity with the earlier theater:

Traditionally, Chicano theater has not dealt with the condition of our families [. . .] It tends to romanticize "la familia." I feel we need to kind of touch the wounds a little bit, look at the sore spots in us.[9]

Theater provides a public medium for aggravating the wounds to effect a cleaner healing. It can also help bridge the gap between the educated class of Chicanas/os and working-class people who do not usually go to the Eureka

Theater, and who have to be brought in by assertive outreach. *Shadow* speaks across borders *within* "Chicano" about the poetry and the complexity of working-class Chicano lives. Its blend of fantasy and realism and especially its melodramatic form play off spectators' familiarity with popular televisual genres such as the *telenovela*.[10]

Shadow, set in Los Angeles in the late 1960s, tells the story of the members of the Rodríguez family: Manuel, the father, in his early fifties; Hortensia, the mother, in her mid-forties; Rosario, Hortensia's sister, in her mid-fifties; and the two daughters, seventeen-year-old Leticia and twelve-year-old Lupe. A son, Rigo, is referred to by the other characters but does not appear onstage. Moraga's previous writing focuses on Chicana negotiations of their culture's privileging of males; *Shadow* similarly explores the harmful impact of machismo on Chicano men. The playwright states that *Shadow* was born out of a

fascination with how Latino men value each other so much. There's a certain way in which, in the face of that, women are sort of like functionaries, objects in the dealings of men's relationships with themselves. (Lovato, 24)

The title's "shadow of a man" functions on multiple levels of the text in relationship to both male and female characters. Through the characters and their interactions, the play demonstrates how Chicana/o sexual and gender identity is constructed through the male ideal in the context of the family.

In the case of the father, Manuel, "shadow" refers to the particular concept of masculinity that orders his self-perception. From the beginning of the play, Manuel appears to be eaten away by some private misery. He is merely a "shadow of a man" plagued by heart trouble and alcoholic absenteeism at work. Alternately abusive to and dependent on his family, he is emotionally and sexually shut down to his wife. Gradually, it is revealed that Manuel is heavily invested in his relationship with his *compadre*[11] Conrado. When Conrado's departure from Los Angeles was imminent some thirteen years before, Manuel gave up his place in Hortensia's bed for one night to Conrado.

While this bonding of two male subjects through the body of a woman may seem like a classic example of male traffic in women, it backfires for Manuel when he is consumed by jealousy of Hortensia, who has come closer to Conrado than he ever can. He becomes obsessed by his sense of failure to live up to the masculine ideal that Conrado embodies. He wants to be Conrado at the same time that he desires him; both are impossible scenarios. In this sense he lives in Conrado's "shadow" and is eventually destroyed by a construct of masculinity that holds out the promise of wholeness in the love between men yet has not yielded that wholeness (Noyes, "Desintegration," 27). The twist that Manuel's love for Conrado gives to the standard erotic triangle prompts Fornés to say: "all family plays, of course, are different, yet this play, to me, makes all other family plays seem the same" (cited by Barber, 1).

The Rodríguez family has lived with this secret for thirteen years. For Manuel, that night is both proof of his lack of manhood and emblem of his loss of Conrado, who left L.A. after all; for Hortensia, it is a constant source of shame and guilt. For both, Lupe serves as a constant reminder, since she takes after her biological father Conrado. Manuel has developed a special attachment to Lupita, not so much for any qualities of her own but because she is all of Conrado he has left. The catalyst that brings this situation to a head is the son Rigo's decision to marry "out." The fact that Rigo never appears on stage communicates his abandonment of home, class, and culture. The play's action opens a few days before Rigo's wedding and traces its aftermath through the following months.

The first time the audience sees Manuel, he comes home drunk and mourns the loss of his son, including Rigo's rejection of Mexican-marked displays of affection between men in his process of assimilation (49). Hortensia tells her sister Rosario how Rigo pushed Manuel away when he tried to give him a welcome-home embrace, preferring to shake hands (45).[12] But Manuel also grieves for another kind of loss—that is, his need to see himself reflected in a brown man's eyes:

You usetu sit and converse with me. Your eyes were so black, I forgot myself in there sometimes. I watched the little fold of indio skin above your eyes, and felt those eyes hold me to the ground. They saw. I know they saw lo que sabía mi compadre, that I am a weak man, but they did not judge me. Why do you judge me now, hijo? How does the eye turn like that so suddenly? (49)[13]

This passage connects Rigo's wedding, which stands for his rejection of the family, and the final festering of the wound inflicted by Conrado's departure. Manuel's comment about Rigo's gaze anchoring him to the ground, to his identity as a man, echoes in a later monologue remembering Conrado:

I look across the table and my compadre's there y me siento bien. All I gotta do is sit in my own skin in that chair. (*Pause.*) But he was leaving. I could smell it coming. I tried to make him stay. How did I let myself disappear like that? I became nothing, a ghost. I asked him, "Do you want her, compa?" And he said, "Yes." So, I told him, "What's mine is yours, compadre. Take her." (*Pause.*) I floated into the room with him. In my mind, I was him. And then, I was her too. In my mind, I imagined their pleasure, and I turned into nothing. (71)

Only when he could see himself reflected in the mirror that is Conrado could Manuel feel content to be "in his own skin." The phrase "And then, I was her, too" is the closest Manuel can come to admitting not only his desire to be his friend but also his homoerotic desire for Conrado. (Interestingly, Moraga stages this desire with the same indigenist script of her Chicana lesbian characters, presaging her conception of a queer Aztlán in *The Last Generation.*) Given the construction of masculinity under which he labors, Manuel's desire can only spell the dissolution of his identity as a man, just as the absence of a male figure onto which he can project his fantasies of the masculine ideal forces him to confront his own failure to live up to that ideal ("I am a weak man"). Manuel fantasizes about Conrado's fulfillment of the "American success story," building swimming pools in Phoenix (55, 69), and summons adolescent memories of male pleasure untainted by failure: "Sometimes, you know, you want to be a boy like that again. The rain was better then, it cleaned something" (55).

After the wedding, Manuel deteriorates rapidly, talking of nothing but Conrado and withdrawing further from Hortensia, his heart "closed" as a fist (63). In an attempt to return to the past, Manuel asks Conrado to come back. For Hortensia, this action is the equivalent of opening old wounds, an activity in which she refuses to participate. But for Manuel, Conrado's return clearly spells the opportunity to relive the past relationship, free of Hortensia's mediating role. Just as he blamed his son's desertion on Rigo's future wife, he now places the burden of his loss of Conrado squarely on Hortensia's shoulders. The night Manuel goes out to meet his *compadre,* he dresses like Conrado in a dark suit and hat (except that the crease refuses to stay in his pants). Just before he exits, he *"dips his hat slightly over one eye and runs his fingers over the rim of it. He imagines himself a different man, in Conrado's image"* (75).

But witnessing the old attraction between Conrado and Hortensia intensifies Manuel's self-imposed isolation as he relives the consequences of that night thirteen years ago:

She walked around the house like she was something special, like she (*He grabs CONRADO by the balls.*) got a piece of you. You know what that feels like? To have your own wife hold something inside her que no es tuyo? She made me feel like I was nothing. (*Pause.*) I loved you, man. I gave you hasta mi propia mujer [. . .] What does that make me? (81)

By objectifying Conrado in the image of the masculine ideal (clearly it is *Manuel* who wanted a piece of him), Manuel has written himself out of his own script ("How did I let myself disappear like that?"). Hortensia refuses to carry the blame for what happened, reminding Manuel that it was what he wanted. After she sends Conrado away and makes one last futile attempt to reach out to Manuel, he orchestrates his own death with a combination of pills and tequila. His final words are: "She took from me everything I ever loved" (81).

This is a play about desire within the heterosexualized institution of the family, although the take on it is clearly not a conventional one. Moraga's first play, *Giving Up the Ghost*, undertook the project of understanding lesbian desire by looking at heterosexuality—specifically, how the imposition of binary gender oppositions ("man"/"woman," "taker"/"taken") informs mestiza sexuality. At issue in *Shadow* is not whether Manuel is gay; instead, the audience is invited to consider desire along a continuum and to explore the intersections between homosociality (social relations among men) and homosexuality. Cultures that teach men that they are more valuable than women and that they should reserve their deepest love for men create the conditions in which they prefer one another to women. Luce Irigaray answers her own question: "Why is masculine homosexuality considered exceptional . . . when in fact the economy as a whole is based upon it?" (192):

Because they [masculine homosexual relations] *openly interpret the law according to which society* operates. . . . Furthermore, they might lower the sublime value of the standard, the yardstick. Once the penis itself becomes merely a means to pleasure, pleasure among men, *the phallus loses its power.* (193)

The same cultures that promote male homosocial relations through the exchange of women prohibit homosexuality or even homosocial desire that is not mediated through the body of a woman.

The cultural dynamic that destroys Manuel has different consequences for the women in the family. They live in the shadow of Manuel's failure, drunkenness, and violence, and eventually his self-annihilation; they live in the shadow of the absent Conrado, who nevertheless continues to affect their lives; and they live in the far-reaching shadow of the "man" as construct, which teaches them their own non-value. But they are also witnesses and survivors, deriving strength and support from one another. Some of the best writing in *Shadow* is in the ensemble scenes among the girls and women in the feminine spaces of kitchen and bedroom: discussing the *telenovela* (act 1, scene 2), looking at pictures after the wedding (act 1, scene 4), or exchanging fantasies and confidences (act 2, scene 1). Yet the conditioning that teaches men's superiority has repercussions for their ability to love themselves and one another. *Shadow* gives another dramatic form to the thematic cluster in Moraga's writing that addresses the myriad betrayals of self and other women that stem from women's internalization of this belief. In *Ghost*, Marisa says:

What *is* betrayal?
Let me tell you about it, it is not clean, nothing neat.
It's about a battle I will never win and never stop fighting.
The dick beats me every time. (7–8)

On one level this passage refers to Marisa's fear that the woman she is involved with will leave her for a man or the "ghost" of a man (the memory of Amalia's dead male lover or even patriarchy's prohibition of women loving women). On another level, Marisa betrays herself. As a lover of women, she wants to heal their wounds but cannot heal them in herself. As in "Vendidas" and *Ghost*, *Shadow* explores the paradigm in which mothers teach their daughters, first, that they are not as valuable as men, and second, that they are only valuable if they have a man. This primary betrayal sets off the "long line" of betrayals among both heterosexual women and lesbians who do not value one another or themselves. *Shadow*'s focus on betrayal among women prevents the female characters from appearing as victims of machismo. They are constructed as both complicitous and resistant in the construction of gender roles.

In spite of Hortensia's own experience of Manuel's alienation due to his over-investment in a *machista* ideal, she reproduces values and attitudes within her family that subordinate women. When Lupe gets her period, Hortensia instructs her in the modification of her behavior in lines that recall Corky's rejection of this socialization: "No, ya no eres baby.[14] You gotta behave a little difernt now, mija. Tú sabes, . . . con más vergüenza.[15] You can't go jumping around all over the place con los chavos[16] like before" (*Shadow*, 67). Hortensia's perpetuation of the double standard creates conflict between herself and her elder daughter, Leticia, since for Hortensia only a man can have the freedom that Leticia craves: "If God had wanted you to be a man, he would of given you something between your legs" (76–77). Leticia rejects this definition of woman as "lack" when she asserts, "I have something between my legs" (77).

Hortensia's phallocentric view is best dramatized in her proud display of her baby grandson's penis for her daughters to adore: "A sleeping mountain, with a little worm of life in it. Una joya" (61).[17] In this scene, Hortensia teaches her daughters, in an act of fundamental betrayal, that women's only access to value and power (the phallus, in her eyes) is bestowed through a man, or through the birth of a male child. When Leticia comments that maybe she won't have children, Hortensia responds, "Then you should of been born a man" (61), defining "woman" exclusively in terms of her reproductive function. Frustrated in her relationship with Manuel, which fails to give her what she wants (fulfilled desire, value), Hortensia looks to her son, Rigo, to give her the kind of power or prestige her daughters never could, but he abandons the family. She then attempts to hand down this lesson to her daughters in the scene with the baby described above.[18] It is too early to know its effect on Lupe, but Leticia at this point resists the message that only the penis confers value, at the same time as she recognizes her place in the world as female and powerless.

Responding to criticism that her work is male-identified because it gives the penis so much attention, Moraga has stated that she is merely calling power by its name. The "dick" in her writing does not represent biological superiority but the symbol of masculine power; for women to write their female bodies as sites of power it is necessary to break down the violence perpetrated in the name of the phallus. At the OutWrite '91 conference, Chicano poet Ronnie Burk commented on the slogan brandished on placards during protests against the Gulf War: "The war is a dick thing." Similarly, the "dick" referred to by Marisa in *Ghost*, and Hortensia's penis adoration in *Shadow*, are crucial components of the construct of "man" that must be changed.

Given the importance awarded the "son," Hortensia's verbal and emotional response to Rigo's class and cultural rejection seems muted. She is unwilling to connect with the depth of her loss, and instead of criticizing Rigo for his defection, she first blames his *gringa* wife-to-be (45–46), then Manuel, who has no trouble identifying the reason for Rigo's departure from the house: "Because he's a gabachero!" (50).[19] Hortensia says Rigo left out of shame for what Manuel has become (50). Although Hortensia ostensibly refers to Manuel's drinking, there is an undertone that insinuates Rigo's perception that his father is less than a "man." Manuel, sensitive to this nuance, replies immediately: "¡Soy hombre!" (51).[20]

Another silence in Hortensia's character centers around her loyalty to Manuel. Verbal expressions of love are absent, but caretaking actions and words abound. The text's construction of Hortensia's decision to stay with Manuel in spite of the emotional and sexual estrangement between them suggests yet another message inherited from mothers and passed down to daughters: the wife's obligation to stay in the marriage at all costs, subordinating her own needs to the supposed welfare of the family.

But Hortensia has not entirely sacrificed her needs in silence; in fact, it is her demand for recognition as a subject, and as a desiring subject, that leads to open conflict with Manuel. In a scene between Hortensia and Rosario, it is revealed that Hortensia was more attracted to Conrado than to Manuel but married Manuel because, as Rosario puts it, "Conrado was not the kina man you marry" (64). Hortensia chose stability and tranquillity, but she remembers the erotic tension around Conrado: "I remember how when Conrado touch me . . . jus' to grab my hand nomás, and los vellitos on my arm would stand straight up.[21] (*Pause.*) I've never felt that with Manuel" (64). Her sister Rosario is an independent woman, but when she describes her life ("Ahora, tengo mi casita, mi jardín,[22] my kids are grown. What more do I need?" [64]), Hortensia rejects Rosario's implied celibacy ("I need more, Chayo" [64]). The younger woman makes it clear that celibacy, whether inside or outside of marriage, is not enough for her, rejecting the idea of a marriage in which she is both invisible and unloved (63).

In the encounter with Manuel that follows this conversation, Hortensia demands his touch and his recognition of her existence:

Manuel. (*He stops.*) Touch me. (*Pause.*) Yo existo. (*Pause.*) Manuel, yo existo. Existo yo.[23] (*He walks past her.*) Nothing's changed, has it? I look at your back and it tells me nothing's changed [. . .] (*tenderly:*) You know how good I know this back? (*Lightly touching him, he stiffens.*) I know it mejor que tú. ¿Sabes que tienes[24] a scar right here? (*Touching it.*) ¿Y un lunar allí? (*Touching.*) ¿Y otro acá?[25] (*Pounding his back.*) ¡Mírame, cabrón! Why don't you look at me? ¡Mírame! (64)[26]

Manuel brutally repulses Hortensia's bid to be both subject and object of desire in their marriage. Motivated by his own sense of failure over his "secret" (lack of masculinity), he projects this shame onto Hortensia: "Nobody knows our secret, but they all know and they're all laughing at what they see inside my head [. . .] You make me sick, ¿sabes?[27] I can't stand for you to touch me!" (65). Hortensia perceives her own desire through Manuel's rejection of her and preference for Conrado. In the scene in which she forces Leticia and Lupe to help bathe her with vinegar (66), Hortensia releases the shame and guilt at having desires at all (fulfilled and unfulfilled) against herself and her daughters. The desiring female body can only be filthy and is in need of redemption and purification through sacrifice.

Like Hortensia, the character of Leticia, her elder daughter, is both complicitous and resistant in the socialization of her desire, her resistance learned in the awareness of race. From her first appearance she is identified with the Chicano movement and its race politics, both in her clothing ("*She is wearing late*

'6os Chicana 'radical' attire: tight jeans, large looped earrings, an army jacket with a UFW (United Farm Workers) insignia on it" [47]) and Hortensia's words ("Allí viene la política" [47]).[28] Leticia criticizes the *telenovela* that Hortensia, Rosario, and Lupe are watching for representing Mexicans as blondes (47); later, when the women look at pictures of Rigo's wedding, Leticia is acutely aware of the racist treatment of her family as well as her brother's attempts to "get over" (56–58). She avenges both by comparing European Americans and Rigo's wedding disfavorably to Chicanos and traditional Mexican ones. The bride's family had disinvited Rosario and the rest of Rigo's extended family, pretending that it would be a small ceremony. Leticia comments: "They were afraid that if too many Mexicans got together, we'd take over the joint. Bring out the mariachi, spill guacamole over everything" (57).

Immersed in the politicization of her ethnicity as an activist Chicana, Leticia has become radicalized by both racial and gender experiences. Her character captures the contradiction of fighting for justice around issues of race within the movement, while only the men, whom she refers to ironically as "Raza gods" (78), have the power. This insight has enabled her to articulate the gender inequality reproduced in her own home, as in the earlier dialogue with Hortensia ("I have something between my legs"). Far from cutting herself off from her family and culture because she has allied herself with feminist values, Leticia's feminism emerges fundamentally out of her specific experience as a Chicana; she responds to white patriarchy as well as to Chicano machismo.[29] Rather than being less Chicana for her feminist politics, Leticia is the most culturally identified of all the characters. The stage notes for Leticia's character metonymically link skin color and political consciousness, as if the clothes of the activist signify racial belonging within the performative logic of making race legible on stage. Moraga inverts the racial logic of the cultural nationalists' anti-feminism, darkening Leticia's skin color as an expression of her politics:

She is no less brown, she is too dark almost, darker than her family wants her to get. She reflects a changing culture, and that makes her la nueva Chicana. Her feminism has nothing to do with white women, who may superimpose that reading on the material because white women think they invented feminism. Emotionally, she has had to distance herself from her family, to avoid being swallowed up by it, but that doesn't make her any less Mexican. (Lecture at the University of Washington, 1990)

Leticia seems to echo Hortensia's belief that women can come into power only through men when she tells her mother about her first sexual experience, with the difference that she is *aware* of the power structures behind male/female re-lationships: "It's not about love. It's power. Power we get to hold and caress and protect" (78). When Hortensia asks why she gave away her virginity for noth-ing, Leticia expresses her desire not to have her worth and her sexuality defined by men: "I wanted it to be worthless, mamá. Don't you see? Not for me to be worthless, but to know that my worth had nothing to do with it" (78).

Rosario, perhaps because by her mid-fifties she has organized her life in-dependently of a man's desires, has the clearest and most pragmatic insights into the ways "man" throws his shadow over woman. Justifying her husbandless status to her sister, Rosario says: "But after you see the other side of a man, your heart changes. It's harder to love. I've seen tha' side too many times, mija" (63–64). In Rosario's analysis of marriage, the man fails to "see" his wife and lives out of touch with his feelings:

It's not that men don' love. They jus' don' stop to see a woman. Us women do all the seeing for them. If a man sighs for no reason, we already know the reason. We watch their faces y sabemos cuando se vuelvan máscaras[30] [. . .] We know better than them what they feel . . . and tha's enough to make us believe it's love. Tha's a marriage. (63)

The flip side of Rosario's analysis is her incisive perception of Manuel's homo-social desire and the way it affects marriage and family life:

Sometimes a man thinks of another man before he thinks of nobody else. He don' think about his woman ni su madre ni los children, jus' what he gots in his head about tha' man.[31] He closes his eyes and dreams, "If I could get inside tha' man, then I'd really be somebody!" But when he opens his eyes and sees that he's as empty as he was before, he curls his fingers into fists and knocks down whatever he thinks is standing in his way. (75)

Rosario resists the mindset of suffering and sacrifice taught to the poor, both men and women. She cautions Lupe against her obsession with sin and the devil; when Lupe protests that she cannot control what she thinks, her aunt disagrees. Yet she validates Lupe's road to self-understanding through wrestling with her own private demons: "Only los estúpidos don' know enough to be afraid. The rest of us, we learn to live con nuestros diablitos. Tanto que if those little devils werent around, we woont even know who we were" (45). Catching Manuel wallowing in self-pity before Rigo's wedding, drinking beer and listening to Mexican love songs, she warns him: "If you listen too much to that music, you start to believe there's something good about suffering" (55). When Lupe wonders if her father is a saint because he "suffers inside," Rosario makes it clear that she believes his suffering is self-inflicted (68).

Lupe, lacking Rosario's years and Leticia's politics, is much more vulnerable. Like Corky in *Ghost*, Lupe embodies some autobiographical elements of Moraga's early struggles with Catholicism and sexuality. But, whereas the tough little Corky rebelliously confronts gender roles and rejects feminine socialization, Lupe is more fragile, more open, and more anxious to please. In the role assigned to compliant daughters in the patriarchal family, she tries to provide for the needs each parent finds unmet by the other. Most disturbing is Manuel's attachment to Lupe. When he comes home drunk and quarrels with Hortensia, he seeks out Lupita as a special source of comfort:

MANUEL: *(going to LUPE)*: ¡Lupita! ¿'Stás durmiendo, hijita? *(He lays his huge man's head on LUPE's small shoulder.)* You'll never leave me, ¿no, mijita?[32]
LUPE: No, papi.
MANUEL: Eres mi preferida, ¿sabes?[33]
LUPE: Sí, papi.
MANUEL: You're different from the rest. You got a heart that was made to love. Don't ever leave me, baby.
LUPE: No, papi. I won't.
   He begins to weep softly. Her thin arm mechanically caresses his broad back. A muted tension falls over the scene. (52)

Although there is no textual evidence of incest, the inappropriateness and invasiveness of Manuel's actions imply a potentially violent blurring of boundaries for Lupe, the "huge man's head" contrasting grotesquely with the little girl's "small shoulder."

Hortensia's internalized shame results in a similar confusion of roles in her relationship to Lupe. This first occurs in the transfer of guilt from Hortensia to Lupe in the reenactment of a scene in which she almost drowned her as a baby, overcome by guilt at Lupe's resemblance to Conrado. The second confusion of roles, following fast on the heels of the first, mirrors the kind of reversal that occurs between Lupe and Manuel. After Manuel rejects Hortensia's demand for recognition as desiring subject, she spills vinegar over herself in the bath in response to her perceived "filth." Leticia and Lupe manage to calm her; as Lupe strokes her mother's hair and gently dabs at her bruises, Hortensia tells her: "Now, I'm your baby ¿no, mija? Now you have to clean my nalguitas jus' like I wipe yours when you was a baby [. . .] You girls are all I got in the world, you know," to which Lupe sadly replies, as before to Manuel, "Sí, mami. Sí" (67).

Besides distorting the parent/child relationships, the secret gnawing at the heart of this family manifests itself in Lupe's fascination with sin and the devil. Although Lupe is unaware of the relationship between her obsession with the devil and the problems in her family, the image of the shadow of the crucifix, and later her choice of the word "shadow" in describing the devil to Rosario, reveal this thematic connection to the reader/spectator: "He's like a shadow [. . .] I jus' feel the brush of his tail as he goes by me" (44). The connection is strengthened when she tells her aunt: "Sometimes I jus' feel like my eyes are too open. It's like the more you see, the more you got to be afraid of" (45). In the way children have of reading situations correctly through nonverbal cues and other kinds of information, Lupe sees more than she can express and understands the truth everything around her denies. This burden is expressed in her childlike equation of suffering and saintliness in Manuel, as discussed above.

Lupe's fear of having eyes that are "too open" and "keeping secrets" in the context of a punitive religiosity stems from her developing sexuality. A passage from *Loving in the War Years* sheds light on Lupe's refuge in the church in the face of familial and sexual realities beyond her comprehension and control: "The strange comfort that the church would be standing there, just around the turn from the cemetery [. . .] That the end of mass would find a palm placed in my hand [. . .] The comfort and terror of powerlessness" (121). At the crossroads of consciousness and sexuality, Lupe prefers the oddly comforting disempowerment the church ensures, which frees her from the necessity of thinking or choosing for herself.

Paradoxically, the church also offers outlets for sexuality and subjectivity. Toying with the idea of taking "Magdalene" as her confirmation name, Lupe uses the classic biblical narrative of the sinner's repentance to safely indulge in a voluptuous lesbian fantasy (miming the action while painting Leticia's toenails):

And then she kneels down in front of Jesus and jus' starts crying and crying for all the sins she's done [. . .] But suddenly the tears become like bath water, real soft and warm and soothing-like. She's got this hair, y'see, this long beautiful dark hair and it's so thick she can make a towel out of it. It's so soft, it's almost like velvet as she spreads it all over Jesus' feet [. . .] Can you imagine what it musta felt like to have this woman with such beautiful hair *wiping* it on you? It's jus' too much to think about. And then Jesus says [. . .] "Rise woman and go and sin no more." Now that's what I call forgiveness. That's . . . relief. (70)

This appropriation of the religious imagery of salvation for the expression of female desire is familiar to readers of *Ghost* (see chapter 5).

On another level the rituals and seasons of the church, designed to establish the individual's relationship with God, facilitate the development of a private, internal life.[34] Although this relationship is ostensibly with God, it is ultimately about the subject's own spirituality, which can continue to exist in adult life independent of organized religion. It is in the space of this interior world that Lupe expresses, in her wonderful monologues, her desire for knowledge and the intimate connections between that desire, sexuality, and spirituality.

Lupe enters her interior world for the last time at the end of the play to explore her feelings about her friend Frances:

I've decided my confirmation name will be Frances cuz that's what Frankie Pacheco's name is and I wannu be in her body. When she sits, she doesn't hold her knees together like my mom and the nuns are always telling me to. She jus' lets them fly and fall wherever they want, real natural-like, like they was wings instead of knees. (*Pause.*) And she's got a laugh, a laugh that seems to come from way deep inside herself, from the bottom of her heart or something. (*Pause.*) If I could, I'd like to jus' unzip her chest and climb right inside there, next to her heart, to feel everything she's feeling and I could forget about me. (*Pause.*) It's okay if she doesn't feel the same way, . . . it's my secret. (84)

There is something alarming about the young girl's desire to get inside of someone else and forget about herself, recalling Marisa's self-betraying gesture of turning away from herself to another, Amalia, in *Ghost*. Closer to home, it recalls Manuel's intense desire, perceived by Rosario, to get inside Conrado's skin in order to "be" somebody, and his need to see his identity simultaneously anchored and erased in the eyes of the brown male other. Lupe's confusion about where her identity starts and stops is apparent earlier in her fascination with her reflection in her own pupils, echoing Manuel's pondering the loss of his reflection in his son's eye: "You can see yourself in there . . . in the darkest part [. . .] Two little faces, one in each eye. It's like you got other people living inside you. Maybe you're not really you. Maybe they're the real you and the big you is just a dream you" (53). The undecidability concerning the borders of her "real" identity is not surprising, considering that other people, especially Manuel, are attempting to live through her.

Yet Lupe's choice of a love object outside the family is progressive, doubly so in that, for a girl, Frances is relatively free of the feminine socialization that imprisons Lupe in a caregiving role. And, while looking away from herself may parallel Marisa's problems in adult life, there is also something hopeful about Lupe's desire to enter someone's body, as an expression of the basic human need for communion.[35] In this sense Lupe expresses the fundamental theme of the play: desire. *Shadow* traces the erotic hunger for passion and wholeness of each of the characters who form a family onstage, even to the youngest child.

Shadow's staging of painful aspects of Chicano culture responds to Moraga's belief that a theater that does not provide the opportunity for self-criticism, for looking within in addition to externally oriented protest, does a fundamental disservice to the community it serves (*Open Window*). This self-criticism is part of the interrogation of the cultural construction of gender roles and the creation of a space within Chicano culture for the recognition of diverse and fluid sexual identities. Moraga's writing fills the need for a "healing theater" (*Open Window*), a theater that extends the possibility of transformation by constructing Chicana/o subjects in all their complexity. Whether focusing on Chicana sexuality in *Ghost*, or the Chicano family in *Shadow*, Moraga examines the contradictions, the mixed messages, the positive as well as the negative. For Moraga, criticizing her culture is "an act of love" (quoted in Lovato, 23).

"The Miracle People"
Heroes and Saints and Contemporary Chicano Theater

Heroes and Saints is a powerful representation of the pesticide poisoning of the fictional people of McLaughlin (modeled after McFarland, in California's San Joaquin Valley): the cancers and deaths, particularly among children, and the gamut of emotions from denial, rage, grief, and faith to the desire for social justice.[1] The environmental justice movement has identified race as the most powerful factor in the public's exposure to toxicity.[2] Magdalena Avila pointed out in her keynote address to the 1993 National Association for Chicano Studies convention that, as of 1987, three out of five commercial hazardous waste landfills in the U.S. were located in black and Latino communities. Perhaps because pesticides target the female reproductive system so devastatingly, women have assumed vocal leadership in the fight against these practices. For Avila, Chicanas are providing crucial direction in the nineties phase of the environmental justice movement, drawing from what she calls a "reciprocal working process" among academics and frontline activists. With their screen prints, altar installations, and computer animation, Chicana artists—Ester Hernández, Cecilia Concepción Alvarez, Yolanda M. López, and Barbara Carrasco—and writers such as Helena María Viramontes with her novel *Under the Feet of Jesus* and Moraga with *Heroes* participate in this reciprocal process of generating knowledge about and activism against environmental racism.

The play's focus on each character's personal experience of pesticide poisoning *in the flesh* expands the meaning of the political within Chicano *teatro* and contributes to the opening up of Chicano identity and the term "Chicano" itself. While *Heroes* engages the concrete conditions and political issues of the people of McLaughlin in ways that are familiar to audiences of Chicano theater, the characters' *embodiment* of these issues invites spectators into the realms of the subjective, the sexual, and the erotic, where they may feel less "at home." By undermining a clear-cut "inside" and "outside" in its examination of the issue of environmental poisoning, *Heroes* explores the interfaces of individual and collective identity, as well as borders within the individual. Texts like *Heroes* and Anzaldúa's "*Cihuatlyotl*, Woman Alone" (*Borderlands*, 173) imagine the struggles of the Chicana subject to reconcile her desire for autonomy as well as community, not by passively accepting cultural consensus but by actively negotiating the meanings of cultural values and behaviors.

Cornel West provides a distinction between pleasure and joy that is useful in illuminating this individual/collective dynamic in *Heroes* (quoted in Dent, 1). According to West, pleasure is inward and individual, as in sexual pleasure or the pleasure we experience in watching a film, dancing, or listening to music; joy has to do with love, solidarity, and the struggle for justice. West poses the experience of joy in terms of social communion: that which brings people together as community and allows the individual an access to the collective experience. In Gina Dent's readings of Alice Walker's *Possessing the Secret of Joy*, the movement from pleasure to joy involves a shift from "the notion of political agency to the examination of how we come to know, to decide, to act" (11). In other words, the movement from pleasure to joy introduces both ethical and epistemological concerns (how must we act; how do we know what we know). Dent reads West's take on the experience of joy (as a collective's alternative way of knowing itself) through Audre Lorde's notion of the erotic as "our deepest knowledge, a power that unlike other spheres of power, we all have access to, and that can lessen the threat of our individual difference" (Dent, 2). These critics suggest that the mythic potential of joy provides an opportunity for us as a community to know ourselves and accept one another's differences. It is essential, then, to understand what conflicts must be resolved before we can enter its realm (Dent, 2).

The assertion of individual and collective agency at the end of *Heroes* ostensibly moves us into the realm of joy as understood above. The main character of *Heroes* is Cerezita, whose pesticide poisoning is figured through her representation as a bodiless head. In a commanding image at the end of the play, Cere and her wheelchair are transformed into an altar displaying the Virgin of Guadalupe. After speaking to the people from her altar, Cere wheels herself into the heavily guarded fields and dies in a flurry of gunfire. Moved by Cere's murder as well as her image and her words, the people rush into the vineyards:

MARIO: Burn the fields!
EL PUEBLO (*rising with him*): ¡Enciendan los files! [. . .] ¡Asesinos! ¡Asesinos! ¡Asesinos! (149)[3]

Cere's sacrifice is especially for the "hunerds and hunerds a pounds of Razita" (111) named in the activist Amparo's speech at a televised protest, that is, for the future generations. Throughout the play, a young girl, Bonnie, plays with her doll; as she bandages its head, takes its temperature, and finally prepares it for burial, she acts out a heartbreaking parallel to the devastation she witnesses around her: "We knew she wouldn't make it. The cancer got her [. . .] She bled through all her openings: her mouth, her ears, her nose . . . even through her pee hole, she bled. It was outta control. [. . .] I gotta bury her. I'm making her coffin" (130–131). Echoing the importance of Corky and Lupe in Moraga's first two plays, Bonnie stands for all the children damaged, both physically and emotionally, by pesticide poisoning.

To understand, in Dent's terms, how Cere comes to act as she does because of what she knows, we must look at the specific cultural repertory in which she performs. In *Heroes*, the conflicts preventing access to joy are particularly dense in relation to gender roles and sexuality within the family, countering the image of organic nurturance in the cultural and racial reproduction of *la raza*, the people.[4] Other conflicts center on the inclusion or exclusion of certain bodies from the collective, according to their approximation to or distance from an ideal imagining of "Chicano."

While *Heroes* maintains a clear-cut distinction between "us" and "them" in the context of environmental racism, it undermines this binary in the treatment of the Chicano family in the play. As in the critique of gender and sexuality, that of the family, ultimately of benefit to all, stems from a lesbian sensibility based on experience:

Since lesbians and gay men have often been forced out of our blood families, and since our love and sexual desire are not housed within the traditional family, we are in a critical position to address those areas within our cultural family that need to change. (*The Last Generation,* 159)

The family in *Heroes* is presented as the matrix of the personal, lived experience of the political: the pesticide poisoning. Rather than presenting positive images of the Chicano family, *Heroes* explores the ways families both constrain *and* empower. The characters may be further "contaminated" there by repressive attitudes toward gender and sexuality, but it is also where they learn to love and where they may learn to resist. As elsewhere in Moraga's writing, the authoritarian father figure is displaced, and the mother is depicted as the primary agent of cultural transmission, for better or for worse. Just as Moraga refashions the iconography of cultural nationalism—*La Virgen,* the People—so, too, does the mother function as martyr, conserver of values. While the family is represented as disintegrating under the pressures of economic and social devastation, AIDS, and poisoning, it remains the central unit of social organization and microcosm of "the People."

Trapped in frustration, denial, and shame, Cere's mother, Dolores, is responsible for the poisonous reproduction of gender roles that teach men's superiority and women's sinful physicality and lack of value. Dolores cannot understand why a man, her son, Mario, would choose to give up his privileged heterosexual status and assume what is, for her, the devalued feminine position. She even encourages Mario to marry and live his gay life on the side:

Why you wannu make yourself como una mujer?[5] Why you wannu do this to the peepo who love you? [. . .] Necesitas familia, hijo.[6] What you do fuera del matrimonio[7] is your own biznis. You could have familia. Eres hombre.[8] You don' gottu be alone [. . .] God made you a man and you throw it away. You lower yourself into half a man. (123–124)

Mario's homosexuality is the ultimate blow for a woman who, convinced of her own powerlessness, hoped at least for a vicarious experience of power through her manly son. As Moraga writes in "A Long Line of Vendidas":

Sometimes I sense that she feels this way because she wants to believe that through her mothering, she can develop the kind of man she would have liked to have married, or even have been. That through her son she can get a taste of male privilege, since without race or class privilege that's all there is to be had. The daughter can never offer the mother such hope, straddled by the same forces that confine the mother. As a result, the daughter must constantly earn the mother's love, prove her fidelity to her. The son—he gets her love for free. (*Loving*, 102)

Unable to accept alternative forms of Chicano masculinity, Dolores rejects Mario. She goes so far as to identify AIDS as divine punishment for his transgressive sexuality: "God makes this sickness to show peepo it's wrong what they do [. . .] Tú eres el único macho.[9] I want you to live" (124).

Dolores casts Cere's sexuality in a sinful mode as well. She calls in the priest, Juan, to hear Cere's confession after she catches Cere looking at pictures in an anatomy book: "Jus' cuz you don' got a body doesn' mean you can't sin. The biggest sins are in the mind" (113). Even though, for Dolores, the bodiless Cere can still commit sins, she believes that her daughter's path to sainthood is practically guaranteed, unburdened by female flesh and the temptations of the world ("Tú eres una inocente.[10] That's how God wanted it. There's a reason he made you like this" [113]).

Insisting on the notion of "family privacy," Dolores hides Cere from prying eyes. She does this in part because she attributes her husband's abandonment of the family to her earlier outspokenness about Cere and about the effect of industrial poisons on fetuses.[11] Dolores has since retreated from public activism and, like Cere's father before her, keeps her "hidden como algo cochino" (103).[12] She conceals Cere behind a curtain when people visit and physically confines her within the private sphere of the home by controlling Cere's ability to move by herself in her electric wheelchair.

In addition to framing a critique of the family, the play crosses certain borders meant to control sexuality and the body. Diverse Chicana/o bodies occupy the stage: the gay son Mario, the woman confined to a wheelchair, the frocked priest, and the nursing mother, Cere's sister Yolanda. Their erotic desires and physical exchanges migrate unsettlingly across neat categories (straight/queer, celibate/sexual, lover/sibling, erotic/political). The gender of the object of Cere's desire is less important than her need to feel as though *she* has a body:

It wasn't your body I wanted. It was mine. All I wanted was for you to make me feel like I had a body because, the fact is, I don't. I was denied one. But for a few minutes, a few minutes before you started *thinking*, I felt myself full of fine flesh filled to the bones in my toes [. . .] You're a waste of a body. (144)

Mario shares his homoerotic memories of his cousin Freddie with Cere, who has no fantasies based on her own sexual experience: "God, Freddie was beautiful. Dark. He had cheekbones to die for, like they were sculpted outta some holy Mayan rock" (104). Within the category "gay man," Mario further disrupts binary representations of sexuality by combining both "butch" (*"He is well built, endearingly macho in his manner"* [95]) and "femme" identifications ("Me chocó[13] the first time I seen your hands digging into Yolie's purse like they belong there" [123]).

As a Chicano gay man, Mario experiences a multiplicity of assaults on his existence as an individual and as a member of a collectivity. He longs to leave the valley. This freedom is associated with whiteness:

When I was in high school, I used to sit out there in those fields, smoking, watching the cars go by on 99. I'd think about the driver, having somewhere to go. His foot pressed to the floorboard, cruisin'. He was always a gringo. (114)

The faceless white men who come to McLaughlin to pick him up and take him to the city are inscribed in this scenario of racialized escape:

YOLANDA: That was one sleazy-looking gringo in that car.
CEREZITA: Mario doesn't like him.
YOLANDA: Well, for not liking him, he sure sees him a lot.
CEREZITA: He gives him things.
YOLANDA: That I believe. (105)[14]

Like the "gringos" of his youthful memories, these drivers who take him along the highway away from the valley are white, while the sick lovers he tries to save through sex mirror his brownness:

And when you love your own sex, and they got your own hungry dark eyes staring back at you, well you're convinced that you could even cure death. And so you jus' keep kissing that same purple mouth, deeper and harder, and you keep whispering, "I'm gonna wipe all that sickness outta you, cousin." And then weeks and months and maybe even a year or two go by, and suddenly you realize you didn't cure nothing and that your family's dissolving right there inside of your hands. (141)

By merging his present lovers with the "Mayan god" (104) cousin of his youth, Mario juxtaposes the two kinds of families that demand his commitment ("I've had to choose" [141]).

Described as both "mujer" and "half a man" by Dolores, Mario struggles to construct his masculinity outside the "blood family" pattern established by his father and Dolores. Yet he identifies with Dolores in the need for a man that allows them to be exploited:

MARIO: We've always been lonely, 'amá. You and me waiting for someone to come along and just talk to us with a little bit of kindness, to tell us how fine and pretty we are, to lie to our face.
DOLORES: Me das asco.[15]
MARIO: Why? Because I remind you of you. What love did you ever get from my dad? He had a sweet mouth, that's all. A syrupy tongue that every time he dragged himself home, could always talk you back into loving him. That's not the kind of man I want to be. (123–124)

Mario relates his refusal to live the lie of heterosexual marriage with male lovers on the side to his rejection of a certain construct of masculinity embodied by his father: "I can't do that 'amá. I can't put my body one place and my heart another. I'm not my father" (123).[16] Choosing not to live his sexuality in the shadow of Dolores' desire to see him a certain way, or in an endless migration along the highway between valley and city, Mario moves away from the family in the hour of their worst need ("Having a life. One life, not two" [113]).

The confrontation between Dolores and Mario preceding his departure exemplifies the unsettling effect on spectators of the redefined structures of identification in Moraga's dramaturgy, which raise fears about homosexuality and AIDS, as well as worry that Dolores' judgment might support homophobic attitudes toward gays and AIDS. Some spectators were dismayed that Mario does in fact end up with AIDS in the play, fearing a reinforcement of Dolores' attitudes in the general public.[17] Heroes risks these multiple alienations to represent the articulations among race, AIDS, and environmental pollution as interactive systems of domination that affect Chicanos. Having escaped the valley for the city, Mario trades one threat for another: "The city's no different. Raza's dying everywhere. Doesn't matter if it's crack or . . . pesticides, AIDS, it's all the same shit" (141).[18]

The character of Father Juan, the "half-breed," engages thorny issues of sexuality, the body, the Church, and Chicano racial identity. The Church's dual role in both supporting the community and inculcating passivity in the face of gender and socioeconomic oppression is a recurring theme in Chicano theater history. While it enriches the representation of Chicano priesthood, Heroes' exploration of Juan's struggle between his sexual desires and his vow of celibacy takes the spectators into taboo territory. His ambivalent sexuality is twinned by his ambivalent racial identity. As Dolores fails to understand why Mario chooses to relinquish his entitlement as a man, Mario wonders why Juan chooses to stay in the valley when he could pass for white and become one of those "gringos" driving along the highway oblivious to McLaughlin's existence:

MARIO: You don't know what it's like growing up in this valley.
JUAN: I was born in Sanger, Mario.
MARIO: Yeah? Don't show [. . .] Why did you come back, Father? All you'd need is a nice Buick, a full tank of gas and you'd be indistinguishable on that highway. (113–114)

Juan has to tell people that he's Mexican ("DOLORES: ¿Habla español? JUAN: Soy mexicano. DOLORES: ¿Verdad?" [98][19]) and his racial indeterminacy seems to create a site of equally ambivalent desire in Mario ("AMPARO [*aside*]: Half y half. MARIO [*suggestively*]: Like the cream?") that resonates in Juan as well. Dolores senses the erotic tension between the two:[20]

DOLORES: Mario, why you standing around sin ropa?[21] Go put some clothes on.
MARIO: All right. I was just helping the man. I mean, the priest.
He puts the water onto the dispenser, then exits. JUAN's eyes follow him. (99)

Perhaps because Juan's "in-betweenness" echoes his own locations and desires (valley/city, white men/brown men), Mario sees the priest as his potential undoing were Juan to embrace his whiteness, abandon the valley, and become "indistinguishable" from the other travelers on the highway: "Just don't stop to pick me up. Your type can destroy me" (114).

Juan's ambivalence has potentially damaging ramifications for Cere as well. For both sexual and political action, Cere needs a body or someone with a body to help her; her lack of action is not due to any lack of strength of will or desire on her part. In Father Juan she glimpses the potential body that would allow her desires to converge. The scene in which Cere and Juan read the multiple definitions of "tongue" together, with its erotic overtones, presents the multiple dimensions of their relationship, a cluster of potential roles for Cere in the play, and the limitations and conflicts that hamper their ability to act and speak:

JUAN: "Tongueless."
CEREZITA: "Lacking the power of speech."
JUAN: "Mute. Tongue-tied—disinclined or" . . . (*He looks up at her.*)
CEREZITA: "Unable to speak freely." (109)

The growing attraction between Juan and Cere accompanies his increasing determination to take overt political action by helping Cere crucify the dead children in the vineyards to draw attention to the people's plight. When Juan arrives at her house to prepare for the action, their political and erotic excitement merges in an embrace. He kisses her, but *"suddenly, JUAN's face takes on a distanced look"* (139–140). As Cere pleads with him to remain present, he comes to orgasm against the back of her wheelchair and runs from the house (140). Unfortunately, in Father Juan, Cere has found a potential sexual/political partner who is paralyzed to act due to his vow of celibacy as well as his own personal struggles with the dichotomy of mind and body, traditional Catholicism and the more progressive theology of liberation. Filled with shame after the incident with Cere, Juan flees, driving north along Mario's highway. Like Mario, Juan deserts his people in their time of need.

Both come back by the end of the play and join in the final act of communal rebellion. In fact, Juan accompanies Cere into the vineyards with the little coffin containing the most recent child victim of the pesticide poisoning. Mario is the first to raise his fist in the air and call for the burning of the fields after they are shot at.[22] At the same time, the representation of Mario's and Juan's struggles and desires within the larger struggle of the community keeps them from disappearing into an undifferentiated whole. The effect at the end is that these marginalized subjects—the "half-breed" priest with the ambivalent relationship to his body and his Church, and the gay man forced to choose between familial and communal loyalties—enter into the mythic construction of "Chicano" struggle on the stage.

Cere represents the most severe degree of "difference" from the "ideal" Chicano body and the most extreme conflict that must be resolved before the people of McLaughlin can enter the communal realm of joy. Until fairly recently in the arc of Western history, the disabled and deformed have been hidden away in the privacy of the home like Cere. The increased visibility and participation of physically challenged people in the public sphere stems from their own history of activism for equal rights. By making a person (of color) in a wheelchair the key player in the community's struggle, *Heroes* breaks ground in Western theater and redresses the absence of satisfying representations of this group of people. On a symbolic level, Cere's leadership in *Heroes* suggests that the repressed or shameful part of oneself or one's community, when confronted and embraced, can become a major source of empowerment for all. Given the shame and secrecy surrounding homosexuality, the representation of Cere's empowering emergence into the public sphere can be seen as another instance of a lesbian sensibility in Moraga's dramaturgy.[23]

Moraga found a dual inspiration for the bodiless Cere. One was a boy born with no limbs in the cancer cluster town of McFarland. Moraga first met the people of McFarland and saw this image of the limbless child in the UFW film *The Wrath of Grapes* (1986). Her other source of inspiration was the character of Belarmino in *The Shrunken Head of Pancho Villa* (1964), by leading Chicano playwright Luis Valdez. In Valdez' play, the son of a Chicano farmworker family becomes a kind of barrio Robin Hood. Another son is only a head and does not speak until his brother returns from jail as a disproportionately large body with no head, suggesting that the experience of incarceration has deprived him of his ideals or incapacitated him to "head" the Chicano movement. Valdez draws the image of the head from the legend according to which the body of Pancho Villa was disinterred and decapitated; the head was never found. Although Belarmino signifies many things in Valdez' text, one of his meanings clearly has to do with the possibility of the Mexican revolutionary tradition inspiring leadership for the Chicano movement. At the end, Belarmino tries to convince his mother to place him on top of his brother's headless body (in this sense he is as dependent as Cere on the mother for the ability to act).

By making the non-realistic choice to represent Cere as a head instead of a torso with no limbs as in the UFW film, *Heroes* plays surrealism against melodramatic realism, the cultural against the political, in dialogue with Luis Valdez and the Chicano theater movement. This choice depends on the magic of theater for its success, and the two excellent productions the play has enjoyed so far prove that Cere "works" magically onstage; she is both wonderfully human and awesomely mythic as stipulated in the stage directions.

The larger-than-life, non-naturalistic mode of much Chicano theater calls attention to the nature of the field of representation itself. In the case of Cere, Moraga's dramaturgy breaks with the traditional representation of woman onstage. In this she joins other artists in the project described by Lynda Hart as an "effort to free the female body from its overdeterminations as a body saturated with sex, site of pleasure for (an)other, subjected and devoid of subjectivity" (Introduction, 5). Hart goes on to delineate the particular significance of this project in the field of performance,

where the female body on stage is easily received as iconic, seemingly less arbitrary than a linguistic sign, and even more so than photographic or televisual images, exceptionally susceptible to naturalization. Indeed, the female body on stage appears to be the "thing itself," incapable of mimesis, afforded not only no distance between the sign and referent but, indeed, taken for the referent. (5)

By representing Cere as only a head, Moraga makes it impossible for spectators to read this woman onstage as the "thing itself," as the female body whose sexualization is both "natural" and transparent. Instead, Cere stages her own body, reclaiming subjectivity, sexuality, and political agency in the process.

Cere brings the erotic and the political together in her intense *need* to act on both sexual and political levels. She struggles throughout the play against Dolores' denial of her physical access to the outside. Simultaneously, she resists all attempts to construct her as a disembodied, pure soul by stubbornly anchoring her principal relationships on the physical plane (with the exception of the mother on whom she is dependent for sustenance and mobility). From the beginning she is shown organizing the children to crucify the little corpses in the fields to draw media attention to the town's predicament. Just as Moraga and other Chicana artists involved in the environmental justice movement develop an esthetic that both mirrors and transforms the horror of the lived reality of pesticide poisoning, Cere orchestrates a metatheater within the play to make a visual and political statement as compelling and horrific as the brutal truncation of the lives of the children. She breaks taboos surrounding the respect owed the dead, so that "nobody's dying should be invisible [. . .] Nobody's" (139).[24]

As "her most faithful organ," Cere's tongue at this point in the play has the potential of agency in both sex and speech, including "speaking in tongues." This fusion of the functions of sex and speech in one organ recalls Moraga's reconstruction of the lesbian body in *Loving* (see chapter 1), lending the "tongue" scene between Cere and Juan the lesbian sensibility available in all her published work, and further troubling the borders between lesbian, gay, and heterosexual. The attraction between Cere and Juan in the context of collective political action establishes the erotic as a potential force in the struggle for justice, while recognizing symbolically the potential transformative energy of the theology of liberation within the ranks of the church. Juan's desertion returns Cere once again to the confines of the family, for (since the growers have begun to have the fields patrolled) it has become too dangerous to continue to let the children be her arms and legs by sending them into the field to crucify the dead children's bodies. She renounces the sexual dimension of the erotic and opts for visionary speech to move the people to action.

But to put her tongue at the service of collective action, Cere must have access to the public sphere. Dolores has virtually imprisoned her in the house by moving the wheelchair's control mechanism beyond the range of Cere's mouth. To get through Dolores to the outside, her emergence must take the form of *La Virgen* and Mexican Catholic martyrdom, since this is the only way Dolores can understand and accept, and therefore allow, Cere's action.

In the half-darkness, the CHILDREN surround CEREZITA and begin to transform her as BONNIE cuts away at CERE's hair. Moments later, they scatter. The lights rise to reveal DOLORES standing in the doorway. A brilliant beam of light has entered the room and washes over CEREZITA. She is draped in the blue-starred veil of La Virgen de Guadalupe. Her head is tilted slightly toward the right, her eyes downcast in the Virgin's classic expression. DOLORES is riveted by the sight. The raite[25] *is covered in a white altar cloth with the roses of Tepeyac imprinted upon it. The cross rests at the base of the raite. The light, brighter now, completely illuminates CERE's saintlike expression and the small cross. DOLORES drops to her knees.* (144)

Cere's strategic transformation into the Virgin of Guadalupe communicates the powerful constraints of gender on the body: to be a hero, Cere must become the saint her mother wants her to be. Cere's goals and the means she chooses to attain them—the death of a martyred saint, the crucified children—are designed to bring about change by making the people's poisoning public knowledge. Confronted with her physical limitations, Cere sacrifices the body she could have had through sex to become the tongue and the image of a community's political struggle.

The process through which Cere comes to know, to decide, and to act, then, is figured simultaneously through the multiple registers of the text. The constraints within which she chooses are not only imposed from without, but also from within the culture, the family. In this sense, the play is as much a *critique* of political heroism and saintly martyrdom as an enactment of them. While Cere assumes the role of martyred saint as a tactical move, the meanings of the Virgin of Guadalupe in Chicano culture support her individual agency.

In addition to religious meanings, the image of *La Virgen* shapes and reflects Chicano/Mexican understandings of gender, and, as the supreme symbol of national mestizo identity, plays a significant role in images of a "people" or a "nation." Alongside her role as model of passive femininity is her militant role as leader of popular rebellions, like the one activated in the people of McLaughlin by Cere's act. The action of the play mirrors recent events in the small town of Watsonville, where, after the Mexican cannery workers were hit hard by a difficult strike in the mid-1980s, *La Virgen* appeared in 1992 to one of the leaders of the strike as "una valiente campesina." People still throng to the shrine that marks the site, attesting to the power that can be derived from faith in *La Virgen* in times of need. The eruptions of the divine across a historical fabric of colonization and oppression—as old as *La Virgen* at Tepeyac or as recent as *La Virgen* at Watsonville—signify the people's resistance to oppression and perform a healing function within an embattled context, establishing places of power as focal points for the community. In *Heroes*, Cerc's miraculous transformation works within this tradition, linking collective political action to the realm of faith.

Figuring the transformative powers of communal joy through Cere's strategic self-construction as the Virgin of Guadalupe highlights the contradictory representation of religion and spirituality. In this sense, *Heroes* is part of a larger undertaking by Chicana artists such as Yolanda M. López and scholars such as Susana Gallardo,[26] addressing gender, racial, and class discrimination in the Catholic Church's practices and reclaiming the ideals of spirituality and "community" underpinning the Church's authority. Gallardo's research on a radical alternative Catholic group in East San Jose suggests Chicanas' ambivalent insider/outsider positioning vis-à-vis the institutionalized Church, neither completely marginalized nor included, accepting nor rejecting. Similarly, in re-envisioning the traditional icon of *La Virgen*, López both recognizes how certain meanings invested in this figure have been used to subordinate and oppress,[27] and draws on what Amalia Mesa-Bains calls the "transfigurative liberation of the icon" (137) to foreground or rewrite other meanings that empower her as a Chicana in her shifting and multiple identities.

While their ends may be similar, the differences between López' famous "Self-Portrait as the Virgin of Guadalupe" and Moraga's play illuminate the particular representation of religion and spirituality in *Heroes*. One is actually the reverse of the other: López makes the Virgin over in her own likeness, while Cere takes on the likeness of the Virgin. Both empower themselves through this figure and her collective meanings, but whereas López secularizes the icon, Cere infuses the traditional image with the secular and the political. In *Heroes*, religion provides the vehicle for a vision of an alternative syncretic practice fusing activism and spirituality that complements the text's critique of institutional Catholicism.

Dolores calls upon God to authorize her most damaging judgments about everything, especially her children (Mario's homosexuality and Cere's deformity). Her attitude toward the "Holy Rollie," while presented humorously ("They turn from the Catholic God. They 'Chrishins' now" [100]), reveals the intolerance and narrow rigidity of her belief system that necessitate Cere's ploy. Mario sums up her religiosity succinctly when he tells her, "Your god's doing all the seeing for you" (124). The other character closely allied with organized religion, Father Juan, if not so much an obstacle in her path as is Dolores, ends up doing very little to help Cere accomplish her goals. Both these figures are recuperated in the syncretic fusion of religious ritual and political action at the end of the play.

The funeral procession, with Father Juan in full vestments and accompanied by altar boys, the tiny coffin draped in white, the prayers and the holy water blessings, the church bells, the sounding of the drum, and the singing of hymns, sets the stage for Cere/*La Virgen*'s appearance:

Upon the sight of la virgen, the prayer is interrupted. A hush falls over the crowd [. . .] El Pueblo bring forth pictures of their dead and deformed children in offering to la virgen [. . .] The singing continues as they pin milagros to the white cloth of her raite. (148)

Beyond Cere's pragmatic and tactical appropriation of *La Virgen* to accomplish her goals, one senses that the spirituality at work here has less to do with "God" than with what Moraga has called "the faith of activists" (see chapter 1).[28] Ensconced on her altar as the Virgin of Guadalupe, surrounded by the visual images, sounds, and gestures of Catholic ritual, Cere in her speech incites the "miracle people" to "flood this valley con coraje" (148). By linking the land and the maternal, she foregrounds *La Virgen*'s indigenous aspect of Tonantzín, the deity of fertility: "name this land *Madre*. Madre Tierra" (148).

The religious ritual provides something like a blessing for the incursion into the fields, akin to the blending of the religious and the political in the public activities of the United Farm Workers Union. A recent film of the march commemorating the first anniversary of César Chávez' death documents the embedding of religious practices in this struggle, including the banner of the Virgin of Guadalupe, Masses, prayers, fasting, and foot washings as a sign of service and humility. In setting this religious tone for the UFW, Chávez drew on a variety of precedents, including the teachings and example of Saint Francis of Assisi and radical Irish priests, Gandhi's philosophy of nonviolent direct action, and a number of papal encyclicals affirming the right, and even the moral duty, of the working class to organize on its own behalf.[29] The blending of politics and religion in the UFW and in the theatrical world of *Heroes* highlights the inextricable relationship between cultural practice and Catholic religion in certain Chicana/o communities and shows that rather than hindering political movement in the classic Marxist understanding, religion can be marshaled in the service of resistance to oppression and exploitation.

After Cere/*La Virgen*'s inspired speech to the crowd, Juan gives a final blessing: "*EL PUEBLO kneel as JUAN blesses them and all those witnessing the play*" (149). At this moment, Mario and Dolores embrace in reconciliation, and as Cere passes her mother on her way to death, Dolores blesses her daughter's action. The inclusion of the spectators in the final blessing before Cere and Juan move out into the vineyard extends the blending of political practice and religious ritual beyond the confines of the performance time and space.[30]

The experience of joy—such as the mass recognition of the divine in an oak grove near Watsonville or the assertion of communal outrage and resistance in a difficult strike—takes on the somber shading of martyrdom in *Heroes*. Alluding to both revolutionary heroism and the Catholic tradition of the virgin martyrs, Cere's self-sacrifice for the good of the community also makes secular and feminine the central ritual of Catholicism—communion—that reenacts the redemption of humanity's original sin through Christ's self-sacrifice in *his* humanity on the cross. The opening of Cere's final speech captures the play's hybrid crossing of the feminine Virgin and the masculine "body of Christ": "Put your hand inside my wound" (148). While visually embodying *La Virgen*, Cere's words evoke those spoken by Christ to Saint Thomas, encouraging him to have faith in the miracle of redemption by touching the wounds left by the crucifixion. As the congregation unites in the mystical body of Christ by partaking of the host, the people come together as a collective political force through Cere's embodiment of their struggle.

The persuasive force of women's speech permeates *Heroes*. The play's textual insistence on the multiple definitions of "tongue" and the ultimate privileging of "speaking in tongues" resonates, in the Chicano imaginary, with La Malinche, called simply *la lengua* (tongue) for her use of language, as Cortés' translator, in the "betrayal" of her people.[31] Amparo and Cere redeem the power of women's speech in the historical and political process, evoking Chicanas known for their oratory power such as Dolores Huerta and María Moreno.[32] Just as her image as *La Virgen* represents collective empowerment, Cere's words, "Put your hand inside my wound," construct the paradox of communion: having no body, her wound can only be the valley itself ("Inside the valley of my wound, there is a people" [148]).[33] Through her words, reinforced by the symbolism of her name, Cerezita Valle, she becomes the valley and the people become one in her. The striking visual image of Cere as *La Virgen* is complemented by the poetic power of her final words. The reduction of her tongue's multiple potential to visionary speech can be seen as a sublimation of sexual desire, or as the "use" of the erotic, in Lorde's sense, in "our acts against oppression" (58). In the world of the play, Cere's appearance as the Virgin, her death, and her rhetorical evocation of the historical resistance of the "miracle people" move the people of McLaughlin to political action.

The evocation of Central American genocide and warfare in Cere's rhetorical construction of the "miracle people" introduces another strategy of representing "Chicano" that coexists in some tension with the evocation of *La Vir-*

gen and the religious rituals embedded in UFW-style environmental activism. The dramaturgy attempts to hold together the solemn quietude of the funeral procession with its static, surreal tableau of the Virgin/head, the hyperbolic melodrama of the violent offstage killings, and the deaths of the Salvadoran people evoked in Cere's speeches. The representation of the parallel killings clearly raises the stakes in the struggle against environmental racism; however, it is not clear esthetically or politically whether the play entirely succeeds in pulling off this bold juxtaposition of representational strategies.

Heroes works with a repertory of specifically Chicano images to represent the people's entry into joy—that alternative sphere of knowledge where collective experience and acceptance of internal diversity are possible. In Valdez' play, the Mexican revolutionary's head covets the Chicano male leader's body. Cere, the head, also longs for and ultimately finds a body. In Moraga's text the desired body is the collectivity, as in the ritual of communion which unites the congregation in the mystical body of Christ. The mythic dimension of the play draws on multiple cultural repertories, recalling the iconographic importance of the colossal Olmeca heads as well as the centrality of sacred sacrifice in Aztec and Mayan cultures. In both Catholic and indigenous traditions, sacrifice is the meeting place of the human and the divine: to ensure natural cycles and cosmic balance, to redeem original sin through Christ's humanity. *Heroes* instills the power of material reality into the sacred, imagining sacrifice/communion as the struggle for social justice. Moraga blends the experience of joy with sacrifice to produce a secular narrative of individual and collective liberation as an alternative to the narrative of *la raza* as family (reproduced in *Shrunken Head*). The spiritual *parentesco* or kinship between Cere and Amparo in their outspoken activism and their powerful use of language traces the outline of an alternative family.

But, as in all her writing, Moraga's symbols in *Heroes* are multiple and strenuously resist binary either/or readings. Cere cannot return to rebel against a decision that makes her one with her community at an awful price, as Tashi does in Walker's *Possessing the Secret of Joy.* Cere's loss of self in the collectivity is at once empowering of that community and deeply troubling, given the traditional teaching that women should sacrifice themselves for others.[34] The gender ideology of the religious symbol of the virgin martyr stresses woman's passivity, obedience, piety, and chastity; in this way, women's "passion and yearning" can be channeled into a kind of permissible heroism that reinforces the devaluation of the female body (Perry, 37). By figuring female self-assertion as a negation of the self, the model of the virgin martyr restricts the *kinds* of self-assertion deemed appropriate for women (Rose, 267). While Cere escapes the constraints placed upon her by culture, her mother, and her lack of a body, the mystical site of self-sacrifice can only offer a kind of agency that paradoxically cancels out the subject. *Heroes* both evokes and mutes the feminine images and discourses of *La Virgen* and the virgin martyrs through the simultaneous re-gendering of the Christ/communion figure. Cere not only acts as martyr and linguistic intermediary, the traditional functions of both La Malinche and the Virgin, but also assumes the masculine role of redeemer.

The loss of the individual self is also the fulfillment of desire (to be one with another). The search for this communion drives all Moraga's writing, as articulated in this beautiful passage from *The Last Generation*:

All writing is confession [. . .] The admission of our [. . .] overwhelming desire to be relieved of the burden of ourselves in the body of another, to be forgiven of our ultimate aloneness in the mystical body of a god or the common work of a revolution. (61)

The objects of desire may be multiple, but the propelling force is the need to transform personal and cultural betrayal into more inclusive forms of community.[35]

The emphasis on the desire for social justice joins *Heroes* to the Chicano theater tradition, even as *Heroes* expands the meanings of political struggle. This is why I think Moraga works within, in a new form, the mythic constructions of "Chicano" as "nation" here and in *TLG*:

I cling to the word "nation" because without the specific naming of the nation, the nation will be lost [. . .] Let us retain our radical naming but expand it to meet a broader and wiser revolution [. . .] Without the dream of a free world, a free world will never be realized. Chicana lesbians and gay men do not merely seek inclusion in the Chicano nation; we seek a nation strong enough to embrace a full range of racial diversities, human sexualities, and expressions of gender. (150, 164)

We may be opposed to essentializing constructions of racial identity, but it is difficult to renounce what Greg Tate has called the "romance" of identifying as black or Chicana/o in the world (quoted in Dent 10, 13). It is the pleasure and the possibility of joy in being part of a collectivity and the potential for struggle as a people that gives meaning to and sustains the notion of "Chicano" in Moraga's writing.

The love of "Chicano" is a fantasy, part of how we identify with the ways we are imagined and represented. Moraga's imagining of "Chicano" out of a lesbian sensibility in *Heroes* and Valdez' search for leadership in *Shrunken Head* are equally a fantasy, not the "right" or "real" way we are.[36] We can no longer remain innocent about the politics of our representations (Hall, "New Ethnicities," 448) and how the fantasy and love of "Chicano" can function to exclude many who would be part of the collective. The emergent critical consciousness of diversity *within* ethnic communities, exemplified in texts such as *Heroes*, veers sharply from the nature of the pleasure some Chicano *teatro* offers, but I agree with Dent that it may "bring us closer to the collective domain of joy" (18).

PART III

The Written Identity

"I Long to Enter You Like a Temple"

Sex, Salvation, and Shamanism

In Moraga's writing, the representation of lesbian sex becomes the vehicle for waging the intimate struggle with gender conditioning on a most vulnerable level and explores the impact of socially defined power dynamics on lesbian sexual relations.[1] Her literary and dramatic representations delve into the differences between butch-femme sexual styles and the *chingón/chingada* polarity, the Mexican variant of active/passive normative heterosexual roles as described by Octavio Paz in *The Labyrinth of Solitude* (see chapter 1). Moraga uses her reading of Paz as a platform to propose some alternative sexualities within this cultural context. In this chapter, after situating Moraga's butch-identified position within the feminist movement of the 1970s and 1980s, I examine certain passages from *Loving in the War Years* that illuminate Moraga's understanding of the *chingón/chingada* polarity and display some of the representational strategies that sidestep this rigid active/passive binary. *Giving Up the Ghost*, her first play, and the mixed genre "La Ofrenda," published in *The Last*

Generation, directly engage the cultural legacy of the *chingón/chingada*, especially how it interacts with and may be undermined by the flow of butch-femme desire.

Moraga writes from a butch perspective, representing the conflict between the power of giving sexual pleasure to a receptive lover ("libidinal force") and the fear of exposure and vulnerability ("gender dysphoria") (Halberstam, "F2M," 104). During the lesbian "sex wars" of the 1980s in the context of U.S. lesbian and feminist history, she positions herself as butch-femme advocate.[2]

In the 1950s and 1960s, the nineteenth-century sexological definition of the lesbian as gender invert (a man trapped in a female body) was losing ground to the notion of lesbianism as a female variant of homosexuality largely parallel to gay men's attraction to men and described as "sexual preference" and later "sexual orientation" (Whisman, 50). Internal divisions were already drawn at this point when members of the first lesbian organization in the U.S., the Daughters of Bilitis (founded in 1955), actively discouraged butch-femme identification in their program of gaining legitimacy for lesbians through assimilation. In the 1970s, lesbian-feminism defined lesbianism "as a form of female revolt and woman-bonding, dissociating it from male homosexuality" (Whisman, 51), in phrases that rallied a "Lesbian Nation": "If feminism is the theory, lesbianism is the practice" and "a lesbian is the rage of all women condensed to the point of explosion."[3]

The construction of lesbianism as the "quintessential feminism" involved the women's music industry; separatist lesbian communities, such as Oregon's Womanshare, that lived on "women's land," excluding even male children; women's centers; rape crisis hotlines; battered-women's shelters; the lesbian feminist press; and the tendency to define the "real" lesbian in terms of feminist politics:

> As this women's culture became more clearly articulated, its borders became less and less permeable. For if the personal was political, then no part of one's life — including preferences for clothes, food, or even sex — was off-limits to scrutiny by the movement. (Whisman, 52)

In their opposition to the system of patriarchy, particularly the notions of "power over another" and the objectification of women, lesbian-feminists, or "cultural feminists," believed that "lesbian sex must be consistent with the best of lesbian ethics" (Faderman, 250), reflecting a utopian model of "equal power" in which penetration, butch-femme, or S/M erotic stylings of images of domination, control, and violence were taboo. Cultural feminists recognized that all desire, including lesbian desire, is socially constructed within the matrix of normative heterosexuality, but they believed it was important to deconstruct those desires rather than incorporate them into lesbian sexual fantasies, publications, and practices (Faderman, 250–251).

By the late 1970s and early 1980s, the feminist movement was fractured by the critique by women of color and lesbian "sex radicals" who rejected lesbian-feminism's prescription of what they called "vanilla sex," which prohibited penetration, pornographic videos and magazines, sex clubs and strip shows, and sexual role playing (including leather S/M and butch-femme). While the cultural feminists insisted that such practices violated feminist principles, the radicals argued that the cultural feminist position reproduced traditional concepts of gender by insisting on universal differences between men and women, and that "non-vanilla" sexual practices were feminist because they "encouraged women to fight repression by examining sexual feelings that had been taboo for women" (Faderman, 252). Cultural feminist activism produced (short-lived) anti-pornographic legislation such as that enacted in Minneapolis and public confrontations such as the one at a Barnard College conference in 1982, where Women Against Pornography picketers denounced the inclusion of panels featuring speakers like Joan Nestle, Amber Hollibaugh, Pat Califia, and Dorothy Allison.[4]

The early 1990s saw a shift from the gender-based Lesbian Nation to the Queer Nation, with an emphasis on fluidity of sexual identity; coalitions among lesbians, gay men, and other sexual minorities (particularly around AIDS); and a critique of the "second-class citizenship" of working-class people, women, and men and women of color within Queer Nation. Many young women in the 1990s identify more as queer (including bisexual and questioning) than lesbian. They have more in common with their male counterparts than what they perceive as the puritanical and identity-politics-oriented "lesbian" and "gay" movements of the 1970s and 1980s, even as they remain ignorant of their analyses, struggles, and gains from which they benefit, directly or indirectly.[5]

Some may lament and others may celebrate the proliferation and fracturing of identities, movements, and communities in the 1990s, symbolized for Arlene Stein by the coexistence of "the dolled-up dykes and lesbian mothers" (xv). Lisa K. C. Hall's description of a gathering of friends at an "imaginary cafe" captures an even broader gamut of self-stylings in a vision of potential connections and coalitions within a "multiply gendered queer community":

a faggot-identified dyke in her "I'm Not a Boy" T-shirt, a Radical Faerie friend in his camouflage khaki tutu, a Queer National in his "Dykes from Hell" shirt obtained from his sisters in LABIA, my queer yet heterosexual boys o' color auxiliary, my students who major in women's studies and go to sex clubs, where we try to avoid each other—and of course me in my newly acquired "It's *Mr.* Faggot to You" T-shirt. Artists, activists, academics, and the unaffiliated creating slices of community that have never existed before. I will always retain my fascination with "identity" and "community" because they're always in process and always provisional. Our identities never become final because new experiences continue to affect the way we see ourselves and these new identifications in turn affect the kinds of experiences we can have and the kinds of communities we can create. (229)

The 1990s appear to be the decade that has definitively put the term "lesbian" itself under rigorous and continual scrutiny, redefining it as an ongoing impulse of self-invention. The vision is no longer one of creating "lesbian" as if it could exist exclusively outside of mainstream structures, but, as Stein puts it, of acknowledging "how much we are embedded in the culture from which we have tried to escape, and how important it is for us to learn to live with the contradictions—while pushing up against them" (xv).

Since the beginning of the 1980s, Moraga's writing has made crucial contributions to shaping this emergent consciousness through consistent re-creation of the category "lesbian" within and against the grain of a multiplicity of contexts. As co-editor of *This Bridge Called My Back* (1981) and coauthor of such pieces as "What We're Rollin Around in Bed With" (1983), with Amber Hollibaugh, Moraga's representation of lesbian sex is located at the juncture of gendered, working-class, bicultural, and racialized identity in a context of butch-femme sexual acts.

While the sex radicals believe that "until women are free to explore their own sexuality any way they wish, they will never be truly free" (Faderman, 250), they consistently pay little attention to the historical significance of sexualized and racialized representations of women of color. Moraga's writing sites this struggle for women's freedom in and on the racialized body. Her writing proposes plural sexualities in the representation of racialized desire, exploring the difference between her culturally informed desire and formulations of "correct" sexuality supposedly devoid of power exchanges: "The fact of the matter was that all these power struggles of 'having' and 'being had' were being played out in my own bedroom. And in my psyche, they held a particular Mexican twist" (*Loving*, 126). In her exploration of the "sex of race" and the "race of sex" (*Loving*, 125), Moraga's writing attempts to liberate a space for imagining a Chicana lesbian desire that is both "twisted" and erotically empowered by culturally specific sexual, psychic, and social meanings. Texts such as *Ghost* and

"La Ofrenda" examine the culturally charged context in which active or passive sexual roles are rigidly assumed but also the potential for imagining a different erotics of "having" and "being had" within this cultural context.

A passage from *Loving* couches Moraga's culturally deviant and sinful desire for women in the language of the *chingón/chingada* polarity: "in order not to embody the *chingada*, nor the femalized, and therefore perverse, version of the *chingón*, I became pure spirit—bodiless. For what, indeed, must my body look like if I were both the *chingada* and the *chingón?*" (120–121). A gender rebel, the writer as a young girl rejects the passive position of the *chingada*, yet cannot imagine herself as a lover of women outside the construction of the *chingón*. The answer to her question ("what, indeed, must my body look like?") is found in the dream of herself as hermaphrodite discussed in chapter 1. This potentially empowering figure embodies an imagined alternative to the mutually exclusive active/passive dichotomy, but the frightened young girl suppresses it and moves away from her body and her sexuality into the spiritual realm of the Church.

Another passage in *Loving* tells how years later a sexual encounter brings home the self-limiting consequences of the *chingón/chingada* polarity, condensing the fear of being open and vulnerable like the *chingada* in the expressive image of tender pink flesh:

All this changed, however, when I thought I saw in a lover, a woman, the chingón that I had so feared to recognize in myself: "the active, aggressive and closed person," as Paz writes, "who inflicts [the wound]." I had met my match. I was forced to confront how, in all my sexual relationships I had resisted, at all costs, feeling la chingada which, in effect, meant that I had resisted fully feeling sex at all. *Nobody wants to be made to feel the turtle with its underside all exposed, just pink and folded flesh.* In the effort to avoid embodying la chingada, I became the chingón. In the effort not to feel fucked, I became the fucker, even with women. In the effort not to feel pain or desire, I grew a callous around my heart and imagined I felt nothing at all. (124–125)

The imbrication of butch-femme and *chingón/chingada* poses the problem of the impoverishment of the desiring subject in Moraga's writing. Her texts return again and again to worry this knot. The question is not of giving up a preference for a particular sexual position (butch), but of engaging the internalized unfeeling *chingón* who "fucks" women (in the double sense of the word) and fears love.

Through poetic lyricism, character, form, and imagery Moraga elaborates an erotic language to set against a phallocentric assumption of penetration as domination, according to which "only penises do the penetrating" (Cvetko- vich, 133). This language represents non-binary giving and taking in sex within a butch-femme erotics in which non-orgasmic penetrators such as fingers and hands are primary. In this sense, Moraga's texts are part of a project described by Ann Cvetkovich: "It would then be impossible to appeal to some biological common ground to explain the meaning of penetration, but even more impor- tantly, new social and sexual imaginaries could be enabled" (133).

But these new imaginaries, unlike earlier lesbian-feminist utopian repre- sentations of lesbian sex, are "non-redemptive" (Cvetkovich, 139). Moraga's writing represents the friction between the desire to save women through sex and the failure of this project. These representations expose the fear, pain, and difficulty involved in making oneself physically and emotionally vulnerable or receptive. Cvetkovich proposes that a sex-positive position be able to embrace this difficulty, as well (134). What follows will attempt to show why the nega- tive is important in Moraga's writing, even as she retains the utopian impulse necessary to imagine alternative sexualities and social relations.

Moraga's strategies of lesbian representation include the simultaneous cri- tique and appropriation of dominant signifiers, from gender roles to the icons of Mexican and Anglo culture. In spite of, or perhaps because of, its repression of the body and sexual desire, Mexican Catholicism becomes an important source for the writing of a unique brand of sensuality. Moraga's work character- istically infuses Mexican and Catholic archetypes with the heat of a racialized lesbian desire:

I dreamed of church and cunt [. . .] The suffering and the thick musty mysticism of the catholic church fused with the sensation of entering the vagina—like that of a colored woman's—dark, rica, full-bodied. The heavy sensation of complexity. A journey I must unravel, work out for myself.

I long to enter you like a temple. (Loving, 90)

In this quote, penetrating the lover's body merges with entering the church, represented through an array of sensory images. The "complexity" of these entries provokes the "journey," referring to the sexual project in Moraga's writ- ing to understand lesbian sex as a "microcosm of all human relations" (TLG, 160). These dreamed movements through space—the entries into church and the dark female body, the journey to unravel the complexity of lesbian sex/ Mexican Catholicism—capture the writer's desire to invest lesbian sex with the values awarded the Church. As elsewhere in the writing, this passage speaks of

Moraga's understanding of the positivity of lesbian sex as well as the inescapable cultural and social contexts that produce the psychic "suffering" referred to in the quote. The "journey" involves the realization of the embeddedness of lesbian sex in these contexts as well as the potential to put new images and meanings into circulation as part of new social and sexual imaginaries.

Closely related to this positive-negative lesbianization of the signs of Mexican Catholicism is the notion of love among women as possible "redemption." In *Ghost*, the possibility of release from sexual and other constraints is framed in religious and racialized terms (held out by mestizas to mestizas). Marisa envisions lesbian sex as a potential liberation from the prison of cultural assumptions: "And I wanted to say but didn't . . . 'Sí. La mujer es mi religión.'[6] / [. . .] If only sex coulda saved us" (56). Marisa speaks her words as a kind of secular confession, directed to the audience. Amalia rejects the confessor role, forcing the responsibility for self-forgiveness on Marisa: "Your thoughts are yours. / They speak of you, not me" (27). While *Ghost* develops the idea of "salvation" in women's love of women, this is clearly a non-utopian representation of lesbian sex, since it voices the demons and hurts that raise barriers between women and ultimately lead to the failure of Marisa's relationship with Amalia in the play. Among these barriers are Marisa's female *chingón* identification, embodied in the pain she experiences in her legs. Amalia's desire to be taken by *and* to take Marisa may teach the *chingón*-identified Marisa to let herself be loved and feel loved by women.

The title of the first act of *Ghost*, "La Pachuca," highlights Marisa/Corky's identification with the tough, rebellious, and chiseled self-stylings of that Chicana/o subculture and captures her conformity to the closed female *chingón* position. The title of the second act, "La Salvadora," is more ambivalent. While it refers to the redeeming power of Amalia's desire to take Marisa, it also suggests that Marisa's love(making) can save Amalia, make her feel again, and cure her socially inflicted wounds. Femme activist Joan Nestle "claims that the butch's power to take the femme gives her herself" (Cvetkovich, 140). This process of giving and taking—that is, the pleasure of attending to the lover's pleasure while taking her and the far-from-passive reponsiveness of the lover in receiving that attention—presents an alternative to pervasive degrading/degraded connotations that encode sexual practices.[7] In Christine Cassidy's theory the term "active receptivity" signifies a psychic and social as well as sexual state (quoted in Cvetkovich, 141). And since sexual relations "physicalize and embody" social and cultural relations (Cvetkovich, 141), both Marisa and Amalia embody the possibility that active receptivity and a giving-taking may open them to themselves and to a "connection with the world" as well (Cvetkovich, 128–129).

Ghost's particular project of representing butch-femme desires in one character further unsettles sexual dichotomies. Marisa and Amalia gradually become one in poetic imagery that develops the notion of a complementary giving
and taking. At the end of the first act, both women speak of the changes going on
inside them. In the second act, the two women are progressively fused. Marisa
sees in Amalia "the other river," which contrasts textually with the image Amalia
uses to describe her male lovers as dead bodies floating down a river. Marisa
asks, "was the beautiful woman / in the mirror of the water / you or me? /
Who do I make love to? / Who do I see in the ocean of our bed?" (27). The
identification of the two women in the subversion of the expected binary positions of active and passive also suggests the potential for self-love, for being
both subject and object of the same racialized desire, mestiza self-love. While
Ghost foregrounds the characters' versatility with regards to sexual positioning,
other texts written by Moraga indicate that such versatility is not a generalized
ideal.

But this is a project whose contours are only hinted at and not fulfilled.
Marisa thinks of Amalia as a liberating blessing in the *Dedicación* that opens
the play:

I am grateful to her   to something
that feels like a blessing (1)

But she is not able to hold on to her. The Dedication also states, "don't know
where this woman and I / will find each other again." Conversely, Marisa hopes
to save Amalia through sex, associated with religion and worship, but the text
does not resolve the question of Amalia's salvation. At the end, the question of
whether Amalia will be able to feel and be open to a connection with the world
is still posed as a question. In the Dedication to the second act, the poetic voice
carefully sets aside the idea of salvation in her memory of Amalia but retains
the notion of the liberating angel: "and I still remember / that / woman / not
my savior / but an angel / with wings / that did once lift me / to another / self"
(33). For Marisa, her pleasure and belief in sex as salvation are constrained by
her experience of homophobia, racism, sexism, and controlling heterosexism.
By incorporating pain, difficulty, and failure in the re-imagining of a sexual and
social world, *Ghost* represents a non-redemptive vision that obliges the reader
or spectator to account for the conflictive social and cultural contexts providing
the arena for sexual experience.

"La Ofrenda" also represents the psychic, social, and sexual consequences
of the *chingón/chingada* polarity as well as the attempt to resignify this cultur-

ally inflected active/passive binary through the redemptive power of lesbian sex. But here the blending of salvation and sex is conceived less in Catholic imagery than in a repertory of indigenous symbols and evocations. Divided into four sections, "La Ofrenda" blends prose and poetry, resisting generic classification. This formal undecidability is an apt form for the project of undermining the rigid connotations adhering to sexual roles.

The undecidable form also echoes the indeterminacy of knowledge that opens the text: "Strange as it may seem, there is no other way to be sure. Completely sure. Well, you can never be completely sure but you can try and hold fast to some things" (77). What the narrator, Lola, wants to know is difficult to pin down precisely, but it has to do with desire, sexual roles and practices, love, and commitment (individual and collective). In the representation of this desire for knowledge, the text makes a move familiar in Moraga's writing: that of de-centering the mind as seat of knowledge and privileging the body. Here the sense of smell reorients other texts' focus on the heart: "Your eyes can fool you [. . .] But not smell. Smell remembers and tells the future. No lying about that" (77). Zigzagging between different moments of the past and the present, the narrative form supports the role of memory in reinventing the past to better understand the present. Through the body (the recollection of smell), not the intellect, Lola will use that knowledge to plot her life into the future.

Knowledge rooted in the body is quickly associated with love and the resistance to love practiced by the guarded lesbian sexual subject who has assumed the role of female *chingón*. In the quote from *Loving* (125) cited above, the "callous" around the heart protects her from exposure and at the same time prevents her from "feeling sex at all" (125). In "La Ofrenda" Moraga employs the metaphor of the locked heart and how smell can open it, leaving the *chingón*-identified lesbian subject open to herself and the world: "Smell can make your heart crack open no matter how many locks you have wrapped 'round it [. . .] Like love" (77). Like smell, love can penetrate her defenses. Yet no facile binary formulation of love or smell is offered: "It can be your best friend or worst enemy [. . .] Smell is home or loneliness. / Confidence or betrayal. / Smell remembers" (77–78).

After this introduction and the initial characterization of the *chingón*-identified narrator, Tiny appears in the second section. Tiny exemplifies Lola's initial expression of relative trust in body-based knowledge in the introductory section. A butch lover of women, Tiny's desire is mapped by the body, not the intellect. By "following her nose," rather than allowing the mind to mediate her decisions about whom she desires, Tiny ends up in potentially confrontational situations with men, through unauthorized use of their sexual property: "when the scent happened to take her to the wrong side of town or into the bed of the wife of someone she'd wish it hadn't in the morning" (78). While, in this passage, the "wife" may be the femme partner of another butch woman, bringing Tiny into potential conflict with another "big bad bitch" (79) like herself, a later textual instance reveals Tiny's penchant for pleasuring the women who belong to men. As opposed to the narrator Lola's (unspecified) political activity in an academic setting, Tiny's "contribution to La Causa was to keep the girlfriends of the Machos happy while they were out being too revolutionary to screw" (80). The dynamic is similar to Marisa's in *Ghost*, who competes with men for heterosexual women but feels ultimately that "the dick beats me every time" (8). "La Ofrenda" explores the ways in which Tiny is "beaten" by the persona of the *chingón* that she has internalized to the detriment of her (female) self.

While Tiny allows herself to be placed in physically threatening situations through her desire for women, the text specifies that she will not fight, introducing "blood" as one of the story's central metaphors: "'The only blood I like,' she'd say, 'is what my hand digs out of a satisfied woman.' We'd all tell Tiny to shut her arrogant mouth up and get her another drink" (78). The initial presentation of this theme opposes blood let in violent confrontations over women to the blood originating in the secret, inner recesses of a woman's body, brought to light through sexual pleasuring. In contrast to cultural feminist claims that butch-femme reproduces the power imbalances of heteronormativity, perceived as active male subjects taking pleasure through a passive woman's body with little consideration of her own pleasure in the act, the sexual power of the butch is defined by her skill in making love to the femme (Nestle, "Butch-Femme Relationships," 100–101, 104): hence, the "satisfied woman." The text packs the term "blood" with other meanings, notably the *sangre* that defines (biological or non-biological) family, and finally, "blood" on Lola's hands, not from lovemaking but from betraying Tiny, herself, and the women of the "race" as well.

After the introduction of the blood imagery, the text turns to the shifting identities of the two characters, Tiny and Lola, through time, signified by their changing names. During the grade school years, their rites of passage are culturally marked through the auspices of the Catholic Church. For First Holy Communion, Tiny is "Christina Morena," otherwise known as Tina, who stands in front of Lola in line. Tiny leaves that identity of Tina behind as physical changes bring a new body, a new name, and a new sexual identity, called simply "the life," lesbian existence: "By Confirmation, Tiny'd left most of us girls in the dust. Shot up and out like nobody's business. So Christina, who everyone called Tina, turned into Tiny overnight and that's the name she took with her into 'the life' " (78). Just as little Tina becomes big Tiny, the narrator also passes through various identities, marked nominally. Lola considers Tina's new name, Tiny, "better" than her own given name, Dolores (after the Sorrows of the Virgin), which corresponds to Tiny's "official" name, Christina, associated with school and church calendars.

Unlike Tiny, Lola navigates an intermediate phase of being called "Dottie" to get to *her* name in "the life": Lolita. Although Tiny calls her Lola, the claiming of the diminutive at this point in the narrative foreshadows the narrator's attraction to her "Lolita Lebrón" persona of radical Chicana, while "Dottie" signifies the possibility of "passing":

> Dottie, they used to call me years later in some circles, but it never stuck, cuz I was the farthest thing from a freckled-faced bony-kneed gabacha. Still, for a while I tried it. Now I'm back to who I was before. Just Lolita. Stripped down. Not so different from those Holy Communion days, really. (78)

Tiny is never explicitly associated with any other ethnic group but Chicanas/os, including her objects of desire; one of her potential lovers, "Angie," is racially unmarked. The text describes Lola's lovers as "white" and "black" (but not Chicana). The text suggests that Lola passes through a "white" phase, signified in the text by "trying" the name Dottie for awhile ("in some circles"). She says she rejected the name ("it never stuck"; "Now I'm back to who I was before") based on perceived physical differences between herself as a Chicana and "gabachas," or white women (freckles, bony). But the text continues to map Lola in two differently racialized spaces: the (Latina) lesbian world of the bar, Cha Cha's Place, and the world of "sophisticated college girls" where Lola carries out her political work related to La Causa. While this latter world may be peopled by Chicanas, other "college girls" of color, and Tiny's cuckolded "machos" working for the revolution, the college environment is implicitly white. Lola seems to spend most of her time in that world, yet she is aware of fundamental differences between herself and the "college girls" who drive her back to Cha Cha's: "Cha Cha's Place where you only saw my ass when the sophisticated college girls had fucked with my mind one too many times" (80).

Lola travels between the political scene at the college and the apolitical scene at the lesbian bar, where she is known as "Lolita Lebrón" after telling the lesbians who frequent the bar about Lebrón's armed action against the U.S. Congress in the cause of Puerto Rican independence. In spite of her distance/difference from the women who frequent Cha Cha's Place, Lola feels loved and respected there, as she seems to want to be, for the political work the bar dykes deride. On the other hand, she suspects "maybe it was only Tiny who respected me and all the others had to treat me right cuz of her" (80), invoking once again Tiny's persona as "big bad bitch."

What is remarkable about the passage about names (78) is Lola's unproblematized assumption that she's now "back to who I was before" (78), an ambiguous phrase which could refer to who she was before being Dottie in certain social groups, or to someone she was in an even earlier period in her life: "Not so different from those Holy Communion days, really" (78). As in other texts, "La Ofrenda" validates Catholicism as part of cultural identity by recuperating Lola's Catholic school days into her adult lesbian life. But more telling for this text, the passage masks the character's actual tendency to radically separate those youthful school days from her adult life.

In this misperception of continuity, Lola's tendency to continue seeing Tiny as she was then is mitigated by her sense of "growing up" as a kind of loss (80). In the last paragraph of the second section of the text, Lola continues her narration of opaque half-revelations:

But it was me she wanted. And I needed my original home girl more than I needed any other human being alive to this day. Growing up is learning to go without. Tiny and me . . . we grew up too fast. (80)

She asserts their mutual need—Tiny wants Lola and Lola needs Tiny to be a supportive "home girl" who will listen to her, respect her for her political work, and ensure that the others pay her at least the token respect that minimizes their differences. The equation of "growing up" and "going without" hints at Lola's *chingón* identification, her inability to love. It also refers to what will be revealed only in the third section of the story, where Lola confronts the reality that they *have* "grown up" (82), a knowledge already equated with privation.

From the time "when we were kids, teenagers," the narrator dredges up a memory of love and unrequited desire in an erotic encounter between them: "we came *this* close to making it with each other" (79). Although Lola loves Tiny, she refuses to be lovers with her, precisely *because* she loves her "like the way you love *familia* like they could do anything [. . .] and you'd still love them because they're your blood. Sangre. Tiny was my blood. My blood sister" (79). For Lola, making love with Tiny would feel like incest. And while Lola says she left Tiny sexually unfulfilled because Tiny would "rather pretend she didn't" (79) desire Lola, the narrator now glimpses her error in believing Tiny's *words* ("what was coming outta her damn mouth") instead of trusting her own body: "I was too stupid to smell out the situation for what it really was" (79). She is faced with Tiny's corporeality, "her damn solid square body like a tank" (79) and her curses (what is coming out of her mouth): "Fuck fuck chinga'o, man, fuck!" (79). Lola says she rejected Tiny because Lola wanted to hear "words of love, commitment, tenderness. You know, luna de miel stuff" (79). But it is Tiny's vulnerability, sitting on the toilet with her pants around her ankles, "her knees squeezed together like they were nailed shut," and *pain* that makes Lola bolt: "I ran from her as fast as my cola could take me" (79). Even before the full revelation of the sources of Tiny's pain later in the text, the reader is invited to imagine the cause of her suffering: the violence of social and psychic realities fundamentally linked to who she is and how she looks.

Lola's reaction to Tiny's need points up Lola's own limiting constructions of self and desire: while she protests that she could never have sex with Tiny because they are like family and insists that she, Lola, was the one who wanted tenderness, love, and commitment, the narrator's analysis of the situation also reveals that the text of Tiny's body did in fact speak what the words coming out of her mouth did not, and the meaning of *that* text was enough to make Lola run. It is Lola who fears intimacy, who separates sex and love to the point that if she has sex with someone she loves, it feels like incest. For Lola, "sister" and "lover" are incommensurable identity categories. The object of Lola's desire must remain unknown and desirable in its racialized unknown-ness, as is the case with the women she chooses: "But I never loved anyone like I loved Tiny. No body. Not one of those lean white or fine black ladies that spread their legs for me and my smooth-talking" (80). Even in the category of "sister," she realizes she has let Tiny down, as she says a little later: "We weren't meant to be lovers, only sisters. But being a sister ain't no part-time occupation" (80).

Lola's conception of sexual roles and styles is another reason for her to reject Tiny. Both Lola and Tiny are butches attracted to femmes (Lola's white and black lovers "spread their legs" for her); in Tiny's case, married heterosexual women. In this erotic scenario, Lola is not attracted to butch Tiny. Since Lola is a *chingón*-identified butch, Tiny's desire for Lola is threatening on various levels. If Tiny desires to "have" Lola, Lola must reject assuming the *chingada* position. But if, as we find out later, Tiny's desire is to be had *by* Lola, Lola's culturally constrained erotic position is still called into question, for knowing that a "big bad bitch" like Tiny could want to be taken means that Lola herself might harbor similar desires. Tiny makes herself vulnerable by allowing Lola to think that Tiny is one of those butches joked about in Joan Nestle's phrase: "Get a butch home and she turns over on her back" ("Butch-Femme Relationships," 103).

This first teenage encounter leaves both women scarred. Although Lola continues to insist on her unparalleled love for Tiny, she feels guilty of betraying Tiny by not accepting her desire to be desired. In the text, this sexual/love betrayal is associated with Lola's distancing from Cha Cha's Place, from the barrio, from what could have been a supportive, strategically separatist community, or *sitio* (place), in Emma Pérez' terms (161).

The crucial third section of "La Ofrenda" relates a subsequent erotic encounter that takes place in Tiny's bedroom fifteen years after the trauma of the first. Now, Tiny uses her desire for another woman as a medium through which to express once again her vulnerability, born of her desire to be desired by Lola. Tiny takes off her clothes, ostensibly for her buddy Lola's detached assessment of her physical attractiveness and potential for pleasing women. Lola is incapable of looking at her, protesting—"This is too cold. It's fuckin' scientific, no one looks at people this way"—until Tiny reminds her that Lola *does* look at people this way (81). This information about Lola's sexual practice fits in neatly with what Lola herself has revealed earlier (the women she "has" for their racialized sleekness and leanness, but does not necessarily love).

Knowing that Tiny expects an honest answer, Lola looks for a long time. She is caught in an impasse because she looks with a split vision, with her "two good eyes, the blue one and the brown one" (81): "I try to isolate each eye, see if I come up with different conclusions depending on which eye and which color I'm working with. Figure one is the European view, the other the Indian" (81). This passage provides, retroactively, yet another reason for Lola's rejection of Tiny fifteen years earlier and reveals the ways in which Lola's desire for women is not only informed by sexual roles but is also racialized and shaped by mainstream images of the ideal female body ("magazine beautiful" [82]). Seen through the "blue" eye, Tiny the "tank" is not desirable, while Lola's desire for the "lean white or fine black ladies" is constructed from the position of the "European."[8]

The painful predicament is broken, not by *seeing* Tiny as desirable through the "brown" or "Indian" eye, but through smell. In the opening section of "La Ofrenda," the narrator expresses her distrust of vision: "Your eyes can fool you [...] But not smell" (77). This shift from racialized visual perception (the European and the Indian eyes) to the sense of smell remits the narrator and readers to the cultural, everyday context of U.S. Mexican life written on bodies and sensory memories. The shift is signified by the break from prose to poetic form in the text. Giving up on Lola, Tiny reaches for her pants: "And then I smell her, just as she reaches over me. Her breast brushing my shoulder, a warm bruised stone . . . something softening. I inhale. Grab her arm. 'No, wait. Let me look at you'" (81). Tiny's smell softens Lola's calloused heart and allows her to see that Tiny is beautiful—not "magazine beautiful" like the women Lola usually desires, but "Mexican beautiful" (82).

Tiny's beautiful brownness contrasts with the commodity consumerism of magazine advertising; she is identified with the blonde dresser she stands in front of, but this commodity has become a familiar mainstay in Mexican homes and a marker of that cultural milieu ("very popular among Mexicanos in the fifties"). The dresser further contributes to the theme of continuity and change: "I know that dresser. For years now. It didn't change, but Tiny . . . she did [. . .] the fifties have gone and went, and in the meantime my Christina Morena went and changed herself into a woman" (82). The dresser and the fifties are emblematic of the continuity in Lola and Tiny's relationship and of how Lola has kept Tiny (and partly herself) captive in her school-day memories ("it had never occurred to me that we had grown up" [82]).

To symbolize and center Tiny's transformation and that of the two women's desire, the text continues to play with names and weaves together a cluster of poetic images that dominate the last two sections of "La Ofrenda." For example, the feminine variant "Morena," or dark woman, replaces the more common patronymic "Moreno." Tiny undergoes yet another change of name, a return to the name of the schoolgirl that Tiny is no longer, now significantly weighted to represent the continuity of cultural and racialized identity: "And in front of this blonde dresser is brown Christina. Christina Morena desnuda" (82). Tiny and Tina disappear into the Christina of the Holy Communion line, who emerges refigured into a woman who "looks like her mother and my mother with legs like tree trunks and a panza[9] that rolls round into her ombligo como pura miel" (82).[10] Smell and matrilineal cultural associations feminize Tiny's body, which facilitates Lola's desiring her.

The expressive switch into Spanish is characteristic of "La Ofrenda," marking key moments in the narrator's opening up and her journey back to her body. Here it communicates the cultural specificity of her awakening desire for Tiny, reconstructing the terms of "family" and the (brown) mother that appeared earlier in the text. In her explanation that she didn't have sex with Tiny before because it would feel like incest, Lola thinks first of the mother: "It'd be like doing it with your mother. No, your sister" (79). In this second encounter, Lola's desire for Tiny is stirred precisely by the connection with the (Indian) mother, redefining "family" and "home" ("hogar") through metaphors and similes that describe Tiny's body and Lola's desire for that body through the dense language of poetry: "The hair below the hill of her belly is the same color as her head. A deep black. Denso. Oculto como un nido escondido. Un hogar distante, aguardándome" (82).[11]

Sensing the nature of Tiny's desire ("She needed me to touch her"), the narrator reproduces an earlier dialogue between the two friends, revealing that not only is Tiny a butch, she is a stone butch: "She never let any of 'em touch her" (82). In the erotic script of the stone butch, pleasure resides in making love to women, not in being touched by them. The concise lines of the transcribed dialogue stand in stark contrast to the poetic lines quoted above that communicate Lola's rapturous discovery of Tiny's beauty.

> "I don't get it. What do you do then?"
> "I do it *to* them."
> "But I mean do you . . . y'know."
> "Get off? Yeah. Sure."
> "How?"
> "Rubbing. Thinking."
> "Thinking. Thinking about what?"
> "Her. How she's feeling."
> "You ever think about yourself?"
> "No one's home."
> "What?"
> "I don't gotta picture, you know what I mean? There's nobody to be. No me to be . . . not in the bed, anyway." (83)

Tiny's rejection of the role of *chingada* and her internalization of the *chingón* role are represented as stemming from a denial of her female self. As in the quote from *Loving* cited above ("In the effort not to feel pain or desire, I grew a callous around my heart and imagined I felt nothing at all" [125]), Tiny never allowed herself to feel pleasure. She finds no sexual role that allows her to be both female and lover of women, and in this sense she erases herself from the erotic script ("nobody to be").[12] To be aroused by a woman's touch on her breasts or sex or to imagine her own pleasure would anchor her desire in her female body and expose her to vulnerability and fear.

It is now unimaginable to Lola that Tiny would not find her *india* female self beautiful. Responding to Tiny's *unspoken* need to be touched, Lola constructs herself as "shaman" as she undertakes Tiny's healing by making her feel her female body, and constructs Tiny a possible female sexual identity of active receptivity through sexual penetration: "So, I put my hands inside her. I did. I put them all the way inside her and like a fuckin' shaman I am working magic on her, giving her someone to be" (83). The project of giving the active receiver of sexual pleasure her self is joined here to the re-signification of phallocentric penetration through the representation of hands as non-orgasmic penetrators. Through this act, Lola also breaks through the non-feeling female *chingón* role into a pleasuring-pleasured butch taking and giving.

To create a new erotic position for Tiny, Lola must silence Tiny's mouth, out of which the curses engendered by the pain of life experience emerge. The process of opening Tiny through active receptivity, of giving her "someone to be" in and through sex, requires healing the social and psychic wounds inflicted on her through racism and homophobia.

I couldn't kiss her, only between the legs
where the mouth there never cussed
where the lips there never curled
into snarls, smoked cigarettes, spit
phlegm into passing pale stubbled faces
mouthing dagger
dyke
jota
mal
flor (84) [13]

Lola must teach Tiny to speak with her body. "La Ofrenda," switching between prose and poetry, relocates the mouth between the legs as an organ of speech/sex, as in *Loving*. Cutting off Tiny's curses, Lola offers her another language:

"Don't say nothing, Tiny." Open your mouth and tell me something else . . .
She smells like copal between the legs. Tiny, Tina who stood
in front of me in the First Holy Communion line, smells
like fucking copal
sweet earth sap
oozing outta every pore
that dark bark tree
flesh kissed [. . .]
I kissed her where she had never spoken
where she had never sang (83–84)

Significantly, only Lola's admonition not to speak is verbalized as dialogue; the lesson about the "other" mouth (to speak, to sing with the female body) can only be communicated by reconstructing the female body through poetic language.

"La Ofrenda" falls short of representing Tiny's active receptivity in the sexual act. Before this point in the text, Tiny's pleasure is represented as seducing heterosexual women, insinuating that she provides pleasure the men cannot give them, and in "Rubbing. Thinking" during sex, as she imagines what her partner is feeling (83). While Tiny is active, if not verbal, in communicating her desire to be penetrated by Lola, the text is silent on her physical activity or responsiveness when they actually have sex. That the act was indeed pleasurable for them is suggested by Lola's revelation "I am working magic on her" (83). Instead, the text focuses on Lola's role as sexual shaman giving Tiny pleasure as well as "someone to be." "La Ofrenda" is primarily engaged with the process of Lola's own *potential* transformation from a closed-down *chingón* identification to a butch sexual practice that gives while taking. By accepting a degree of openness or willingness to make herself vulnerable, Lola can be receptive to certain pleasures, not necessarily that of penetration. Unlike *Ghost*, in which both characters embody a fluidity of erotic positionings, in "La Ofrenda," only Tiny exchanges, however transitorily, her erotic script of top for that of bottom. Lola remains the top pleasure giver; what the text explores is the shifting meanings attached to this sexual act.

The outright failure of Lola's shamanistic project, set against the social and psychic damage captured in the quote cited above and in Tiny's (and Lola's) inability to follow through on their sexual coming together, points to the non-utopian nature of Moraga's representation of lesbian sex. Lola is ever the unreliable narrator. Revealing that she was rejected by Tiny after this erotic encounter, Lola swears she would have married her, suggesting that the experience with Tiny has helped her resolve the opposition love/sex reinforced by *familia* or kinship taboos: "The girl was family and I knew her. I knew her and *still* loved her" (85). But contradictorily, the narrator also insists she was relieved when Tiny "put on her pants and told me to get out" (85), insinuating that Lola still fears commitment, love, and intimacy *outside* the bounds of the "blood" family, just as before she complained that "being a sister ain't no part-time occupation" (80). While the expression of relief may be part tough bravado in the face of Tiny's closing up again, part of it does ring true. However, the task of meeting Tiny's need both physically and psychically may have proved too daunting for Lola, as insinuated in her phrase, "I was relieved [when Tiny told her to get out] because I wouldn't have to work for the rest of my life loving someone. Tiny" (85). The possibility of an intimate future together as a result of their sexual encounter is too frightening for Tiny, and perhaps also for Lola, let off the hook by Tiny's emotional shutdown. Her professed desire to spend her whole life with Tiny is not convincing. On some level, they are both too "twisted" or damaged by social and cultural forces to help each other in the long term.

Instead, the narrator chooses to resurrect memory. Lola, like Marisa at the end of *Ghost* without Amalia, remembers the unattainable woman in an erotic context: "I close my eyes and I am rubbing and thinking rubbing and thinking rubbing and remembering what this feels like, to find my body, una vega anhelosa, endless llano de deseo" (84).[14] The process of awakening Lola's desire for Tiny has allowed Lola to love herself, just as Lola's desire for Tiny sought to awaken Tiny's love for herself as a brown woman. In trying to work sexual magic to give Tiny back her body, Lola has made magic for herself in the rediscovery of her own body, described in natural images as "vega anhelosa," "llano de deseo." The "offering" of the title is a reciprocal one: "*¿Dónde 'sta ella que me regaló mi cuerpo como una ofrenda a mí misma?*" (84).[15] Even if a permanent relationship between them was not possible, and whether or not Tiny carried forward any empowering relationship with her dark female body, the encounter with Tiny has led the narrator to find her own, a connection she can pull up at will through the memory of Tiny's scent.

The fourth and final section of "La Ofrenda" recounts another, more definitive cause of Tiny's disappearance from Lola's life: her death from breast cancer. Only in retrospective reading do these lines concluding Lola's sexual fantasy in section three take on the dual valence of rejection and death:

Ella
Lejana.
Una vez, mía.
I open my eyes . . . Desaparecida. (84–85)[16]

Lola rages against social discrimination based on race and gender in disease research, and science that constructs breast cancer as a "lesbian castigo" (85)[17] resulting from childlessness, paralleling the representation of AIDS as a punishment for gay men's sexual practices.

Rejecting mandated forgetfulness ("and then we are supposed to forget. Forget the women we discover there between the sheets, between the thighs, lies, cries. But some things you don't forget / smell" [84]), Lola remembers and reinvents. In the recollection of Tiny's scent ("copal"), she celebrates Tiny's memory in a ritual burning of richly scented copal. Shifting into poetry, Lola repossesses the lesbian body from constructions that, internalized, produce self-hate and self-punishment:

I burn copal.
Her name rising up with the smoke,
dissolving into the ash morning sky.
Her flesh softening like sap
over rock, returning liquid
to the earth. Her scent inciting . . .

memory.

I inscribe my name, too.
Tattooed ink in the odorless flesh of this page.

I, who have only given my breast
to the hungry and grown,
the female and starved
the women.

I, who have only given my breast to the women. (86)

Lola's discourse here is very different from that of the "smooth-talking" seducer of objectified "lean white or fine black ladies" (80), signifying the changes in Lola since their sexual encounter and Tiny's death. In their sexual encounter, each of them opened herself. Tiny's memory, written on the body through scent, is the memory of the possibility of opening, softening, and actively receiving and giving in desire.

At the end Lola opens herself in a different way. Her relationship with Tiny connects her with the world. As Tiny gave the narrator her own desiring female body as an offering to herself, so Lola at the end offers her female body to a collectivity of women. Alongside giving sexual pleasure with hands or mouth during sex, Lola opens herself to the social context of lesbians in offering the breast in a maternal gesture of nurturing and love, in opposition to the female *chingón*, and echoing the earlier link with the Indian mother through Tiny. She has not relinquished her butch desires, but her experience with Tiny has feminized her body. The end of the text rewrites the breast as a site of nurturance, not death, creating *sitio* (Pérez, 161) as a supportive community of like-minded and besieged women. In this new "family," love includes sexual and political commitment and a fierce tenderness. In contrast to Lola's former objects of desire, the community of starved women is not racially marked.

The radical break in decorum at the end of "La Ofrenda" (from Lola's tough talk to the lyrical and impassioned imagery of the concluding verses) also calls attention to the construction of Lola as shaman who works magic not only as a lover of women and a nurturing "mother" but also as a writer. The narrator's journey is self-consciously constructed as discursive in the text ("Tattooed ink in the odorless flesh of this page" [86]). Writing is embodied through metaphor, but the adjective "odorless" continues to valorize "smell." During sex with Tiny, a different kind of speech was taught, the language of the body spoken by and through the "other" mouth. At the end, the nursing breast replaces this reconstructed mouth, a move prepared for by the earlier reference to Tiny's breasts, given back to her by Lola. Lola's life-giving breast counters Tiny's, the site of her death-dealing cancer. The mouth is now for suckling, and the butch shaman is represented as the mother/lover/writer in an image bespeaking a resolution of the formerly incompatible terms love/family/sex.

The ending foregrounds once again the importance and mutation of names and identities throughout the text. In telling Tiny's story, the narrator has told her own ("I inscribe my name, too"). Tiny's name, of course, is inscribed as well, but her name is written by the smoke of the copal offering while the narrator's is written on the page with ink. Although the narrator is also associated with nature ("vega," "llano"), the text's ending aligns Tiny with nature (smoke) and the narrator with discursive production, reinforcing their earlier difference. In effect, the narrator is still shaman, this time using writing to represent a transgressive practice, appropriating the authority of writing to tell stories of lesbian life.

The tragic yet uplifting tone of the end must be balanced by the cautious indeterminacy of the beginning; the beginning and end are linked through the lines of poetry that conclude the two sections. Ostensibly, they occur in the same narrative time; the narrator is recalling and telling past events from a position in the present. As discussed above, there is no evidence that Tiny changed or maintained the sexual perspective represented in their sexual encounter. Similarly, it is after Lola's learning experience with Tiny that she calls into question the surety of knowledge ("Can't be sure but can hold fast to some things") [18] and affirms the relative certainties of the body (smell). Even after Tiny, the narrator continues to lock up her heart but remains susceptible to smell (the body), which can open her, for better or for worse, for joy or pain, connection or loss.

Lola writes that she is "back to who I was before" she became the more assimilated "Dottie." Now the reader understands Tiny's role in Lola's desire for the native woman, whom she remembers/writes as nature and mother. The narrator, Lola, finds in nature the metaphors to parallel her experience of Tina's body as "coming home" to her own dark mother, and as she later reveals, to herself ("tree trunks," "pura miel," "nido," "vega," "llano," "copal," "sap," "dark bark tree"). In other texts such as *Loving* and *Ghost*, lesbian sex and the lesbian body are figured through Christian metaphors of "salvation," "redemption," and "temple." Here, tied to the textual emphasis on the Indian, "shaman" replaces "savior," magic and ritual replace salvation, and nature replaces the architectural metaphors for the female lover's body culled from the rites and mysteries of the Church.

Though identifying Tiny as Indian through smell makes her desirable to Lola, Lola is as defined by her language and nationalist symbols as those symbols are reshaped by her writing. She has become Lolita again but not Dolores (militant commitment versus passive suffering). Perhaps she *is* "not so different from those Holy Communion days, really"; she is the same and not the same after the gift of the brown body. Yet it is a different kind of holy communion, read through the ending of the story, of women at the breast (social and political movement, sexual identity/practice and the reproductive body in an alternative, non-procreative family). The opening Catholic imagery here joins the indigenous-as-(magically)-natural that dominates the rest of "La Ofrenda," for Catholic imagery, too, signifies the narrator's desire of "race."

Using Paz's analysis of closed and violent subjects who inflict pain because they are not allowed to feel pleasure, Moraga explores possible internal motivations for that behavior. The psychic and social difficulties of sustaining Moraga's sexual project in her texts provide some clues to this internal aspect of female masculinity.[19] In the writing of butch and *chingón* identifications as both sexual and gender constructions, Moraga's texts undertake a reading of cultural indoctrination and attempt to come to terms with it by representing lesbian sex, specifically butch-femme identifications, as one imaginable engagement with the stigmatization of dominating-dominated polarities.

Whiteness in
The Last Generation
The Nation,
the "Half-breed,"
and the Queer

This reading of Cherríe Moraga's *The Last Generation* (*TLG*) focuses on the text's overlapping constructions of whiteness:[1] in the discourse of cultural nationalism, in the familial context of "directly mixed" racial identity,[2] and in the racialization of desire.[3] I see this essay as part of a larger project studying whiteness as a racial category. This project seeks to dislocate representations of non-dominant groups as "different" vis-à-vis the norm as well as to unseat the pervasive normativity of whiteness itself.[4] For Darieck Scott, monolithic whiteness "can and does begin to fall apart when subjected to a scrutinizing gaze" (307): for example, in interrogating Moraga's desire for a white woman, elucidated in *TLG*, the infinite expanse of monolithic whiteness begins to break down into a series of specificities or subtypes. In Moraga's text, while the political commitment to her mestiza self and Chicano nationalism banishes a whiteness forever "tainted by history" (Scott, 307–308), lesbian desire creates a space in the text to renegotiate the "powerful fiction" of a seamless whiteness as norm and center.

The recuperation of cultural nationalism in *TLG* should be read against the women-of-color project laid out in *This Bridge Called My Back* (1981) and continuing in Moraga's first book, *Loving in the War Years* (1983). This project entails a collective understanding and a political agenda that refuses to choose among aspects of identity (woman, Chicana, feminist, lesbian). The shared vision of *Bridge* produces a "theory in the flesh" that stems from the lived experience of multiple oppression and the construction of a new subject (feminist *and* of color, lesbian *and* Chicana) based on the (re)cognition of difference within (Lorde's notion of self as other).[5] This vision includes not only the theorizing of a multiple and shifting subjectivity and identity (difference within) but a *politics* of unities-in-difference (Anzaldúa 1987, Hall 1990, Sandoval 1991).

In the essay "Queer Aztlán" in *TLG*, the making of a new national subject entails a relational naming of whiteness. The text rejects the additive model of merely including previously excluded categories in Chicano, feminist, and gay communities and proposes instead a new vision of Chicano nationalism. The focus on identity, in particular on that of multiple or mestiza subjects, works in tandem with a nationalist agenda including the defense of native territories on a global level:

Without the dream of a free world, a free world will never be realized. Chicana lesbians and gay men do not merely seek inclusion in the Chicano nation; we seek a nation strong enough to embrace a full range of racial diversities, human sexualities, and expressions of gender. [. . .] In a "queer" Aztlán, there would be no freaks, no "others" to point one's finger at. (164)

The central project in *TLG* of recuperating or revisiting nationalism from a queer perspective expands the notion of social or revolutionary change to include the politics of sexuality, a dimension of liberatory politics often lost in the search for the nation.

In a move already initiated in *Heroes and Saints*, *TLG* draws on a repertory of myths, symbols, and fantasies that construct the ideal nationalist subject as Indian, and an ideal social formation based on the tribe, understanding Aztlán both as a "physical" and as a "*meta*physical" territory (153). The desire to focus nationalism through a queer lens seems to foreground these "codified symbols and imaginary metaphors" (Mercer, 276) in a way that undercuts the ambiguities and careful readings of these narratives and images that characterize Moraga's earlier writing, particularly in *Loving* and *Ghost*.

Here, the emphasis on indigenous ecological concerns (*TLG*, 167, 170) within Chicano nationalist discourse allows the textual conflation of Indian land and female brown bodies, a move that creates space for women within the ideal national subject. Moraga represents the earth as Mother, and draws a parallel between woman and the land through the metaphor of rape: "Like woman, Madre Tierra has been raped, exploited for her resources, rendered inert, passive, and speechless" (172).[6] Through this connection, Moraga can claim that both the female body and the land are "territories to be liberated":

The nationalism I seek is one that decolonizes the brown and female body as it de-colonizes the brown and female earth. It is a new nationalism in which la Chicana Indígena stands at the center, and heterosexism and homophobia are no longer the cultural order of the day. (150)

As victims of male violence (rape and other forms of gay bashing), Chicano gay male bodies have also been colonized: "For women, lesbians, and gay men, land is that physical mass called our bodies" (173). The re-visioning of Chicano nationalism offered here includes an internal critique of Chicano gay men's reluctance to examine their own misogyny and male privilege (161–162). *TLG,* then, modifies the ideal Indian body of Chicano nationalism, changing its gender and allowing for queerness.

An examination of the terms of the new nationalism—"Queer Aztlán"—suggests that they are perhaps hopelessly in contradiction with one another, reminiscent of a previous decade's dilemma of Marxism's and feminism's "unhappy marriage." What are the connections between valorizing queerness and the insistence on "belonging" in terms of a nationalist discourse of land and the Indian woman as conquered/raped territory? What are the contradictions in this set of identifications? What is the dark woman doing in these representations and ways of identifying?

In an important article, Norma Alarcón posits a Chicana feminist project of identification with the Indian woman as a strategic response to the dominance of a particular masculinist nationalism in Chicana/o studies ("Chicana Feminism"). In texts such as Gloria Anzaldúa's *Borderlands,* the valorization of the native woman is used to support a multiple and contradictory identity as opposed to the ideal national subject. Since this project has achieved a measure of success in changing the discourse of Chicana/o studies by the mid-1990s, perhaps now is the moment to interrogate more closely this desire for the dark woman and to look at the tensions these forms of identification produce in Chicanas' work. For example, these discourses may erase the differences and contradictions they are trying to bring into view.

These tensions become obvious in Moraga's writing because of the ways she consistently negotiates the terms of her identity on the field of desire and sexual practice. By naming whiteness, *TLG* allows the processes through which "others" are imagined to become visible. In her writing, Moraga is always seeking out the dark woman: in herself, in her individual and collective past, as the object of desire and politics. In *TLG*, like the feminist projects discussed by Alarcón, nationalist tropes (*mestizaje*, land) are recodified through the devalued female instead of the male. Even as Moraga tries to evacuate her white privilege, there is a sense in which the whiteness in herself that seeks the Indian woman echoes the very system she critiques, a system in which whiteness desires and needs the dark Other to re-create and renew itself. "Indian woman" translates into certain forms of identification involving the whiteness in herself as well as in the nationalist narrative of the conquest as rape of the land and of the Indian woman. Yet the desire for "la Chicana Indígena" is coterminous with the desire for a white woman in the text.

To represent the "full range of racial diversities" promised by its queer nationalist vision, the text must negotiate its own racialized representation of colonization as the rape of the native woman, especially given the text's transposition of these images in the U.S. context in relation to "la Chicana Indígena": "there still is the Rapist Father and he is white and the Violated Mother and she is not" (128); "Chicano Nation is a mestizo nation conceived in a double-rape: first, by the Spanish and then by the Gringo" (153). This construction of whiteness spills over into the personal/familial as well: "I am the product of invasion. My father is Anglo; my mother, Mexican" (54). In "Whose Savior?" the line "I hate white people" is tellingly juxtaposed with "the white people I am" (102). The hated features of the racially mixed (including her own "pink spots") are presented as the product of rape, creating an overlay of national and familial histories.

In its search for the Chicano nationalist body, then, *TLG* constructs the figure of the Chicana Indígena in opposition to the White Rapist Father. This move de-privileges the male heterosexual Chicano subject of Chicano nation, and, according to Norma Alarcón's formulation of a Chicana writing project, both invokes and recodifies "the" native woman, "bringing into focus the cultural and psychic dismemberment linked to imperialist racist and sexist practices." However, in marked contrast with Moraga's earlier writing, the recodification of the native woman within the discourse of rape in *TLG* leaves little room in which to imagine the *agency* of the Chicana Indígena in bringing about the political agenda sketched out in the text's nationalist vision.

This binary construction of whiteness and indigenousness along the axis of rape also contrasts sharply with the nuanced critique, from a lesbian perspective,[7] of La Malinche and the *chingón/chingada* binary that informs her writing. Much of my discussion in previous chapters focuses on the analysis of female betrayal and male superiority contained in the title of Moraga's essay "A Long Line of Vendidas" and how many other texts, including *Ghost*, explore the impact of the narrative of *la chingada* (the violated Indian mother) on Chicana/o subjectivities and gender and sexual identities. Even in *TLG*, the recourse to the "Indígena" as icon of authentic national identity is complemented by a notion of identity as self-invention.[8]

The perception of interracial relationships through metaphors of rape and invasion seems at times to occlude the possibility of loving, consensual interracial unions, just as the emphasis on whiteness as White Rapist Father (conflated with the U.S. government) sidesteps the possibility of multiracial coalitions that include progressive, anti-racist white people. Further, this discourse ignores the possibility of "difference within" the category of whiteness. In *TLG*, whiteness, placed outside the borders of the nation in order to delimit the authentic indigenous body of Chicano nationalism, is also put into play in the erotic register of the text. Similarly, *TLG*'s juxtaposition of white rapist/imperialist father with images of other whitenesses de-centers and fragments the fiction of its monolithic power—no longer One and the Same defined in terms of its Other but another whiteness among others. In *TLG* the overlay on the family of the hierarchical binary of White Rapist Father/Non-white Violated Mother from the lexicon of colonization sets up a useful dissonance; for example, with the representation of the marriage of her (very strong) mother and "soft pink" white father. This layering of representations partially weakens the binary discourse of racialized and politicized rape and rejection in the context of her family and her own body.

In its desire to imagine the racially diverse as subjects of Chicano nationalism, the text negotiates, among other constraints, the Mexican/Chicano valorization of *mestizaje* and the mestizo subject, a valorization which operates within certain strict racial parameters (only Spanish/Indian),[9] and the psychological impact of U.S. notions of "half-breeds" as belonging to neither racial/cultural group (Frankenberg, 125). The difficulties in representing the racially diverse body of Chicano nationalism are further compounded by the shame of having enjoyed the benefits of light-skin privilege and assimilation ("working to maintain that conexión under the constant threat of denial [. . .] I have tasted assimilation and it is bitter on my tongue" [127]):

At the height of the Chicano Movement in 1968, I was a closeted, light-skinned, mixed-blood Mexican-American, disguised in my father's English last name. Since I seldom opened my mouth, few people questioned my Anglo credentials. (145)

The image of the "explorer" in the following quote further captures the contentious relationship of the writer to her "mixed" identity. The metaphor emerges in the memory of a Mexican lover whom the writer would have left "if México had not been so forgotten in me":

Instead I stayed [. . .] until México [. . .] grew dim in my explorer's imagination.

I write the word "explorer" and shudder at the image it evokes [. . .] I am both the "explorer" and the "Indígena." Most Mexicans can claim the same, but my claim is more "explorer" than not. And yes, most days I am deathly ashamed. But of what, exactly? My white family was kept distant from me, not because of its conquests, but because of its failures. (122)

The writer desires her own mestiza self in Mexico and Mexican women; yet her whiteness and her desire to know Mexico position her as an "explorer" vis-à-vis these objects of desire, a subject position she finds intolerable ("deathly ashamed").

The writer's conflicted relationship to a whiteness historically associated with U.S. imperialism fuels the anxiety over cultural extinction expressed in the book's title. Moraga extrapolates from the loss of Mexican/Chicano identity she sees in the children of her siblings and cousins to the fate of the Chicano nation in general. This slippage between the personal and the collective is characteristic of the text and generates some of its most productive contradictions. The equation of "mixed-race" offspring and loss of cultural identity, for example, co-exists with the writer's statement that her political consciousness and activism are a direct result of being "half-breed":[10]

I read all I can for a clue [. . .] some sense of how my mixed-blood identity has driven me to politics, protest, and poetry (112) [. . .] I know full well that my mestizaje—my breed blood—is the catalyst of my activism and my art [. . .] Had I been born a full-blood Mexican, I sometimes wonder whether I would have struggled so hard to stay a part of la raza. (127)

Moraga recognizes the racist power structure that conditions the beliefs and practices surrounding miscegenation and whiteness in both Mexican/Chicano and U.S. contexts, acknowledging that "miscegenation's children wrestle, in one way or another, with the consequences" (*TLG*, 128). She explicitly rejects the term "biracial" because it communicates a refusal to choose between "white" and "color." She considers the term "passive," "without political bite," and biologically based.[11] Instead, the writer reclaims the derogatory term "breed" (126) to construct an identity based on conscious identification with the colonized and devalued pole of darkness. Ever vigilant to the privileges and power that adhere to whiteness, the text explores the consequences of being "miscegenation's child" on the political, psychic, and erotic levels.

In the political context of Spanish and U.S. imperialism, Moraga consciously identifies as Chicana and repudiates white identification. In the essay "Art in América con acento," the writer's refusal "to be forced to identify" with the imperialist U.S. is seen as a political choice (*TLG*, 54). The notion of choice recalls the test of loyalty to the race within Chicano nationalism installed in the wake of La Malinche's racial treason: "ever loyal to the dark side of their mestizaje" (126), "I am of that endangered culture and of that murderous race, but I am loyal only to one" (129). At the same time, the privilege of being able to choose Chicana and refuse white identification is itself seen as a curse. Moraga quotes Emma Pérez on how the privileged closeness of the "half-breed" to Anglo language and culture is a *maldición* (curse) in disguise, affirming: "In the 'choice' resides the curse [. . .] this güera-face has often secured my safe passage through the minefields of Amerikan racism" (126). While the ability to pass as white is constructed here as a privilege and a curse, other texts present a kind of tactical manipulation of perceived whiteness to help the writer and her friends/lovers of color out of potentially violent or threatening situations: "once my light skin and good English saved me and my lover from arrest. And I'd use it again. I'd use it to the hilt over and over to save our skins" (*Loving*, 97).[12]

Moraga's choice to be loyal only to one side shows awareness of "racial identity as socially and contextually constructed, not the essentialist or biology-based idea of identity" (Frankenberg 130), and is consistent with the notion of identity signaled by such terms as "Chicana" or "women of color" which have less to do with absolute racial identities and more to do with understanding "Chicana/o" as a political act of ideological self-definition. This strategy contrasts with the theoretical position exemplified in *Bridge* of refusing to choose "between" or "among" aspects of identity, articulating these at times contradictory aspects in the notion of a multiple subject.[13] In *Loving* and *TLG* the subject chooses to refuse one aspect of identity—whiteness—because of the racialized power relations embedded in the history of colonization in both Mexican and U.S. history. The "half-breed" subject/writer cannot simply put "whiteness" into horizontal play with other aspects of identity that have in common a lack in power and privilege ("woman," "Chicana," "lesbian," "working-class").

But the notion of purity or wholeness persists in the idea that one can choose to be loyal to only one aspect of identity, given the porosity of racial and cultural borders which makes brownness and whiteness "at least partially coextensive" (Scott, 312).[14] The constraints on choice in the construction of racial identity are revealed in the tension between identifying as Chicana but being "read" as white (*TLG*, 97, 125). In another passage, an Indian woman in Oaxaca asks the writer how she knows the Indian name for the moon, being white (120). The body stubbornly persists in spite of political and discursive re-signification: "throwing up all that bitterness, all that self-hatred, all that disgust at my whiteness, my hunger to be part of that memory, that México" (121).

In opposition to a similar scene in Richard Rodriguez' *Days of Obligation*, in which he vomits the colors of the Mexican flag in an attempt to rid his body of the racial markers that separate him from whiteness (xv), Moraga's text reveals the desire to purge whiteness from the body externally perceived as white. For Norma Alarcón, in rejecting a "minoritized identity," Rodriguez refuses to play out some "drama of ancestral reconciliation": "the hidden episteme in Rodriguez's pastoral is the rage at our embodied history, for while his wit may pass muster, his face does not. As a result, the face becomes a weapon along with wit. How else can he tell us that his body is as textualized as his speech?" (Alarcón, "Tropology of Hunger," 150). In Rodriguez' scenario, "those that continue to be 'ethnic' [in the U.S.] . . . are those who are unable to miscegenate, that is, they could not actually pass for or impersonate an 'Anglo-American'" (Alarcón, 148). Moraga constructs herself an "ethnic" identity in her writing in spite of her ability to "impersonate an 'Anglo-American'" that causes her anguish. In a reversal of Rodriguez' scenario, her commitment to Chicano nationalism does "pass muster," but her face does not. As she writes in *TLG*, "if my thoughts could color my flesh, how dark I would turn" (126).

The competing discourses and images of whiteness and racial diversity in *TLG* are marked in part by the use of capital letters for the "magical signs," in Katie King's phrase, of Chicano nationalism—Rapist Father, Chicano Nation, Chicana Indígena, Violated Mother—and the use of lowercase words melding noun and adjective that communicate a different take on identity. At times these words connote a multiracial woman-centered community, as in "black-familia," "coloredgirl revolution," or "whitegirl" (118). The use of "whitefather" or "whitedaddy" underlines something lacking in the white male subject, highlighting the discrepancy between the gendered racial construct and lived experience. Moraga empties out the subject position of whiteness as the White

Rapist Father in the representation of the softshoeing white father with the "soft pink hands" (6), the "orphan father" caught in a humiliating moment of vulnerable exposure, whose penis is a soft, pale "little bird" (93) in contrast to the phallic symbol of male power.

In the images of Moraga's white extended family—as trash, abusive, unpolitical, and no strangers to drugs, alcoholism, and gunshot wounds—the text reverses the expectations of the dominant white subject created in the image of the White Rapist Father. As in Barbara Smith's anecdote about the black students who refused to believe Steinbeck's *The Grapes of Wrath* was about white people (*Bridge*, 117), such representations of whiteness interrupt the conflation of economic and racial categories (e.g., black, working-class, poverty, urban violence) (124):

The white people I am are not rich.
Are freckled
pale
overweight
polyestered and without
class
or good genes.
They do not know how to dress.

They are not romantic.
They are not the rugged-boned women I've seen
in picket-line photos of the thirties
arm 'n arm with negro church women
chicano miners' wives.
[. . .]
The white people I am have sucked dry
the bones of the colored
worn their own resistance down
by a quiet weak-kneedness
made to resemble patience. (102–103)

Such representations of whiteness in *TLG* depart from what Dorothy Allison calls the "myth" of the working class in popular culture:

I have felt a powerful temptation to write about my family as a kind of moral tale with us as the heroes and the middle and upper classes as the villains. It would be within the romantic myth, for example, to portray that we were the kind of noble Southern whites portrayed in the movies, mill workers for generations until driven out of the mills by alcoholism and a family propensity to rebellion and union talk. But that would be a lie. The truth is that no one in my family ever joined a union. Taken as far as it can go, the myth of the poor would make my family over into union organizers or people broken by the failure of the unions. The reality of my family is far more complicated and lacks the cardboard nobility of the myth. ("A Question of Class," 144)

There is a sense in which the unprecedented "owning" of whiteness in *TLG* illuminates the difficulties of claiming *any* despised identity (143).[15] Both desire and denial surround the resistance to working-class prejudice in Moraga's writing, a working-class doubly and differently constructed as white and Mexican. In one of the writer's dreams, the white aunt is represented as working, while the women in Moraga's working-class Mexican family are seen as "brujas":

My aunt is a waitress slapping hash onto a grill and plates onto customers' tables. My Mexican aunts and my mother are nearby. They sit hunched around a low table. They are whispering secrets. They appear very dark, like brujas. This gathering is a holy coven. I stand between this circle of witches and my working-class aunt. She throws a hand on her hip, wipes her brow with the back of the other. "These Mexicans," she says, "are so damn crazy!" (123–124)

Besides refracting white working-class prejudice through the white aunt and rewriting the familiar scenario of "choosing" between aspects of Moraga's identity,[16] the dream constructs a view of the white women in Moraga's extended family as almost an oasis in their straightforward relationship to work, in contrast to the Mexican women's convoluted and coveted interiority ("secrets"), a source in Moraga's writing of both attraction and danger.

In addition to contesting the monolithic character of whiteness through a series of specific and contradictory representations, the text creates points of identification with whiteness for Moraga and for the reader through the white family (father, aunt, grandmother) and desire for a white woman.

A sense of sympathy with the white father is created at the end of "Peloncito" in the image of the "orphan father," the boy who got less attention than the grandmother's bird. The white father's body is asexual, boy-like, even infantile, yet possessed of a secretive, onanistic sexuality of ambiguous object choice (*TLG*, 93).[17] In the realm of the imaginary, identifications and erotic investments can be made through a man whose sexuality is constructed as indeterminate (Romero, 124). The writer identifies with the white father subjected to the judging eye of a Chicana mother who transmits and enforces her culture's gender ideals: "wife at the ironing board: / 'what are you doing, jim, what are you doing?'" (93–94).

The opening line of "If a Stranger Could Be Called Family" ("there *are* men in my life") complements that of "Peloncito" ("There is a man in my life," 93). The white father is represented on the level of (pre-oedipal) images and memories. His nostalgic reverie about his mother's vaudeville days is squelched by the "back-seat wife" (97): "her son waxes nostalgic like an old lover / a young suitor. / 'She was nothing special,' the back-seat wife whispers / 'I don't think they ever put her on the stage even'" (97). Both father and daughter desire and identify with the image of his mother on the stage. It is as if the writer tells his stories for him or at least in his place:

she was nothing nothing
what little legacy we orphans
my father and I have
shattered.

I point to the small theatre across the street.
It is nothing nothing special,
but there I will tell *their* stories
lies, nostalgia, and the whole ball of wax
because we all got a story
we all each one got a story
to tell. (97)

Both anger and poignancy lie in the emphatic repetitions anchoring the identification with the white father in the mother's refusal to validate their experience and their creative potential. This is a very interesting moment in a body of writing that returns again and again to the powerfully charged relationship with the Mexican mother. What does it mean, in the context of Moraga's other writing, to identify with the white father as "we orphans"? Father and daughter are connected, for one, through a "shattered legacy": the stories of her father's life Moraga commits herself to tell, and her own truncated search for the Indian line of the family (130). On another level, they are both orphans of a mother whose primary love was bestowed on her only son. In this sense, the painful relationship with the mother creates another legacy that can be seen as connecting father and daughter across gender or as constructing the white father in the feminized position of (metaphorically) orphaned "daughter." The passing reference to not betraying her father in writing about the White Rapist Father (129) echoes in the loyalty of her formerly abused cousin to the white aunt at her deathbed (124). Moraga and the white cousin are positioned in the same way vis-à-vis the white parent through the image of "her mother's square freckled hand (my father's hand)" (124), unsettling the discourse of "loyalty only to the dark side."

The medium for identification with the "wild" white grandmother is her unconventional lifestyle and her "artist's hunger for love and limelight" (123). The writer's white aunt, who looks like a dyke and sees the queer in Moraga, tells the writer she both looks like her grandmother and has her spirit (123). Regarded merely as "white, and therefore foreign" by the child in her Mexican world, this independent old woman, represented as a surfeit of whiteness vividly offset by a touch of red ("a wild woman in a white Cadillac with white skin and white bleached hair [. . .] with long red painted fingernails" [123]) is reclaimed through the father's re-told history of neglect and the recuperation of the white aunt's stories "censored by my father" (123).

The white aunt is a crucial figure in working though the confrontation with personal and cultural mortality expressed in the title of the book as well as the writer's fear of and desire for whiteness. She reappears after a twenty-year absence, because she believes she is dying "and wants to repair any damages done" (122), an undertaking not unlike the confessional mode of *TLG*. Although this is the most difficult of Moraga's relationships with the white family, due to the aunt's abuse and abandonment of her children, it is also the most productive in the realm of representing the writer's (split) desire/fear of whiteness. The white aunt appears to the writer in a dream: "I cannot see her face, because she stands behind me, holding me, her arms around me like a straitjacket. I panic. She won't let go" (123). This image exceeds the discursive limits of the White Rapist Father, forcing the writer to confront the possibility that her perception of whiteness (in herself and in the white woman she desires) may be functioning in her life like a straitjacket.

In spite of the ruptures in the white male ideal represented by the white father, it is the gender of the white aunt that permits the negotiation between racial/national identity and desire:

My white aunt comes to visit me as all the women in my family have, uninvited through my bedroom door. She will stay until she is given the respect due her. She will stay until she has changed from a faceless entity straightjacketing my every movement into a woman of real flesh and bones and name. (125)

A link between the aunt and the writer's white lover is crafted through the "Betty" incident.

"What's a 'Betty'"? I ask. We are coming out of the theatre, out from the world of Spike Lee's *X* [. . .] My companion answers, "She's a 'bimbo,' a Black man's white woman. She's considered 'trash' by everyone—Black *and* white [. . .] "That's pretty ugly on all counts," I say. Still, I push her away from me that night, that white away from me. *But she will not let go.* (124–125)

In spite of or perhaps because of the weight of a racialized history that impacts their erotic relationship, Moraga is drawn to examining the hold these white women have on her:

My aunt's name is Barbara and I am here to make peace with her in the white women I love, in the white woman I am. All those "Bettys," that "trash," that working-class whitegirl I learned to fear on the "other" side of the family, on the "other" side of me. (125)

In acknowledging and naming these white women as part of her life and part of her, Moraga's writing also breaks down the monolithic power of whiteness as a "faceless entity."

In addition to economic and political ramifications, the conflation of racial and class hierarchies in both the U.S. and Mexico constructs certain racialized ideals of beauty and desirability which have repercussions in the erotic realm. Moraga's position in the feminist "sex wars" of the late 1970s and 1980s rejected the notion that power relations could be absent even in lesbian-feminist "vanilla" sexual practices that avoided penetration or top/bottom erotic identifications (see chapter 5). Then, as in *TLG*, Moraga argued that the same racialized power relations at work in society are played out in the bedroom:

In love, color blurs but never wholly disappears. I have had only one great fear as a lesbian lover—that my eye would turn on my beloved, that I would see her through the stranger's eye, that what I fear in my own desire, its naked hunger, I would recoil from in her open-faced body.
And my eyes have turned over and over again.

> I have never had a race-less relationship [. . .] As deeply as I have feared the power of my infinite female darkness, feared my Mexican muteness, feared my bottomless rage in my brown-skinned lovers, I have feared the mirror of my passivity, my orphanhood, my arrogance and ignorance in the white women I have loved. It is not a pretty picture. (115–116)

The struggle with racialized desires for gay men of color is different from that for lesbians of color due to the phallocentric constructions of gay men of color in terms of a hyper "having" (African American men) or "not having" (Asian men).[18] Still, important parallels exist between Moraga's vision of Chicana feminism as the love of mestizas for themselves and for other mestizas, and Marlon Riggs' take on Joseph Beam's manifesto that black men loving black men is *the* revolutionary act (Beam, 240). In a racist society structured by dominance, the recuperation by the subject of color of the devalued dark body as worthy of love and desire signals liberation.

Moraga's "unwavering faith in lesbians to name from the bed those battles being waged on the street" (*TLG*, 116) acknowledges the erotic as a domain of power, not untouched by social relations, but not reducible to them either. The erotic in the text is never fully contained by nationalist and anti-interracial discourses, but remains shifting and empowering. The ("half-breed") body is privileged as a site for the production of knowledge, theory, and sexual pleasure. In several places in the text, desire negotiates the terms of its fulfillment through the politicized terrains of race and gender. In "The Grass, Not Greener," the writer's mestiza identification creates a distancing effect from her white lover, whom she dreams as mestiza. She affirms "I cannot stay here forever," but doesn't leave, seduced by the beauty of everyday intimacy (110–111). The distancing through racial identifications in "Grass" should be read in conjunction with "Indian Summer," in which the two women's difference provides an erotic crackle in the sparring dialogue, the images of the hose and the water, and the appreciative descriptions by the narrator of this "wild whitegirl" (108). The "wild" in this charged representation of interracial desire positions the white grandmother, also described as wild, as a point of erotic identification. In play with the painful subject position of "half-breed" in *TLG*, a self-affirming erotic identification as butch appears, whose desire is channeled through racial identifications.

In other texts in *TLG*, such as "La Ofrenda," whiteness becomes the field for the negotiation of mestiza desire, a process initiated in *Loving*. The autobiographical trajectory in *Loving* traces a path from assimilating/passing as a white heterosexual, to coming out into a white lesbian community where the experience of racism and homophobia facilitates her identification with her Chicana mother, to engaging with women-of-color lovers and political commitments, ending in a specifically Latina context. Subject and object of the erotic encounter represented at the end of *Loving* share the mestiza position as a point of both political and erotic identification. In the process, whiteness drops out, identified in *Loving* with the former anglicized self and the "queer" white father (Romero, 124). In "La Ofrenda," the offering of the title is reciprocal: Tiny and Lola each give the other her own mestiza body (see chapter 5). As at the end of *Loving*, whiteness (the "blue eye") is represented as an obstacle to mestiza self-love and desire (reconstructed as unilaterally "Indian" in "La Ofrenda") and drops out of sight.

In "Just Vision," as in "La Ofrenda," split subjectivity is constructed in terms of vision and having two oppositionally defined eyes (right/left instead of blue/brown). Where "La Ofrenda" partially succeeds in bridging the differences within and among mestizas and their desire by sidestepping the split in favor of smell, "Just Vision" falters in part because it addresses the daunting task of bridging the split. Both texts should be read in the context of the writer's fear of her "eye turning" on her lover, expressed in the passage quoted above on the racialization of desire and the embodiment of racial power relations in the erotic (*TLG*, 115–116). Two of these texts present an either/or choice (the eye turns or it does not, the eye is blue or it is brown), while "Just Vision" constructs the "third eye" ("seeking both sides to everything / keeping each eye, right and left / from wandering off / too far" [28]). The poem represents the hope of overcoming the various splits in the writer's subjectivity as well as in the social formation. This utopian possibility is figured through images of superhuman strength and salvation: "just to get to the other side, / just to keep the two halves of my self / from cracking" (27). But it is a failed project: "the splitting has already occurred. / There is a faint line of fault / driven like a stake into the spot. Where once was the third eye" (27–28). The word "fault" resonates with the split caused by an earthquake and the connotation of guilt surrounding the racial identifications of the textual subject. The wordplay in the poem includes a vision of a just future and "simply" or "merely" vision as in the poem's epigraph from El Centro Campesino Cultural: "*Your cosmic or third eye is a synthesis of your two eyes. / Neither left nor right views, just vision*" (27). Moraga takes a powerful image from the textual and iconographic repertory of Chicano nationalism to suggest the possibility of transcending the binaries governing our perceptions, including racial binaries.

The third eye reappears in a privileged position in "Codex Xerí," the final essay of *TLG*, in the mythical indigenous context of Olmeca culture.

And we, the Codex-Makers, remove the white mask.
We wait and watch the horizon.

Our Olmeca third eye
begins to glisten
in the slowly
rising
light. (192)

The note of hope sounded at the end of *TLG*, figured through the slow open-ing of the third eye, is couched here in the racialized conquest narrative ("The Chicano codex is the map back to the original face [. . .] Our rapist wears the face of death" [187]).[19] The third eye no longer represents the site of a possible bridging of binaries as in "Just Vision." Here the activation of the third eye is constructed in tandem with the need "to remove the white mask," that is, to refuse white identification or assimilation, and to play a revolutionary role in bringing the destructive and exploitative Fifth Sun to an end. The privileged placement of Codex Xerí at the end of the book illustrates the importance of cultural nationalism in Moraga's recent writing. The notion of "open[ing] the wound to make it heal," found earlier in Moraga's thoughts on the function of her writing for the theater, is part of this nationalist, mythic, and anti-imperialist discourse.

The splitting of vision and body in "Just Vision" ("cracking / down / wide / open / through the center of my skull") contrasts both with "La Ofrenda" and the love poem "Where Beauty Resides," where desire leads to a sense of com-pleteness and peace. In a sense, "Where Beauty Resides" fulfills the promise made to the white aunt "to make peace with her in the white women I love, in the white woman I am" (125), as the object of desire in the poem can be read as white ("the sheets are a steel blue that ignite your eyes"; "shirt slipping over head / you emerge, a radiant medusa" [180]). As in "La Ofrenda," in this text the *indigenismo* of Chicano nationalism is activated in the context of lesbian desire: zero as a symbol of completeness and wholeness in Mayan thought, where the splitting of the subject is healed, including the splitting along racial lines. Here, this Mayan concept is combined with the Buddhist notion of emptiness being the fullest, that is, the most complete state of being. The poem captures the transformative power of desire in the state of completeness reached through sexual intimacy, the longed-after communion and fulfillment of desire in the other (the lover, the community) that motivates all of Moraga's writing. The poem rewrites and appropriates Catholic discourse on lesbian sinfulness: once the writer "would have confessed / the sin of you"; now, the subject emptied of self is "a sacrament, / a flame / a holy sacrifice" (183). The figuring of the desired state of completeness in negative terms (zero, emptied of self) may relate to the conflictive experience of split subjectivity as well as to a state of transcendence or of reunification on a spiritual level. In this dual yet complementary sense, the poem sheds light on Cere's sacrifice in *Heroes*, which also relieves her of herself, not in sex, but in death.

TLG presents the erotic encounter as a microcosm of human relations, a theme elaborated by Dariek Scott: "When we are moved sexually toward someone, there is a profound opportunity to observe the microcosm of all human relations, to understand power dynamics both obvious and subtle, and to meditate on the core creative impulse of all desire" (Scott, 160). *TLG* offers the possibility of communion across the barriers that divide women; internally, as mestiza desiring subjects in "La Ofrenda"; and across the barriers that separate women in "Where Beauty Resides." This in itself constitutes a "just vision" for the future. The "half-breed" subject, uniquely positioned as "split," can negotiate those healing divisions . . . *or not.* It is important to point out that the struggle to resolve these contradictions and conflicts, particularly with whiteness, is ongoing and is not resolved definitively in the text.[20]

A similar tension (to bridge the difference, or not) is apparent in the articulation of "queer" with "half-breed." Lesbian and "half-breed" are linked through the discourse of deviance in "I Was Not Supposed to Remember": lesbian as monstrosity and "half-breed" as freakish mutation (see chapter 1). In a context of transgressive border-crossing (between whiteness/brownness, gender/sexuality, medical examination/sexual pleasure), the lesbian body is seen as monstrous (the tumor as abnormal cell growth, the excessive hairiness, the need for corrective hormone treatment). The self-hatred unflinchingly offered for public view in this poem is one of the "consequences" for the racially diverse of living in a society that sees the "mixed" child as doomed to fit nowhere. The final image of the poem, the hybrid sheep-goat, recalls that of the film *Giant*, representing the white child as a lamb and the Mexican child as a calf, critiqued by Yolanda López in her documentary film on Mexican stereotypes as presenting the two "races" as two completely different species.[21] This is one of the most painful texts in *TLG* that deal with the "half-breed." As with the choice of the term itself, Moraga's writing responds to her deeply felt need to exteriorize and name the most wounding and problematic aspects of her experience.

The dream of the half-human, half-animal children represents another taboo mixing of elements represented simultaneously by lesbian and "half-breed." While all the children have the same father, no reference is made to his race in the text of the dream. Their "deformity" is presented as being caused by a mixing of bloods paradoxically described as "too many with one father" (127), which somehow is the women's fault ("irresponsibility"). In her Indian friend's account of a dream of being raped by a lion, her initial outrage fades as "she realizes that she is the one named to bear the new species—half-beast, half-she" (128). Both Moraga and her friend explicitly reject the role of "virgin mary of the next generation,"[22] casting both their own directly mixed identities and those of the children of the future in the nationalist conflation of brown female sexuality, rape, and race treason ("sleeping with the enemy"): "We are Malinche's children and the new Malinches of the 21st century" (128).

While the "half-breed," as Malinche's child, needs to prove her loyalty to "la raza," she nevertheless continues to produce "unorthodox" mestizo children in the dream. These animal/human hybrids could represent "the full range of racial diversities" (including whiteness) prescribed for the future Chicano nation in "Queer Aztlán," as well as "half-breed" lesbians having babies in racially diverse families without fathers. In the text analyzing the dream, the father is explicitly racialized as the White Rapist Father, which removes the possibility of *racial* hybridity, since the mothers are also white. This contradiction shifts the border-crossing into the area of gender treason. Even though whiteness is subtracted from the miscegenated new breed of the future in the footnote (128), all the mothers are both lesbian and white, and Moraga identifies with both the "hybrid seed" and the mother position in the text analyzing the dream: "As mixed-blood women, we are the hybrid seed she carried in the dream and the mothers of a new generation" (128).

The representation of this new breed reveals the impact on Moraga's subjectivity of various anti-interracial discourses: racial differences as biological and essential, as well as the shame of a racial mixing bearing "the burden of history" (Scott, 307) and presided over by the White Rapist Father. But it is also a powerful image of becoming, capturing the position "between" (Scott, 306) and portending a future harmony between humans and the earth in resonance with the nationalist tribal ideal put forth in the Chicano nationalist agenda in *TLG*. The image of the half-human, half-animal children also contests the "authenticity" of the traditional "magical signs" of Chicana/o racial and national identity with an ongoing process of self-invention.

In the coextensive imagery of the text, certain signs cluster around a monolithic whiteness or an Indianness represented as "real" or "original," while others stem from the awareness of identity as constructed and open-ended. The two registers of the text are not rigidly separated, but overlapping. For example, the utopian and ethical impulses of the nationalist discourse are crucial in investing the notion of self-invention with a political vision of the future and a commitment to activism. At the end of "Queer Aztlán," Moraga offers a political agenda for the new nationalism (174) which blends the old (the defense of remaining Indian territories) and the new (the internal critique of mestizo culture). She states that "our freedom as a people is mutually dependent and cannot be parceled out—class before race before sex before sexuality" (174). *TLG* brings "difference" into the concept of nation and constructs identity within this awareness of the self as other.

Alongside Chicano nation, with its fixed racial boundaries of Violated Mother/Rapist Father, the text offers other, more mobile identifications of community: "whoever we I am with" (115). Again, the "half-breed" subject is constructed as ideally positioned to move across borders:

> We light-skinned breeds are like chameleons, those lagartijas with the capacity to change the color of their skins. We change not for lack of conviction, but lack of definitive shade and shape. My lovers have always been the environment that defined my color [. . .] Everybody so contagious, I pick up their gesture, their joke, their jive. We invent ourselves. (116–117)

This protean quality coexists with the rejection of whiteness and the attempt to fix identity in only one community. The image of the "new breed," for all its complicity with dominant nationalist and racial discourses, also functions as a symbol of the potential of the "half-breed" and queer, like the concepts of the chameleon, zero, and the third eye, to "bridge a world of opposition" (128).

The multiple meanings of the title of the essay "Breakdown of the Bicultural Mind" (breakdown as in no longer running or an emotional or nervous breakdown; break down as in an analysis) include the personal and psychic costs of anti-miscegenation and racialized power hierarchies, the analysis of the component parts of these discourses and practices, and the implication that "bi" is no longer functional or operable. The image of the faceless white aunt standing behind the writer, her arms around her "like a straitjacket," deconstructs the social taboo against bipolar "racial mixing" and shows it to be insufficient to contain or explain the concomitant disavowal and desire of whiteness.

TLG makes visible variously empowered and disempowered whitenesses that are "internal" as well as "external" to the writer as a subject and as a body. It represents a range of emotions (rage, shame, compassion, desire, forgiveness, denial, acceptance, rejection) in confrontations with whiteness as self and whiteness as other that get played out in various interactive contexts—lover, parent/family, nation—wherein these responses to whiteness(es) can be seen as appropriate or inappropriate, possible or impossible. *TLG* also brings into view the various disciplining discursive frameworks—colonialist, nationalist, lesbian-feminist—which allow or make inconceivable particular ways of seeing/being white(ness). Such productive contradictions reveal how the text is both constrained by and exceeds the discursive worlds that delimit it.

Writing the Lesbian Mother

"Waiting in the Wings"

The structure for this final chapter on Moraga's writing stems from the title of her essay "Waiting in the Wings: Reflections on a Radical Motherhood" (1994).[1] In the prologue, Moraga outlines the major themes of her "own queer story of pregnancy, birth, and the first year of mothering" (6). The phrase "Waiting in the Wings" evokes the urgency and sense of destiny in her baby's conception, premature birth, and maleness, which are linked in the text to "survival in the age of AIDS" (6). "Radical Motherhood" refers to the politics of lesbians having and raising babies together, including the writer's relationship with her white lover, blood family, and extended queer family. "Reflections on . . ." introduces the theme of writing. At the end of the prologue, Moraga states that her essay is also "a poet's journal (I see now in retrospect), for even giving birth does not satisfy the artist's hunger" (6). In my analysis of this essay I reshuffle the priorities of Moraga's title, considering the issues of radical lesbian motherhood before studying the cluster of themes contained in the phrase "Waiting in the

Wings." And I begin *in media res*, extracting "Reflections on . . ." from its mediating position between the meanings invested in her son ("Waiting in the
Wings") and the politics of lesbian mothering, to foreground issues of writing,
with a focus on the relationship between Moraga's life and her work.

"Reflections on . . ."

At a fall reading following the publication of *The Last Generation* (1993) at
San Francisco's now-defunct feminist bookstore Old Wives' Tales, a woman inquired in an aggrieved tone as to the status of *TLG*'s meaning now that Moraga
was no longer childless, as if by giving birth the writer had somehow betrayed
her readership or annulled the "truth" of what she had written (see chapter 6).
In reply, Moraga blandly reminded the audience that *TLG* was a book, to be
distinguished from her life: in the writing of the life, it becomes text. Yet she acknowledged the intimate relationship between her experience and her writing.

In "Wings," Moraga discloses that to resume her public appearances as a
writer after the premature birth, precarious first months, and safe homecom-
ing of her son makes her feel "thoroughly exposed and noticed, so protective
of Rafael, protective of myself, the secret of our struggle for his survival" (65).
What interests me here is this separation of the public and the private, the life
and the writing of the life, caught in the image of the "secret." Moraga's desire
to escape the limelight, to keep her private life private, conflicts with the intensely autobiographical nature of her writing, and it is the nature of the autobiographical dimension in her writing that ultimately undoes the public/private
dichotomy. For Ramón Saldívar, "Moraga's autobiography disrupts facile conceptions of a private and a public self as she constructs her life story amid the
historical conditions, material circumstances, the analytical categories of race,
class, and gender that are the crucial mechanisms in the maintenance of power"
(188). In writing about her most intimate experiences, Moraga has created a
public voice for Chicana lesbian identity politics,[2] making demands for entitlement as "citizens" in multiple social arenas of historical exclusion and marginalization: U.S. mainstream society, Chicano nationalism, white middle-class
feminism, and the gay/lesbian movement. Moraga's writing claims a public
space to voice the need for an intensified political response from the Chicano
community in general and specifically from Chicana/o gays and lesbians. For
many of us, her writing has been extremely valuable for calling attention to the
public and legal aspects of the lived intersections of race and sexuality; specifically, in "Wings," to the lack of legal rights for lesbian couples and mothers.[3]
While critical attention to the issues addressed by her writing tends to over-

shadow its formal elements at times, for this reader it is precisely *how* she writes that gives power to *what* she writes.

The incident at the reading from *TLG* highlights the nature of Moraga's public persona and impact as a writer, for her value as a public voice of Chicana lesbian issues is most potently activated in the settings of lectures and readings from her work. The venues of Moraga's public interventions are bookstores, conferences, and, most commonly, university campuses, ranging from ivy league and state universities and colleges (on both coasts) to smaller regional schools. No matter what department invites Moraga to speak on campus, the audience is generally made up of Chicana/o students (mostly heterosexual). The gay/lesbian audience is mainly white, while Chicana lesbians from communities outside the university are also present.

These are risky contexts for Moraga in her public persona as Chicana lesbian writer, and, by virtue of her multiple identity, she is never sure which part of her persona will be at risk. I focus here on the vulnerability she experiences in these public settings as a lesbian, particularly when she reads texts such as "La Ofrenda" that deal explicitly with lesbian sex and lesbian erotic stylings in the gender roles of butch and femme. In her 1995 keynote address at the U.S. Latina Feminisms conference at Cornell University, Moraga talked about how she began feeling "like a pervert" as she read this story at a small Christian college, internalizing the revulsion and rejection of the audience, which was overwhelmingly white and heterosexual, with a minority of students of color and an even smaller group of gays and lesbians.[4] Chicana lesbians in the audience have to deal with these negative reactions as well. I have been in settings—for example, an evening of artists and poets at the National Association of Chicana and Chicano Studies conference in San Jose in 1993—where people around me openly expressed disgust at what Moraga was reading.

At every public reading, Moraga must make politically strategic decisions about what to read and whether or not to come out by what she chooses to read. At times she chooses not to publicly identify as a lesbian, if she senses the audience will not be receptive. Since many who enjoy her work under these circumstances buy her books after the reading, she is in effect coming out in private to people whose respect and sympathy she has already won. After another reading at a small college in California's Central Valley, in which she chose to come out to a predominantly Chicana/o audience with little or no exposure to lesbian themes, a man aggressively informed her that she didn't "look Mexican," using his rejection of her as a "breed" instead of sexuality to disconnect her from the "community." Yet, on the same night a closeted Chicano gay man who was HIV positive approached to thank her for reading a speech by the gay character Mario from *Heroes and Saints*, remarking that this was the first time anyone had ever spoken to him, as a gay man. These are the public contexts, requiring the highest personal investment, that have the biggest potential pay-off, in terms of Moraga's project as an activist-writer, of claiming the rights of "citizenship" within a variety of communities, especially within the Chicana/o community.

The "secret" captures the dilemma posed by Moraga's desire for privacy and the confessional, bare-all, autobiographical nature of her writing. Embodying the most intimate and taboo, the secret becomes the liminal and discursive site of the collision of the private and the public, engaging the conflict between her increasing weariness of the ways the public invades her private life and the factors that impel her public persona as a Chicana lesbian writer. These factors include the intangible drive to externalize her interior life as well as her culture's deepest taboos; the link between these subjective experiences and the politics of identity; and the professional, and, therefore, economic identity embodied in the Chicana lesbian persona. The "secret," particularly in "Wings" but with a rich intertextual context,[5] expresses the paradox of something that, by definition, needs to be kept private and is simultaneously being exposed for public consumption in writing. In "Wings," the secret divulged becomes a privileged site for the textual construction of the new lesbian self as both mother and writer. The secret plays a major role in each section of my analysis: in rewriting lesbian parenthood, in the radical representation of birthing through lesbian sex, and in the scripting of the lessons learned from the son at once ancient and infant.

Besides inhabiting the space between the writer's literary, public persona and her private, personal life, like the secret, the essay's "reflections on" have to do with writing as the locus of self-production. I have spoken of what Moraga's writing means to me as a Chicana lesbian in terms of gaining a public voice; another major contribution is what her writing shows about identity as constructed and always changing in an ongoing, open-ended process. In Moraga's essay, this self-construction is accomplished through a textualization of the body and identity. The layered and changing process of textual production of the self is visible in the forms, process, and metaphors of writing itself. "Wings" is a palimpsest of journal entries and recorded dreams, corresponding temporally to the events chronicled, that have been written over, bridged, and filled in retrospectively in a time of greater distance and reflection.[6] This textual fabric is further interwoven with *Loving in the War Years*, *TLG*, and the plays, which, while less directly autobiographical than the essays, have similar thematic concerns. *Loving* plotted the writer's course from white to brown identification, to a mestiza lesbian self as desiring subject of mestiza lovers. *TLG*'s metaphor for the process of self-invention was the chameleon, referring to the "light-skinned breeds" who change color and transform themselves.

"Wings" features maps of Moraga's navigation of a new subject position—motherhood—that has been defined in ways that exclude lesbians. This exclusion has resulted from the equation of motherhood and heterosexuality in mainstream society, on one hand, and from particular constructions of lesbian identity and sexuality in the lesbian community, on the other hand, which in turn have been affected by the gender notions of the dominant culture. In "Butch Mothers, Femme Bull Dykes," JoAnn Loulan traces the oxymoronic resonances of "butch mother" to the conflicting associations of mothers with passivity and butches with dominance, assertion, aggression, and self-reliance (249). For Loulan, the rejection of the mother role for butches is related to an underlying fear of female/male stereotyping that ultimately restricts our ability to imagine a full range of lesbian sexualities (251).

The restricted vocabulary available to refer specifically to our sexual identities ("butch," "femme," "androgynous") highlights both the stifling effects of the male-centered heterosexual paradigm which has left us "outside the conversation" (Loulan, 251) and the need to "reinvent categories to help us understand who we are" (252). "Wings" represents such an attempt to create language for new genders and sexual identities, not so much in the sense of naming or a new terminology but a textualization of experience that allows for "some combination of presumably incompatible terms" (Halberstam, "F2M," 100). In the trajectory of Moraga's writing, "Wings" constitutes yet another phase of her relentless examination of the impact of cultural constructions of gender, race, and sexuality on her subjectivity, and the use of her authority as a writer to carve out a space of legitimacy and visibility for her experience.

My own interest in writing about "Wings" has less to do with the actual experiences of insemination and conception, pregnancy, childbirth, and mothering in Cherríe Moraga's life than with the way she imagines them in her writing, and the usefulness of that process in my own understanding of how identities are constructed through textualization and invested with particular meanings on a personal and collective level.

Of particular interest is the essay's provocative redefining and recombination of "woman," "(butch) lesbian," "mother," and "writer."[7] Since cultural constructions define "mother" and "lesbian" as mutually exclusive categories, there is no one for Moraga to be as both: *It is hard to write when there is no one fixed now to be* (49). The parallel to Lola's giving Tiny "someone to be" in "La Ofrenda" is striking (see chapter 5). While Lola gives Tiny "someone to be" as "Indian woman," ostensibly through sex, Lola also presents herself to the reader as a writer, explicitly at the end of the text ("I inscribe my name, too. / Tattooed ink in the odorless flesh of this page" [86]) and in the telling of the story itself ("this page"). In Moraga's process of writing herself "someone to be" as lesbian mother and writer in "Wings," lovemaking and images of a "natural" female Indianness give way to metaphors of journeys and maps, involving not *"miles of physical territory"* but *"an interior map"* she does not yet know how to read (8).

On the trip to the hospital after her water has broken, the writer attempts to chart her way by the indexical signs of a world gone suddenly oblique and strange; lying face up in the back of the moving ambulance, the writer tries "to 'read' the route from the shape of streetlights overhead, the curve of free-way interchanges, the palm and sycamore trees overhead lining the backstreets" (33). Her body becomes an unfamiliar text as well: *"I experience pain often in my womb, my vagina. I don't understand the signs"* (8). The two pink lines on the pregnancy test are unmistakable, yet she cannot convince herself that *"such insignificant markings"* could *"pronounce something as irrevocable as a human life"* (9). Having expected a female child, she writes that she must "ex-cavate" the meaning of her child's maleness *"from the most buried places in my-self* [. . .] *I understood the female, the daughter. The son holds a message I will learn to decipher with my heart"* (16).

In writing "who to be" as butch lesbian mother, Moraga reveals how all her identities have been unsettled through the experience of pregnancy, birth, and mothering. Angered by the crudeness of her brother's curiosity about her pregnancy, she wonders *"what canyons of ignorance I would have to transverse to have my brother understand who I am in this"* [21]). Yet the fact remains that she herself is not entirely clear about how to negotiate this new identity:

Coming home will never be the same, coming home with this child. I now always will return a mother. "Mother," the term takes the shape of my being very gradually. I hear the word fall from my sister's mouth and she is not referring to our mother, but is speaking to my son of me. We laugh at my still virgin-response. The intellect not quite caught up to biology. (73)

In the face of irreparable alteration, the writing provides a path to the new self.

While much of the perplexity Moraga records in "Wings" must seem like old hat to women who have borne many children and never questioned their right to the role of mother, Moraga's writing brings home the power of internal-ized social constructions that fly in the face of common sense and biology. At the beginning of the essay, Moraga writes: "I had come to my motherhood along the long hard path. Nothing has been a given for me, not even my womanhood" (6). Since having children is defined in the context of heterosexual marriage, Moraga's lesbian identity seemed to preclude being a mother. And because of her butch erotic identification, she confesses that even the category of "woman" seemed foreign to her. Besides butches' erotic positioning as active lovers of "women," their role includes protecting them:

> buried deep inside me, regardless of the empirical evidence to the contrary, I had maintained the rigid conviction that lesbians (that is, those of us on the more butch side of the spectrum) weren't really women. We were women-lovers, a kind of "third sex" and most definitely not men. So having babies was something real women did, not butch lesbians, not girls who knew they were queer since grade school. We were the *defenders* of women and children, children we could never fully call our own. (3)

Butch lesbians' lack of "bona fide motherhood" is complemented by a lack of bona fide "fatherhood" as well, as her experience co-parenting a lover's child taught her: "I [. . .] raged against my predicament, my lack of bona fide motherhood *or fatherhood*, and the absolute impotence of being the lesbian lover of a mother" (4). While the loss of that child with the end of the relationship was a devastating blow, the experience of co-parenting taught her that she was "woman enough to mother a child" (5).

In this way, the text opens up a range of positions that include an understanding of a female or lesbian masculinity that is not tied to the specifically sexual (as is the lesbian designation "Daddy"), not equated with men, and not seen as "an extension or discursive effect of maleness" (Halberstam, "F2M" 95). In "Wings," Moraga tells the story of a friend who gets called "Daddy" by her lover's son and teaches/passes on "masculinity" to this male child ("he learned how to be a boy from Maria. He learned masculinity from Maria and she was a wonderful male role model, the best of fathers with a woman's compassion" [22]). The essay calls the meanings of "masculinity" as well as "fatherhood" into question. The verbal echo of authenticity when Moraga affirms that she is *"bona fide pregnant"* (10) redresses the previous lack (of authentic motherhood, of legitimate fatherhood) and mirrors how the act of conception brings together previously warring parts of herself.

Similarly, the possibility that one might fulfill both gender roles for the child compensates for the biological impossibility of lesbians making babies together ("Our blood doesn't mix into the creation of a third entity with an equal split of DNA. Sure, we can co-adopt, we can co-parent, we can be co-madres, but blood mami and papi we ain't" [22]). In the discursive context of the essay, "bona fide pregnant" constructs Moraga as butch lesbian, father and mother at once. The textual site for this process is what is called a "secret" in the text: the children of lesbians "hunger for 'normalcy' (that mami and papi business)" (22). In the political struggle for the rights of lesbian and gay families, same-sex parents are understandably less than eager to publicize their children's desire to have one mommy and one daddy like everyone else. But in "Wings," this secret made public activates the redefinition of parenting roles and identities in the text.

If becoming a mother secures in some way Moraga's lesbian womanhood, it throws the category of writer into crisis. The connection between the tensions lesbian/mother and writer/mother is the overarching experience of becoming a mother (and one threatened with the death of her newborn) that overshadows all other aspects of her identity and compels the textual project of redefinition. The conflict between the subject positions of "writer" and "mother" is presented in a variety of contexts: from her shock upon learning of her child's maleness ("*All day today I have been unable to write*" [16]), to the inadequacy of words to express the depth of emotions and experiences of pregnancy and especially of the baby's prematurity ("*I am afraid to write of these times, afraid somehow language will lessen what I know*" [40]). The writing and the pregnancy are presented as two forms of creativity that enter into a kind of alignment, at times paralleling, at times competing with each other ("*My body taking on the full shape of creation does not lessen my need for art*" [28]).[8]

The main conflict between "writer" and "mother," however, lies in the sidelining of writing in the around-the-clock demands of the baby's intensive care. Once her son has been sent home from the hospital, Moraga is shocked by how quickly she feels her identity as a writer threatened by the all-consuming demands of motherhood (68):

I miss the immersion into my writing terribly, fear I will not be able to retrieve that impassioned momentum. The baby cries [. . .] Somehow I feel that something has broken in me and yet I am forced to proceed along as if everything were normal, as before. I am a mother now and I do not yet know how to fully inhabit that place in the world [. . .] My writer's heart feels stolen by the struggle for my baby's survival. (66–67)

The tension between "writer" and "mother" is caught in the deployment of similar phrases to express her feelings upon her son's release from the hospital ("free at last" [66]), and the search for release from mothering to work ("free to continue writing" [69]) that haunts the pages of the essay, as Moraga "steals" whatever time she can to write: "But now, coming out from under that sea of terror, I need the work, the writing more passionately than ever. I need to know I am more than these tasks of motherhood, more than mother. I need to remember that I am a writer" (68). The physical and spiritual exhaustion carried forward from a taxing eighteen-month period from pregnancy to her son's discharge from the hospital makes it difficult to access the dream life and contemplative spaces that have always served as a crucial and rich source for her writing. With a tone of self-irony that both mocks and authorizes her need for this space as a writer, she describes as "high drama" her outburst and stormy exit: "*I have no internal life!*" (89).

Becoming "mother" changes the way Moraga writes: "*Not because of the time constraints (which are awesome) but because my soul is never completely empty in the same way. I am conscious of another entity always pulling on me*" (78). Writing affects mothering and mothering transforms writing:

> I don't know how "Medea" emerged, even in the rough form she presently wears, but the writing did not feel the same. It did not take a piece of me in the same way earlier writing has. The writing isn't any less challenging, but now a hole has been created where once I was childless. Now "Medea" passes through me differently. The art comes to me differently. I can't say how exactly. (80)

This notion of having a child creating "holes" in the mother, drawing on Castañeda's *Teachings of Don Juan*, also appears in one of Dolores' speeches in *Heroes*:

> When you got a baby, when you feel that baby come out entre las piernas,[9] nothing is the same after that. You are chain to that baby. It doesn' matter how old they get or how far away they go, son tus hijos[10] and they always take a piece of you with them. So you walk around full of holes from all the places they take from you [. . .] Como se puede sentir una mujer[11] whole and strong [. . .] with so many empty places in her body? (130).

The parallels between these two passages suggest that before giving birth, Moraga had experienced writing in a way similar to Dolores' speech on her experience as a mother ("they take a piece of you"). Now that having a child has created that "hole," Moraga constructs her writing in a different way. The key to the adversarial relationship between writing and other relational identities (as mother, as lesbian lover), revealed as the essay develops, has to do with the writer's stance toward irrevocable change and transformation (78). In the final section, "Waiting in the Wings," I will discuss how this resolution is related to the issues of "choice" and control that surfaced in Moraga's decision to have a child.

Radical Motherhood

The construction through writing of Moraga's "queer motherhood" enables her to see herself as both queer and mother, subverting binary divisions that police the border between "gay" and "straight," "butch" and "femme," active and passive. While the need to "map" unknown territory discussed above has to do with learning how to occupy the subject position of mother for which her life as a butch lesbian has left her unprepared, Moraga also infuses the experiences of conception, pregnancy, and birth with a lesbian sensibility that profoundly alters the traditional representation of these privileged markers of heterosexual womanhood. True to the centrality of the erotic as both practice and metaphor throughout Moraga's work, much of this redefining has to do with writing sex into these sacred realms of heterosexual privilege, breaking taboos in mainstream representations of procreation that tend to divorce sexuality from pregnancy and childbirth once conception has occurred. It is only fairly recently that pregnant women could be shown on TV, and Dan Quayle's confused outrage over Murphy Brown/Candace Bergen's single motherhood is a reminder of the popular perception of the reproductive female body, especially the pregnant woman, as indecent, as well as the need to sanitize its representations. If single motherhood is upsetting in our conservative climate, lesbian motherhood is even more controversial.

In "Wings," the insemination itself, accomplished through the turkey baster method practiced by many lesbians,[12] de-centers both the male-dominated medical profession and scientific technologies as well as the primacy of heterosexual intercourse. The scene is written as a new kind of lovemaking involving the donor, the lesbian lover, and the butch writer in a new, softer role:

when Ella and Pablo sat around me on my bed after the insemination, a comforter covering me, my legs propped up in the air with pillows, I felt "made love to" [. . .] The insemination had nothing to do with sex or orgasm or excitement [. . .] Still for all its awkwardness, I can say that the experience was probably the best loving I'd ever known. I am still awed by the fact that these two people loved me enough to go through whatever embarrassment to help me conceive [. . .] Very simple . . . and unromantic. And yet, I felt "made love to." And whether pregnant or not, I knew I would never forget what that softness felt like, my legs up and open to receive whatever destiny had decided for me. I close my eyes and dream Pablo as a sweet twin lover. I put my mouth and nose into the hollow of Ella's neck, breathe her in and I am sustained. Momentarily, there is tranquilidad. (7)

At the same time that Moraga's essay "queers" the privileged signifiers of female heterosexuality, it also constructs the experience of having a child as changing the way Moraga is lesbian in the world.

In the discourse of sexuality in Moraga's writing, there is a way in which "butch" monopolizes the category of "lesbian" and is constructed, as discussed above, as "not woman." The flip side of this construction is that "femmes" are "women" but also "not (really) lesbians."[13] Recent publications have addressed these issues from a femme perspective, documenting the invisibility of femmes as lesbians, the discrimination they endure within the lesbian community because of their appearance and erotic styling within the butch-femme polarity, and the need to explore femme identity and sexuality apart from their relation to butches.[14] As butch lesbians can redefine masculinity in ways that sever it from men and maleness, femmes redefine femininity by withdrawing it from heterosexual circulation and interrupting the simple equation between gender identification and sexuality, femininity and heterosexuality.

For many writers on the topic, coming out to people as a femme "means opening your mouth and telling them you are a lesbian. Butches, often through dress and demeanor, announce themselves without speaking" (Morgan, 46). As Jaime M. Grant puts it, "I understand, as a lesbian who passes for straight in almost every public setting, that my lover does visibility work for me every day. . . . She takes the anti-lesbian hits meant for all of us" (97).[15] The mediating function of speech and "choice" in the femme's rejection of "passing" recalls issues of racial/ethnic "passing" discussed in chapter 6 ("Since I seldom opened my mouth, few people questioned my Anglo credentials" [TLG, 145]): "As a femme, she's always passed effortlessly, that is, until she opens her mouth and the lesbian feminist rolls out without restraint" ("Wings," 61). While at times "Wings" reinforces the butch-femme polarity with the attendant implication that the butch is the "real" lesbian, it also undertakes a rewriting or reversing of these roles within the context of lesbian parenting and butch motherhood. In "Wings," the softening described in the insemination scene allows Moraga to textualize herself and her body in ways that blend butch and femme.

When her lover's mother wonders why a male-to-female transsexual could still want to have sex with a woman, now that she has "a vagina with feeling"

(28), Moraga is wounded to the quick *in her butchhood* that sexual pleasure and penetration for women remain so irrevocably identified with the penis. When she and her partner argue over this incident in terms of Moraga's supposed "man-hating" and "dick-centered resentment" (compare Marisa's "the dick beats me every time" in *Giving Up the Ghost* [8]), the writer retrenches in a butch positionality that constructs femme as other, even as the writing conveys an ironic self-awareness: "*I go to sleep wallowing in my queer sense of isolation/alienation even from my lesbian lover. She's a femme, I think. She doesn't really understand*" (29).

Immediately following this text, Moraga details the "feminization" of her butch body and self:

> *Ella tells me daily how much more feminine I look. I see it, too, my hair longer than it's been in fifteen years, my hips and thighs and breasts rounding from this pregnancy, the softening taking place throughout my body, the tears.* (29–30)

This recombination of butch and femme extends to a modification of the butch role as defender of women, allowing her to depend on a woman: "*I cling to Ella in a way I never imagined [. . .] Seeing Ella's goodness to me in my pregnancy has opened my heart to her in a way I know cannot be reversed. She has allowed me to depend on her. For the first time in my life*" (23, 27).

Through the tender scene of impregnation Moraga also rewrites and redeems the nationalist narrative of rape that plays such a central role in *TLG*. The loving multiracial triangle (white, brown, and "half-breed") replaces the violent binary of (white) violator/(brown) violated that plays itself out over and over in the bedroom, especially in scenarios of cross-racial desire. Furthermore, by inscribing her narrative of pregnancy within that of "*this continuing history . . . of conquests and culture clashes, of the regeneration of raza and the creation of new razas*" (23), by identifying herself in this narrative with the Spanish conquistadores "*whose hairiness I inherited*" (23), and by allowing herself to become impregnated by a "man of the race," Moraga reverses the assignment of racial and gender meanings to the positions of active and passive, impregnator and impregnated in the narrative of La Malinche. At the same time, the closed butch body is opened and filled. The result of these rewritings is not a total transformation of heterosexual narratives of conception, lesbian constructions of "butch" and "femme," or nationalist myths of racialized rape and conquest, but a "queering" that both continues and transforms them.

Barely two months pregnant, Moraga describes the experience of masturbation in words that suggest a rewriting of the end of *Ghost*, when Marisa "puts her fingers to her forgotten places" and fantasizes about Amalia, the elusive and now vanished object of desire. In "Wings," the woman called forth in the ona-nistic fantasy is the writer herself, joined, even in erotic sensation, with the child within her:

> **New York City.** *This morning as I am thoroughly alone, I put my fingers to that nostalgia (my new york days, my new york lovers) and remember, but it is no past woman I discover there, but more the eruption of the older me. How do I describe that at the moment of orgasm, I feel the infant inside me curl up into a hard fist, no vio-lence, but a hard ball of intensity swelling in my womb? And I cry for this life, this miracle.* (17)

The discovery of the self as both subject and object of desire is sited in the textualization of her queer pregnant body.

The involvement of the fetus in the writer's sexuality spills over the bound-aries of the "normal," as when she transgresses heterosexual incest taboos (and lesbian same-sex eroticism) in the construction of Pablo as her "sweet twin lover." This transgressive border-crossing also occurs in her writing of the sen-sual reveling in her boy child that colors her dreams:

> *the baby is born already a grown boy, like little Peter; then older like Pablo. So beautiful, so sensual. I touch him all over; I can't believe he is mine, although I am so disappointed that he was born a boy. I touch his penis inside his pants. I know I have gone too far, but I am delighting so much in his beauty.* (12)

Just as the lines between public and private are blurred by the exposure of auto-biographical "secrets," the writing crosses the lines between taboo and accept-able representations of lesbian motherhood and sexuality. The installation in the oniric realm of the representation of the fetus (and Pablo) as both exten-sion/mirror of her own body and ("masculine") object of her desire explores and expands the writing of sexuality and erotic identifications.

The loving triangulation in the act of insemination reappears in the deliv-ery room. Significantly, both obstetrician and Moraga's mother are absent in the writing of the scene. Moraga is supported by her lover and her sister, who make a "marvelous delivery team": her sister the experienced Lamaze pro after having four babies, her lover adding her physical strength to relieve the pain in Moraga's lower back ("No light-weight lover for me, the girl is pure power"

[36]). Moraga does not flinch from recording her body's intense sensations as the baby is being born ("I" [. . .] "feel the urge to defecate; my vagina is pure fire, a horrible burning" [37–38]). Afterwards, the experience blends with sexual pleasure:

> Relief, my body is engulfed in a pleasure . . . an animal pleasure, a pulsing, an aliveness like nothing I've known [. . . .] They don't bring the baby to my belly as they do in the movies. (38)

The explicit reference to her experience diverging from representations of childbirth in popular culture underlines Moraga's redefining of the scene of female heterosexual privilege as woman-centered and lesbian. "In the movies," the unbelievable pain of childbirth is signified by the screams of the mother, almost immediately forgotten as her anguish turns to smiles when her infant child is laid on her body. Moraga details the (usually unspoken) proximity of childbirth with bodily processes of elimination and sex, establishing the experience on the level of "animal" sensation and survival in the text.

The textualization of this experience as specifically lesbian includes the feminization of the butch body. Just as she softened and opened in the penetration and filling of her body in insemination and pregnancy, here the delivery is described in terms of sexual pleasure from a position of femme receptivity that constructs her as "woman": "I am a girl and a woman and an animal and estoy temblando [16] like the best of sex, the best of being thoroughly entered and spent" (38). Later Moraga returns to the writing of the experience of birthing as lesbian sex, constructing the connection through the image of the "secret." As in "La Ofrenda," the sense of smell provides the authorization of knowledge:

> [The infant's] smell. His smell that grew sweet with the rise of milk inside my breasts, that grew sweet with woman-sex. Even my sister tells me, "I love that smell. I'll never forget that smell," knowing it four times in her life. She didn't mean some baby wrapped in the new-born warmth of a receiving blanket. She meant birthsmell, the thick-membraned blood-smell passing out between a woman's legs at birth and for a full moon's cycle following. I didn't tell her how close such scent came to that lesbian secret, of how close women came to birth each time we make love to one another and mean it. It is a lesbian sex smell. A mother-smell. A mother-lover; a mother-fucked smell. It is life. (51)

As before with the secret fear of lesbian parenting, the exposure of the "secret" of "lesbian sex smell" makes possible the radical redefinition of motherhood in lesbian terms. The passage from "birthsmell" to "mother-lover, a mother-fucked smell" also traces the rewriting of her experience to include both butch and femme positionalities. She is then both mother-lover and mother-fucked, although the latter is only textualized in "Wings" through the experiences of insemination and childbirth in the context of Moraga's changing, more "feminine" appearance; the femme-eroticization of these areas in the text complements the continuing butch identification in sexual practice (*"I like it and yet in bed feel a strong urge to reassert my butchness, my self as a love-maker"* [30]).

"Radical motherhood" refers on one level to this writing of "lesbian" through "mother" and "mother" through "lesbian" that both facilitates and legitimates Moraga's womanhood while "queering" the privileged categories of heterosexual female experience. On another level, the text documents the radical social practice of lesbian parenting, particularly the obstacles she and her lover encounter in a social and legal system that defines parents as a heterosexual married couple ("We try to get what we can on paper, to protect ourselves against pain, against loss, but the papers don't protect us" [24]).

"Wings" concentrates on the obstacles to lesbian parenting at the hospital during the baby's three-and-a-half-month stay in intensive care. The hospital becomes the site of a literal gatekeeping, for example in the marginalization of the lesbian couple and the refusal to recognize Moraga's lover's right to see or inquire about her son:

Ella called the hospital this morning to inquire about the baby, having to put up with the usual deterrents: who are you? No male voice on the line, but a woman, my lover; seeking to know about our son. "Read the damn chart," she snaps back. "I'm the co-mother." (46)

Throughout this process, Moraga and her lover are aware of and insist on their rights. As in the drawing up of legal papers, their ongoing struggle for recognition and equal treatment at the hospital is a form and practice of resistance. The filing of complaints and writing of letters protesting and documenting their treatment at the hospital calls attention to the fact that "radical motherhood" has legal as well as social dimensions.

Besides the "usual deterrents," they are forced to undergo the harassment of the security guard after hours. The text highlights one particular confrontation, triggered by the dual combination of the guard's homophobia and their impatience to see the baby during a severe medical crisis:

each night, we go through the same interrogation. "Only immediate family," the young man tells us. He is very serious in his fresh-pressed uniform. He is taking his job very seriously. "Yes, we know," I answer for the hundredth time. "She (refer-ring to Ella) is immediate family. Call the ICN they'll okay us." The same old ritual, the same harassment night after night. Then he can't help himself, a grin begins to crack the professional facade. "You say you're both the moms!" He eyes his buddy-co-workers and the street gang begins to form around us. Oh, they're gonna milk this one for all its worth. They are very bored. "I didn't know two women could have a baby together." But I am primed, too. Thinking of Rafaelito swollen beyond recog-nition. *Don't fuck with me tonight, boys.* We had already filed our complaints, called their supervisor who always seemed to enjoy the joke as much as they, spoken with the ICN social worker, and in a few days I would write the obligatory letter to the hospital administrator. Pero, para nada. [. . .][17]

That night I can't take any more. [. . .] "That's right," I say, "you'd be surprised what two women can do together." [. . .] And I storm through the entrance cursing and screaming [. . .] counting in my mind how many times we've gone through this. (60–61)

The violence of Moraga's response and the aggression in her self-presentation ("I would have belted him" [62]) is related to the cluster of concerns intersect-ing "butch" and "mother." A crisis in butch identity as "protector of women" is brought on by the role reversal in her relationship with her lover:

My impotence enrages me. I can't protect her from the pain she experiences each time they make her the outlaw. I'm the dyke in the matter, I tell myself. I'm the one who's supposed to be on the outside. But not now. As Rafael's biological mother, I am surrounded by acceptance at the hospital until Ella walks in and we are again the lesbian couple, the queer moms—exoticized or ostracized. I know this is new for Ella. New and hard. (61)

This role reversal de-centers Moraga as lesbian outsider since pregnancy and motherhood have eased her interfacing with the heterosexual world. Besides her inability to "protect" her femme lover, Moraga sees her partner now experi-encing her former butch role of being "the lesbian lover of a mother," on the outside, with a tenuous relationship to the child. No matter who births the baby in a lesbian couple, because of the biological conundrum discussed above, one lesbian parent will always be placed in the position of non-biological parent.

In this sense, both femme and butch identities are undergoing a transfor-mation: "I know what it is to live with that uncertainty as the 'non-biological' parent [. . .] no other reward than the act of loving in the here and now. Not enough for most of us" (22). The text values as "lesbian" precisely the willingness to take this risk (22). Moraga praises her partner's support and strength throughout the process ("her Amazon strength, her Irish outrage, her basic loyalty during the hardest year of my life" [92–93]). The prologue states that the essay tells the story "of faithfulness between two lesbian lovers (mothers)" (6).

The vacillation between the designations "lover" and "mother" to describe Ella captures the dynamic of acknowledgment and disavowal in the text's representation of this figure. Again, I want to distinguish between the actual person's role as co-mother of Moraga's son and the textualizing of this relationship, in which Ella becomes a crucial figure in the displacement of a series of issues that have to do with the "queer motherhood" discussed above, racial and cultural identity, and the writing of "queer" and "blood" family.

Moraga's decision to have a child was made, not in the context of her relationship with her lover, but in the context of her experience with Joel (the child she lost as "lesbian lover" of a mother), and in the context of the "blood family" issues raised in *TLG*. The loss of Joel brought home the precariousness of the position of the lover who is not the mother: *"Men (and women) come and go, I could hear my mother's refrain, all you really got are your children. But mamá, I lost the child, too"* ("Wings," 5). In "Shadow," Hortensia expresses the same belief:

> No matter what you did, you would always be my children [. . . .] With a husband, it's difernt. You see, this man did not come from your body. No matter cuantas veces le das la chichi, tu marido no es tu hijo. Your blood never mixes. He stays a stranger in his own home. (83) [18]

The intensity and importance of the "real bond" between mother and children (blood being thicker than water) is shown in Moraga's writing to be matched only by its potential toxicity, as in *Shadow* and *Heroes*.

In spite of the reaction of the rather naive reader at the bookstore, for whom Moraga's having a child negated the meaning of *TLG*, her decision can be seen as a logical outgrowth of Moraga's fear of being "the last generation" in her family. In the face of her parents' aging, having a child provides some solace as well as continuity ("Born in Los Angeles, as the generation before him" [78]): *"With each visit, they seem a bit smaller; physically, a bit older; slightly more vulnerable [. . .] I am filled with emotion. This family means so much to me, this family slipping away"* (8).

The primary location in the blood family of the decision to have a child also relates to the issue of commitment in lesbian relationships that Moraga fictionalized through the character of the narrator in "La Ofrenda" and Marisa in *Ghost*.[19] "Wings" marks a turning point in Moraga's writing, from believing that a future can never be dreamt "in any lover, only in family, only in my sister" from whom she believed she would *"never be parted. Not really"* (12), and the gradual realization through her pregnancy that perhaps she could make a future with her partner, captured in the verbal echo of *"never be parted. Not really"* (13).

The difficulty in making a commitment to a lesbian relationship is related to internalized social and cultural forces. Convinced that she is incapable of being a mother, Moraga displays a compensatory butch bravado: "So while my sister was busily making babies every three or four years, I was busily making lovers (yes, about every three or four years)" (3). The co-parenting of Joel both convinces her that she is "woman enough to mother a child" (5) and motivates her to have her own child so she will never again experience the devastation of losing a child. The joining of "butch lesbian" and "mother" in the text once again provides the space for the blending and redefinition of other categories. It is only when she has become pregnant that she can imagine making a commitment to a relationship: *"I know it is this life I carry within me that causes me to imagine a future, a future I could never dream in any lover; only in family"* (12).

Yet her lover's status within this future is indeterminate. In the textual construction of herself as butch mother, Moraga monopolizes the roles of both mother and father, constructing her partner as lover to her, not mother to her son, and Pablo as friend to the child, not father.

How can I explain what brought me to the decision to find a man—a decent young man, already a part of my familia—and not ask him to father, but to simply help me get pregnant and be a friend to my child if he could. "I would never speak badly of you to my child," I told Pablo. "What you're giving us is all I want from you. It's enough."

In a way, I asked the same of Ella on a deeper level, not to be a mother; but only a lover of my child, a lover of me. Probably that's the most noble of gestures, more noble than offering sperm and having the privilege of knowing your bones' memory lives on in another being, without obligation. (21)

The text vacillates between giving her partner the role of mother and taking it away, reinforcing the outsider position assigned her by the hospital as merely lover of a mother.

The indeterminate position of Ella in the text has to do with the biological/non-biological dynamic as well as with the issues of whiteness and racial loyalty explored in *TLG*. This tension is partially resolved through the shifting writing of "faithfulness" in the text: "the faithfulness between two lesbian lovers (mothers)" (6) and faithfulness to the race. I have already discussed how the text partially rewrites the narrative of *mestizaje* by constructing Moraga as white (*"whose hairiness I inherited"*) and impregnated in *"the regeneration of raza and the creation of new razas"* (23). As in *TLG*, this whiteness is both acknowledged and disavowed.

The writer calls attention to the nationalist and racial factors that entered into her choice of donor: "Nation. Nationality. I am the mother of a Mexican baby. I am the worst and the best of Chicano nationalists, I picked a man for his brains and his dark beauty. And the race continues" (23). The first words her partner speaks to assure the writer that the baby is whole and hale at birth highlight his Indian features ("He has an indio nose" [38–39]), and he is referred to twice as having an "African head" (57), once in a context associating her son's determined struggle for survival with racial and cultural identity (72). It is also important to the writer to construct the context of support for herself and her child in racial terms: the women in her writing class are described as *"thoroughly Indian women in their response to me"* (23). She resents the *"white male pediatrician-types with their nurse wives and seven kids 'bonding' their way into my Mexican psyche"* (69), and revels in the "colored queerboy contingent" (85) she envisions as part of her child's support network: "how glad I am to be in their company, to bring my son into their circle of fine and critical minds, smart mouths, and righteous attitude. [. . .] I make a wish like a prayer that my son will always have such men, such hope in his life" (86).

As in *TLG*, the writer struggles to reconcile nationalist concerns with her desire for a white woman. Referring to the "queer contract" among herself; the gay male donor, Pablo; and her partner that delineates her "home," the writer ascribes the attributes of women of color to her white lover in order to place her within this home: "And I gotta whitegirl lover with lovely cullud girl curls and a butt to match and Spanish that don't make a fool outta her" (23). The nationalist emotion evoked by Pablo's dedicatory words written in a picture book he gives her son traces the limits between culture and desire even as the text blurs them anew:

> *Those are the words that keep me from saying so freely to Ella, yes should I pass on, the baby goes to you unequivocally. It is this business of cultura. There is no denying that I had this baby that he might be a Mexican, for him to know and learn of mexicanismo, for him to feel that fuego, that llama, that riqueza I call lo mexicano.*

Pablo said it best: belleza, lucha, cultura.[20] *There was a rush of emotion reading the words, a resonance, an echo I felt, a longing met. And for a moment, I miss that Mexican loving in my life.* (73)

In the desire to be the mother of a Mexican baby, Moraga's whiteness is simultaneously there and not there, much like she constructs her lover as "familia" but keeps her on the outside because of her whiteness.

The desire to have a Mexican baby is also related to the issues of blood family discussed above. The politics of radical motherhood resurface in the difficulty of finding a Catholic priest willing to baptize the baby, *"in spite of the fact that Rafael's mother is a queer and a pagan who calls the Virgin Mary by her Indian name and, on occasion, can be caught worshipping the moon"* (83).[21] The criticism of certain family members, that she gets to have it both ways, echoes her fears of the privileges attached to her light skin: "If I wanted to be on the outside, then I damn well better stay there and not cash in on their territory" (84).

Moraga freely admits the contradiction and reveals her reasons for insisting on the ritual:

> I wanted Rafael to be named in front of his blood family (the ceremony among the queer familia would come later). I wanted him to return to Los Angeles healthy and whole (he had left there on the edge of survival) and be presented to his gente en la tradición de catolicismo mexicano.[22] Call me old-fashioned. At bottom, I wanted to make my mother happy. My sister's kids were never baptized, being Jewish through their father. And my brother's kids, although thoroughly Catholic, are as estranged from our family as my brother. [. . .] Rafael was my gift to my mother, the only real grandchild whose baptism she could claim. At the reception afterwards, she was every bit the proud grandparent, dressed to kill and amazingly tranquila. (83–84)

This "gift" of her male son to her mother needs to be read intertextually in relation to *Loving*'s analysis of the "long line of betrayals" perpetuated from mother to daughter by putting the males first in the family and the culture.[23] In "Wings," Moraga provides the Mexican son her mother always wanted, one who ostensibly will remain loyal to the family, thus proving the daughter's own superior worth and loyalty. For Moraga, taking up the subject position of "mother," even as she reconstructs it, brings her inevitable benefits (especially since the child is male), whether she wants them or not, just as her light skin brings benefits that she interprets as curses in *TLG*. In the context of the relationship with the Mexican mother, there is a sense in which becoming the mother of a Mexican son places Moraga more thoroughly within the "long line of vendidas" as the woman who betrays other women by accepting the privileges that being the mother of a Mexican man confers. Yet her status as (butch) lesbian mother destabilizes this continuity. In this sense, her writing of "the next generation" parallels Cere's strategic channeling of her agency through forms that will be acceptable and meaningful to her mother and community (see chapter 4).

With the newly constructed bond between Mexican mother and daughter through the Mexican son, the long line of betrayals is displaced laterally onto her lover, on the grounds of a racialized motherhood, in a dream that rewrites an imprisonment scenario similar to the one that opens *Loving:* [24] "*I dream that Ella and I are going to slaughter. Along with dozens of women, we are to be executed en masse. There is a war going on and we have been taken captive*" (85). In both texts, the metaphor of wartime captures the perils of lesbian relationships in a homophobic and heterosexist society. The 1995 slaying of an activist lesbian couple in the Medford-Ashland area in Oregon demonstrates with terrifying clarity how closely this metaphor is grounded in reality. Unlike the dream in *Loving,* which posits lesbian faithfulness above life itself (i), motherhood takes precedence in "Wings," as Moraga is allowed to escape, but her lover is not:

> *I realize I have been separated from Rafael, that he is alone in our apartment. I shout this out loud, hoping I will be spared to save my son. This is exactly what happens. A guard hears me and takes pity. He leaves a gate open through which I can escape. Of course, Ella is not allowed out, but to my great relief I learn she, too, is released later.* (85)

In *Loving,* the guard who has befriended the lesbian couple refuses to help them escape; in "Wings," the guard does not hesitate to risk his own neck in the name of motherhood. The dream reveals how motherhood, allied with "man," like her light skin in other contexts, helps Moraga "get over," momentarily mitigating her lesbianness. As in *TLG,* putting the "Indian" first, constructed here as putting the Mexican son before the white lover, produces a sense of discomfort that is expressed in the relief Moraga feels in the dream when she learns her lover has also been released.

In other texts in "Wings," paternal whiteness is depicted as a powerful, even divine calm, a fearlessness in a text obsessed with the fear of death. In one dream, Moraga's father expertly lands a beautiful plane: "*He is brave and spins the plane around and around and upside-down. I am afraid, but soon discover it is not too frightening. All the while, I marvel at the change in my father: his competence, his courage, his command*" (19). In another dream, tidal waves ravage an island, as *"white people, young, moneyed"* rush to the shore (55): *"Then my father appears from out of the water. He is dressed in white. Surfacing from underwater his calm is almost christ-like. He walks toward the shore without fear"* (54). When it becomes apparent that her mother's life is in danger, the *"voice of Ella or my sister"* tells Moraga to save her mother, even though this futile gesture would result in her own death. This text reveals the other face of the triangular team of writer, lover, and sister in the birthing scene: the bond also implies a pact to uphold a set of demands and responsibilities revolving around the sacredness and primacy of motherhood. In the dream, Moraga feels shock and guilt that it has not occurred to her to save her mother. Although she still feels the pressure of these "voices," the dream symbolizes a moving away from the need to "save" her mother (and other women) at all costs as a (butch) lesbian.[25]

Moraga's identification with a (masculine) construction of whiteness as fearless tranquillity and the ability to survive potentially life-threatening situations in these dreams relates to her own need to find the internal resources to make it through her son's premature birth and medical crises. The racialized and gendered assignment of roles in the dream reflects her textual self-presentation as being able to perform the roles of father as well as mother. It also sheds further light on the family scenario in her writing, and what has broken loose to motivate this changing representation of the white father: from disappointing and ineffectual in *Loving*, through *TLG*'s more compassionate portraits of his symbolic orphanhood, to these scenes of paternal empowerment (see chapter 6). In "Wings," the father's unobtrusive reliability and almost spiritual composure contrast with the convoluted, even claustrophobic emotional complexity represented by the mother, as in the dream of the Mexican aunts as witches in *TLG* (123). It is this seductive yet entangling bond that on some level does not allow Moraga to be a woman, that keeps her bound to the mother as daughter. Becoming a mother and writing herself in that subject position permits a maneuver in which Moraga both fulfills a pact with her mother by giving her the Mexican son and frees herself as a woman. This in turn accounts for the representation of her father and at times her lover as touchstones of a kind of quiet strength, less enthralling, perhaps, than the dark women Moraga desires personally, esthetically, and politically, but perhaps for that reason a welcome relief.

The racialized dynamic between the desire to give her mother the Mexican son she has never had and the simultaneous distancing from the desire to save her, mirrors the tension in the parallel construction of "blood familia" (along the lines of race and ethnicity) and "queer familia" (along the lines of sexuality).

"Wings" continues the project, announced at the end of *Ghost,* of "making familia from scratch," as writing becomes the space for the combinations and contingencies of different kinds of families. Even as Moraga affirms the rightness of her son's birth in Los Angeles "among my blood familia" and recognizes her own, her mother's, and her grandmother's features in his face (39–40), she recalls her grandmother's insistence that she conform to a heterosexual paradigm, and claims the name of "family" for her lesbian relationship: "*Abuelita who always asked me, '¿cuándo te vas a casar, hija? Necesitas familia.'*[26] *While my family held me in her lion arms and my son had his guts cut open on the floor just above our heads*" (49–50).

At one point the text presents blood family as the only possible site of commitment and trust, yet it is a space marred by desertions, lacks, losses, betrayals, and failures in Moraga's writing. On the other hand, lesbian relationships are also marked in the writing by the dynamics of heterosexual families that the utopian construction of "queer familia" would hope to eradicate. Moraga fears that the fighting with her partner will cause her to pass on a legacy of unhappiness to her baby, just as she imbibed her own mother's unhappiness with her father "*at her breast*" (68), suggesting that the "long line" syndrome is not unique to heterosexual families.

"Queer familia" is also extended family; she defines Pablo as "already a part of my familia" (21) before the insemination, and her son as "*the child of queers, our queer and blessed family*" (45). During the medical crisis of the baby's ileostomy, her partner calls lesbian friends to come to the hospital because "We need some family with us" (48). Immediately following the passage detailing the importance of the ritual naming of her son in the context of her blood family, the text fills the concept of family with new meanings in the context of her relationship with her lover: "So, Santa Bárbara is a welcomed relief after so much familia. And suddenly Ella and I realize que somos familia (we three) in a way we never have before" (85).

It is the textualization of radical motherhood in the context of queer *familia* that provides a bridge across racial differences. In the fight for her son's life, Moraga and her partner pull together to face the security guards' homophobic insults:

Nobody really gives a damn that two women have their baby in a hospital for over three months, not knowing if he is going to live or die, and they still have to endure insults from testosterone-driven homophobes with no power acting like they got some. (My class and race analysis don't do shit for me when the brothers are standing in the way of my child. The hospital was full of AIDS patients and Ella and

I often wondered how *their* lovers were treated when they came through the same door after-hours.) (61)

While the text emphasizes the exclusion of the "colored queerboy contingent" from the festivities for the twenty-fifth anniversary of Stonewall along racial lines, the hospital guards' abuse of power channels solidarity along other lines having to do with the politics of sexual identity. This shifting of the lines of inclusion and exclusion in communities of support and different kinds of "familias" underlines the text's reluctance to view these categories as fixed or absolute.

Waiting in the Wings

The theme of writing and those represented by the phrase "waiting in the wings" converge in the destabilization of "choice" and related issues of control. The notion of "choice" in "Wings" functions intertextually, in light of the central role it plays in *TLG* and *Loving* with regards to Moraga's "choice" to embrace only her brown side. I place quotation marks around the word because the readings I propose of *TLG* and *Loving* reveal its problems and limitations. For example, *TLG* shows that embracing brownness does not make whiteness go away, and choosing mestiza objects of desire at the end of *Loving* does not put an end to the desire for a white woman.

"Wings" presents Moraga's decision to have a child as a triple-pronged choice whose outcome she believes she can control. This decision involves countering the impotence of the (butch) lesbian lover by having her own child who can never be taken away from her. It also entails having a girl child to finally break the "long line of vendidas" syndrome through a radical lesbian mothering practice. And finally, it involves the cultural nationalist project of having a child who will end the threat of "the last generation": "I had this baby that he might be a Mexican, for him to know and learn of mexicanismo, for him to feel that fuego, that llama, that riqueza I call lo mexicano" (22). "Wings" records the thwarting of the first two dimensions of these carefully laid plans, and while we will have to await Moraga's future autobiographical writing to learn the outcome of the third, there is no guarantee that our children will embrace the racial/cultural identities we hope to pass on to them. The essay traces the process by which Moraga, through writing, relinquishes her desire for control over these outcomes, while partially recuperating the notion of choice at the end.

The first impasse coincides with the news of her child's maleness: *"the news of my son came as a deep shock to me, that sent me to bed to recover"* (16). Plagued by a low-grade fever, she fears that her violent reaction to his maleness will cause her to lose the baby: *"I feared there was no place for my shock at this maleness"* (17). The depth of her disappointment is related to the intimate and inextricable relationship between her life and her work, her lesbian commitment to women and the fundamental feminist project that fuels her writing:

> I must believe that my son can forgive his mother's relentless need to describe the source of our female deformation. It is not mere feminist rhetoric that makes a woman stop dumbfounded in the face of a life of raising a son. It is the living woman-wound that we have spent our lives trying to heal. (17)

This "woman-wound" is represented on many levels in Moraga's work, together forming an analysis of all the interconnected forces that inflict both psychic and physical damage on women on the global, national, and "community" levels and within the family, the couple, and the self. It is the "wound in me/between my legs" in "Passage" (*Loving*, 44). It is Marisa wrestling with the legacy of Corky's rape and the inscription of rigid gender binaries on women's bodies (*Ghost*). It is Lupe and Cere poisoned by family secrets and Cere's exhortation to the people to put their hand inside a wound that is at once the contaminated valley and her absent body mutilated by environmental racism and Catholic repression (*Heroes*). It is the hope that sex might heal the injuries that kill the spirit, voiced by Marisa, Lola, and even Mario ("I've always loved sex, Father, always felt that whatever I had crippled or bent up inside me that somehow sex could cure it, that sex could straighten twisted limbs, like . . . the laying on of hands" [*Heroes*, 141]). It is the vision of a theatrical practice that must delve into the festering places in Chicano culture in order to cure them, a commitment reiterated at the end of *TLG* on the apocalyptic level of the alternative between the destruction or survival of the planet: "The planet is Crow Woman in whose mountain-breasts the missiles of destruction have been implanted. We must open the wound to make it heal, purify ourselves with the prick of Maguey thorns. This Sun will not pass away painlessly!" (191–192).

In "Wings" the "woman-wound" is related textually to a source that recurs throughout the writing: the "orphanhood" caused by the mother's primary betrayal of the daughter in putting the male first. Moraga's desire for a girl child (*"I wanted a female to love"* [17]) was related to the affirmation of her lesbianism as a "daughter who loves daughters" who has always "nursed" and supported other women, including her mother. The sight of her pregnant body effects a kind of healing in which she becomes both subject and object of her desire, both mother and lover of a mother, her self: "*I try to reach somewhere wounded and orphaned inside of me and bring this sudden image of my queer womanhood into its view: I, object of my own desirous lesbian woman-hungry eyes. I, a mama, too, like all the mamas I have longed for and loved*" (6). Besides constructing herself as both mother and mother-lover, subject and object of lesbian desire, by presenting herself as both mother and daughter, Moraga is able to rewrite the breaking of the long line of *vendidas* as a kind of self-mothering that erases her orphanhood: "*I am not now as I once was that orphaned woman walking the cobblestone in the pre-dawn silence. I am she who rises en busca de la luna,*[27] *seeking mother/daughter, seeking light. Moon keeper; I divine*" (21). In this sense, her mothering continues her lifelong loving of women (her self), regardless of the sex of her child.

Her son's extremely premature birth and desperate struggle for survival shatter any cherished notions Moraga may have had about playing the role of defender and protector of a child who will never be taken from her. The biological fact of giving birth to the child does not guarantee that she will not lose him. The passage describing Moraga's shock at her child's maleness vis-à-vis her life project as activist and writer is countered by another in which she experiences outraged identification at their shared woundedness: "When Rafaelito is brought back to the ICN, he is a limp yellow doll, a stripped monkey naked under the glare of heat lamps. He is all wound and he is my son" (48). Later she writes of his radical separation from her as a "wound" (51). These texts expand the scope of her project to include both the woman-wound of the lesbian-feminist and that of mother/son inflicted by a radical prematurity.[28]

Just as she learned to open her heart and ears to her son's spirit in making the decision to conceive, she now relinquishes the desire for control, constructing the experience as a series of lessons to be learned. Moraga writes her child as a quest for meaning, his prematurity suggesting the title's notion of "waiting in the wings":

I tell friends, I almost missed Rafaelito, that he had been there waiting in the wings, and I could hear his voice in the most remote corners of my dreams and in the raising of other women's children. That is how I account for his precipitous birth at only 28 weeks of gestation. He was a spirit who, for some time, was wanting to get here, through me. He was in a hurry. And when I finally opened my heart and listened, he took hold of me right away. I was pregnant with the first insemination and six months later, he was born, weighing only two pounds, 6 ounces. (2)

His fragile yet persistent hold on life textualizes him as wordless teacher of lessons that have to do primarily with death:

Rafaelito came to me effortlessly, our first try at conception. He was, literally, waiting in the wings . . . angel wings, waiting for me to finally decide to call him to this earth. But now I see Rafaelito is not so-easily-won. He enters this life with a delicate deep strength, as living reminder of the precariousness of our lives. (45)

Moraga expands the notion of healing in her work by making sense of her son through the writing of a new self. The news that her friend Tede is dying of AIDS confirms the destiny of the infant's maleness (14–15) in his name, Rafael Angel: Rafael ("the healing angel of god"), Angel ("waiting in the wings"). "This birth, *I think,* may be for them, this male birth for so many dying brothers" (16).

The text does not recuperate the other brother who has been lost to Moraga and her blood family for some time — her assimilated brother who abandoned the family (racially and culturally) and inquired so crassly after her baby's *father.* Instead, her son and Tede are equated through the image of the angel (47): "I remember the passing of my queer queen brother Tede who wrote to me of angels, never knowing I held one with folded wings inside of me" (94). The strongest male-to-male bond in the text is between the "angels" Tede and the boy child, de-centering male fatherhood in Moraga's writing of herself as both father and mother. On the news of Tede's death, the text reiterates the *"queer balance to this birthing and dying"* (45). Further blending the "blood" and "queer" *familias,* Tede, the *"queer recently-born ancestor,"* takes his place among *"all the dead Mexican relatives we remembered and invoked"* (49).

The forces bearing down on the bodies of queer/raza are multiple: the emaciated gay male body and the sexless and wounded infant body are immaterialized as angels through AIDS and prematurity in much the same way Moraga's work writes the adolescent female body out of the script through religion, pesticide poisoning, and rape. In writing the infant as teacher of lessons about these individual and collective losses (42, 55), Moraga gives him at times the face of masculine power and privilege (*"Some days I imagine him a bitter old man, un juez,*[29] *severe and authoritative. I imagine him judging my harshness, my moods, my mean ways"*), at others she thinks of him as *"a young sage-spirit, as delicate as his angelic name"* (18). But the main image for the fear and final acceptance of death is the "animal." The sensations of the growing fetus inside her ("*He is pure animal, nothing human about these sensations. They are the animal I am when I make love, am hungry, move my bowels, fall into a deep unconscious sleep*" [28]) and the "animal pleasure" that follows the birth (38) set the stage for the primordial animality of her infant's struggle for his life ("*His hunger, his desire to survive, his clinging animal heart*" [72]) and her own as his mother: "*For what is survival other than animal? I am an animal only for my child*" (76).

The most intense moment of this crisis provokes the ultimate lesson of motherhood; the knowledge garnered in the animal struggle to hold on to life is further distanced from rational mental processes through the introduction of the transcendent level, adding the spiritual to the reservoir of textual meanings instilled in "faithfulness" along sexual and racial lines:

> there are no guarantees, only faith [. . .] I remember in the grip of fear, thoroughly knowing I have no choice in the matter. My baby will die or will survive and my tightest hold against death can not keep Rafaelito here. [. . .] *Si es tu voluntad,*[30] I find myself saying the unthinkable out loud, passing the decision on to powers unknown. But in that gesture of letting go, I felt Rafaelito move towards us, toward life. (46–47)

The text constructs the essence of the son's lesson as yielding "choice" and control in the terrifying knowledge of the familiarity of death (50).

The lesson of letting go in the face of death joins the AIDS meanings invested in the infant's maleness ("queer balance"). This knowledge is transferred to the familial level of accepting her parents' aging and imminent death through the image of the map: the baby's hands and features with which Moraga can read her family's continuity, even in death:

> *Ironically, as my baby grows older [. . .] he becomes more "baby" and less sabio, less viejito,*[31] *less my mother's aging face, and instead, the seamless face of hopefulness, of future. But his hands retain the memory. Wrinkled, a map of generations revisited* (51).

In this backwards journey, the infant's face resembles her aging mother, her own "*collapsing chin,*" the "*blurring ancient eyes of my grandmother in the years just before her death at 96*" and his own when he is an old man and his mother is dead (40). As the text exposes the "secrets" of lesbian parenting and lesbian sex in writing "lesbian mother," the lessons Moraga learns from her teacher-son are made public in the writing even as they are buried within him: *"the ancient-ness will obscure itself in ounces of baby fat and he will carry this knowledge of this closeness to death (the other side of life) as a great secret inside of him"* (40).

The lessons imparted by the messianic infant are mapped on a national level as well, including the deaths of UFW leader César Chávez, writer Audre Lorde, and filmmaker Marlon Riggs (94). The construction of queer/colored family on the national level helps relieve the binary tension between the "blood" and "queer" families in the text, with their productive blendings and in-ternal contradictions. This national family, not based entirely on either shared racial/cultural identity or sexuality, functions as part of the public space of activ-ism Moraga claims for Chicana lesbians, a shared political project carried out through activism and art.

At the end, Moraga counterbalances the destiny of the birth of her son in the context of the lessons he must teach her with a partial recuperation of "choice" in her own agency as writer and mother: *"I almost missed my call from him . . . had I waited moments longer; a few months more, we might have missed each other in this life. I believe this, that not all is destiny, but choice, too"* (86). Her agency is located in her decision to conceive and the process leading up to it. Moraga's writing in general and particularly here in "Wings" attempts to make sense of, though never resolves, the struggle between the lack of "choice" (what we are born with and into) and agency in fashioning our selves, in her case in writing "someone to be."

The reversal of the roles of parent and child in the construction of the infant son as teacher is counter-reversed at the end (like a good play). This counter-reversal occurs in the space of writing, although the lessons she will teach him are without words, as he has taught her without words:

> *Rafaelito watches me as I write. He is quiet now, not interested in the baby "gym set," dangling over his head. He is interested in the movement of my hand across this page. Black strokes against the soft beige grain of this paper. He watches me. And for the first time it occurs to me that he may have something to learn from me, by my example. My job is not merely to see that he is grown and protected, but also to teach him something, something without words, that may be very beautiful after all.* (76)

Like the de-privileging of the space of writing as the scene of knowledge in favor of smell in "La Ofrenda," "Wings" writes the mother/son less on the semantic level than in the materiality of the "black strokes against the soft beige grain" of the paper. The page itself becomes the epistemological ground for the infant to learn from what the writer does. "Wings" privileges the material practice of art, just as Moraga's writing as a whole deploys sexuality as a means of knowing that is both metaphor and practice.

Complementing the image of the secret, site of the text's most radical rewritings of the self through the hidden made manifest, the son as "gift" captures the millennial tone of jubilation and hope that ends the essay. The gift accomplishes the transfer of learning between the writer and infant son: *"He is all gift to me. But they tell me, I also am a gift to my son"* (25). I have discussed how the text constructs the male infant as Moraga's gift to her mother, a gift that also releases her on some level from her daughterhood:

The gift of this child is how he has opened my eyes. I see my mother's amazing physical beauty, the quality of her skin, still sensual, seamless (the skin of a fifty-year-old at seventy-eight). She dresses in front of me, stands bare-breasted without shame. Is it motherhood that has made our bodies finally shameless to each other? (55)

The son has given Moraga the insights she needs to accept death (*"the gift of bearing witness to a soul's decision to take hold of an earthly life"* [51–52]), and treasure the changing face of family:

There will never be enough time to appreciate the gift of familia. At times I want to split my face and eyes wide open, drink in something so quickly vanishing in the daily growing up of nephews and nieces when breasts appear and voices change and adam's apples suddenly emerge from adolescent male throats and hips hips and hips continue to round in the bodies of little skinny girls turning women as the clock keeps ticking past us. (74)

"Wings" ends with the recognition of the cyclical nature of life and death, which does not cancel out its pain, but does bring a kind of joy:

The deaths that surrounded the birth of my baby have given me great pause. They have been living reminders to me of the fragility of our existence, the endless circle of birth/and/death/and/rebirth that Mexicans have always bemoaned and celebrated dancing drunk with life around the lip of the grave. (93–94)

It is in this space of insight that Moraga is able to resolve the contradiction between her identities as (Chicana) "mother" and "writer." If her son was "waiting in the wings" to teach about relinquishing control and accepting death as a part of life, it is also true that with his arrival, her writing was banished to "the wings": *"so much to write of what I've learned about familia, life, fear of death. But the writing remains in the wings. It takes great effort to move this pen across the page in an attempt to document some thread of what I am/we are experiencing"* (45). Yet it is through writing that Moraga takes the necessary distance in textualizing her experience to arrive at the place where she understands that her work is independent from her son and her son is independent from her:

> *I knew on a most profound level—differently than my deeply intuitive sense of it at his birth—that Rafa is his own man. He is growing up and away from us. And so . . . I don't know . . . I am reminded that my creativity is not dependent on this child. I am left with the work of this writing, this daily act of creation. As I was before Rafa entered our lives. Rafael, too, will have his work to do.* (91)

While the passage just quoted separates writing and mothering to a degree, the epilogue stresses how writing the self as mother changes the self. Although her baby had stopped nursing by the time Moraga was revising the essay, she writes that the experience of scripting his birth and near-death returns the milk to her breasts, "as thick as the day I gave birth" (92).[32] In the nexus of the public and the private, of who she is in the world and on the page, Moraga rebirths herself as well as her son in the act of writing. In this sense, writing and mothering remain complementary as well as competing activities.

"Wings" textualizes the creative experience of conception and childbirth, submitting it to another creative process that finally shapes the wordless "name of [the] son" into letters (91). The messianic connotations of the infant reintroduce the political, as throughout Christian history the joyful hope in the second coming of Christ at the turn of the millennium has signified the dream of both divine and social justice.[33] The text's construction of the infant son as teacher of lessons permits the maximum concentration of transnational, national, and "community" concerns in the personal history, dissolving the private/public dichotomy.

The ending of "Wings" with the maternal breast contrasts with that of "La Ofrenda," in which Moraga appropriates nursing as a marker of maternity to support a lesbian self-presentation as lover and writer but "not mother" ("I, who have only given my breast to the women" [86]). In "Wings," the experience of motherhood becomes text and the writing of the text reinscribes the maternal body. The joyful nursing/writing body at the end of the essay counters the breasts of *Heroes* and *Loving* (and parts of "Wings"), at which infants may suck familial and environmental poison. The double writing (of the text, of the body) occurs in a context that is both private (the "secret" of her intimate life with her "families") and public: she continues to give her breast to the women figuratively, in a writing project that claims a public voice for Chicana lesbian identity politics. Moraga's textual construction of the new self in "Wings" shows the relative autonomy yet interconnectedness of the categories of lesbian, mother, and writer.

Appendix

A Chronology of Major Works by Cherríe Moraga

1981   *This Bridge Called My Back: Writings by Radical Women of Color.* Edited with Gloria Anzaldúa.

1983   *Cuentos: Stories by Latinas.* Edited with Alma Gómez and Mariana Romo-Carmona.
      Loving in the War Years: Lo que nunca pasó por sus labios. Essays and poems.
      "What We're Rollin Around in Bed With: Sexual Silences in Feminism." Co-authored with Amber Hollibaugh.

1989   *Giving Up the Ghost.* Play premiered at The Studio, Theatre Rhinoceros in San Francisco.

1990   *Coatlicue's Call/El llamado de Coatlicue.* Play premiered at Theatre Artaud in San Francisco.
      Shadow of a Man. Play premiered at the Eureka Theater in San Francisco.

1992   *Heroes and Saints.* Play premiered at the Mission Theater in San Francisco.

1993   *The Last Generation.* Essays and poetry.

1994   *Heart of the Earth: A Popol Vuh Story.* Play commissioned by INTAR Theater, New York.
      Heroes and Saints and Other Plays. Collection of plays.

1995   *A Circle in the Dirt.* Play commissioned by The Committee for Black Performing Arts, Stanford University.
      Watsonville: Some Place Not Here. Play commissioned by Brava Theater Center in San Francisco, supported by the Rockefeller Foundation.

1997   *Waiting in the Wings: Portrait of a Queer Motherhood.* Memoir.

2000   *The Hungry Woman: A Mexican Medea.* Play.
      Loving in the War Years: Lo que nunca pasó por sus labios. Essays and poems. Expanded edition.

Notes

Introduction

1. I write this in response to the charge leveled by Ignacio García, who argues that Chicana lesbian feminism has jeopardized the viability of Chicano studies. See his essay in David R. Maciel and Isidro D. Ortiz, *Chicanas/Chicanos at the Crossroads: Social, Economic, and Political Change.*

2. Cherríe Moraga and Gloria Anzaldúa, *This Bridge Called My Back: Writings by Radical Women of Color.* I refer the reader to the following list, which is by no means exhaustive: Norma Alarcón, Ana Castillo, and Cherríe Moraga, eds., *The Sexuality of Latinas;* Norma Alarcón et. al, *Chicana Critical Issues: Mujeres Activas en Letras y Cambio Social;* Gloria Anzaldúa, *Borderlands/La Frontera: The New Mestiza,* and *Making Face, Making Soul/Haciendo Caras: Creative and Critical Perspectives by Women of Color;* Teresa Córdova et al., *Chicana Voices: Intersections of Class, Race, and Gender;* Adela de la Torre and Beatriz M. Pesquera, *Building with Our Hands: New Directions in Chicana Studies;* María Herrera-Sobek and Helena María Viramontes, eds., *Chicana Creativity and Criticism: Charting New Frontiers in American Literature;* Carla Trujillo, ed., *Chicana Lesbians: The Girls Our Mothers Warned Us About,* and *Living Chicana Theory.*

3. See especially Norma Alarcón's influential essay, "The Theoretical Subject(s) of *This Bridge Called My Back* and Anglo-American Feminism" and Chela Sandoval, "U.S. Third World Feminism: The Theory and Method of Oppositional Consciousness in the Postmodern World."

4. The verb "entender" (to understand) denotes queerness, as in "entendida/o" (an "in-the-know" person).

Chapter One

1. The mouth.
2. The center of the heart.
3. Cave.
4. The heart of this woman.
5. You understand?
6. The fucker.
7. The fucked.
8. One of the epigraphs of an earlier version of the play is the sign of the cross: "In the name of the Father, and of the Son, and of the Holy Ghost."
9. *Actos* are political skits, *mitos* theatrical forms incorporating Aztec and Mayan symbolism and philosophies. The pachuco is a member of a subculture of the 1940s, portrayed in Luis Valdez' play and film *Zoot Suit. La muerte* means death, and Quetzalcoatl refers to the Aztec god who, upon exiling himself for a crime he committed, promised to return. This supposedly facilitated the conquest, as Cortés was interpreted as being the returning Quetzalcoatl.
10. See Teresa De Lauretis, *Alice Doesn't: Feminism, Semiotics, Cinema*, p. 132: "Her body . . . has become her battlefield and, paradoxically, her only weapon and possession. Yet it is not her own, for she too has come to see it as a territory staked out by heroes and monsters (each with their rights and claims); a landscape mapped by desire, and a wilderness."
11. The church.
12. The mass.
13. Poor women.
14. In "Vendidas," Moraga grapples with difference in the context of oppression, concluding that "the danger lies in ranking the oppressions. *The danger lies in failing to acknowledge the specificity of the oppression*" (*Loving*, 52).
15.

The tongue I need
in order to speak
is the same I use
to caress
you know.

16. In her gagged mouth.
17. Profound and simple / that which was / never / spoken.

Part II

1. See Yolanda Broyles-González, *El Teatro Campesino: Theater in the Chicano Movement,* for an analysis of Chicanas' creative response to these limitations within El Teatro Campesino, and Denise Chávez, *Shattering the Myth: Plays by Hispanic Women,* for exceptions to this rule.

2. For a critique of the trope of the "race-as-family" to police the political correctness of Chicana/o cultural representations vis-à-vis the dominant culture, see Yarbro-Bejarano, "Sexuality and Chicana/o Studies."

3. "As long as they insist on remaining 'men' in the socially and culturally constructed sense of the word, they will never achieve the full liberation they desire [. . .] By openly confronting Chicano sexuality and sexism, gay men can do their own part to unravel how both men *and* women have been formed and deformed by racist Amerika and our misogynist/catholic/colonized mechicanidad; and we can come that much closer to healing those fissures that have divided us as a people" (Moraga, *TLG,* 162).

4. For more information about this Chicana/o theatrical tradition, see Yarbro-Bejarano, "Teatropoesía."

5. Moraga, "Shadow of a Man," lecture at the University of Washington, 1990.

6. This may be why, as Case et al., editors of *Cruising the Performative: Interventions into the Representation of Ethnicity, Nationality, and Sexuality,* point out: "Acts have a long subversive history in Western cultures. From Plato's *Republic* onward, the 'unnatural' quality of acting was condemned by numerous philosophers and state officials alike. Theaters have been closed by the state and actors' bodies, such as Moliere's, rejected at the cemetery gates as polluted by 'art.'"

7. The Latino Theater in Chicago produced *Shadow* in May 1992.

Chapter Two

1. See, for example, Sandra Harding, "The Instability of the Analytical Categories of Feminist Theory."

2. As in María C. Lugones and Elizabeth V. Spelman, "Have We Got a Theory for You! Feminist Theory, Cultural Imperialism and the Demand for 'the Woman's Voice'"; and Gloria Joseph and white socialist feminist Jill Lewis' *Common Differences: Conflicts in Black and White Feminist Perspectives.*

3. bell hooks, *Ain't I a Woman: Black Women and Feminism,* and *Feminist Theory: From Margin to Center.*

4. Here and throughout the book, I refer to the first, unproduced version of Moraga's first play, *Ghost,* based on staged readings only and published by West End Press in 1986, not the version produced by Theatre Rhinoceros and published by West End Press in 1994 in *Heroes and Saints and Other Plays.*

5. See also Emma Pérez, "Sexuality and Discourse: Notes from a Chicana Survivor."

6. See Alarcón, Cypess, and Del Castillo, among other Chicanas' and Mexican women's projects of rewriting and reclaiming the figure of La Malinche. For a theatrical context, see Yarbro-Bejarano, "The Female Subject in Chicano Theatre: Sexuality, 'Race,' and Class."

7. "Chicana's Feminist Literature: A Re-vision through Malintzin, or, Malintzin: Putting Flesh Back on the Object," and "Traddutora, Traditora: A Paradigmatic Figure of Chicana Feminism."

8. For a critique of applying the mother/daughter model developed by white feminists to women of color, and the beginnings of an analysis of the mother/daughter relationship among black women, see Gloria Joseph and Jill Lewis, *Common Differences*.

9. Revising this in 1995, I would relieve the binary "lesbian/heterosexual" tension by adding a few more commas, including bisexual, transgender, and "questioning." This semantic shift signals the recognition of a broader spectrum of gender and sexual identities.

10. Dudes.

11. The rapist employs the identity of "Mexican," speaking Spanish and exploiting her sense of solidarity and *respeto* (respect) to lure Corky into helping him (38). Once he has her alone and is holding a screwdriver against her body, he drops the mask: *"'Don't move,' he tells me. In English. His accent gone. 'n' I don'"* (40).

12. So what?

13. Flat, wide.

14. With a memory so violent that / it could destroy all these buildings.

15. Moraga's writing on the autonomous yet interconnected structures of gender and sexuality was before its time; in a playful 1990s gender-bending version of recognizing the "man" in the "woman," a femme contributor to Lesléa Newman's *The Femme Mystique* writes, "I am femme because I know there is a boy inside me. The boy is femme, too. The boy wears dresses and shops. The boy cooks and selects the wines. The boy is hungry" (Kay Elewski, 274).

16. Kinda cold.

17. You know.

18. Shorty.

19. See Yarbro-Bejarano, "The Female Subject," for further discussion of the use of narrative form in the Chicano theater movement.

20. In the 1989 Theatre Rhinoceros production of the play, Moraga orchestrated the three characters' monologues from the first published version analyzed here around a series of new scenes between Marisa and Amalia that develop their relationship in linear fashion from beginning to end. Intertwined with this story line, the monologues still summon the "ghosts" that haunt the characters' desire and their relationships. The new dramatic structure intensifies the conflict between the two women and the triangular relationship between Marisa, Amalia, and Amalia's lover Alejandro. It also highlights the characters' self-destructive investments in these memories and how they affect their ability to love themselves and each other.

21. Emphasis in original.

Chapter Three

1. An earlier version of *Shadow* was published in *Shattering the Myth*.

2. See particularly the section "Between the Lines: On Culture, Class, and Homophobia," and Moraga's introduction to this section (*Bridge*).

3. On "nation," see Paul Gilroy, *"There Ain't No Black in the Union Jack": The Cultural Politics of Race and Nation*, and Homi Bhabha, ed., *Nation and Narration*, especially Bhabha's introduction and essay "DissemiNation" (291–322). On Queer Nation, see numbers 11 (Winter 1991) and 12 (Spring 1991) of *Out/Look*. Number 12 includes a critique of its exclusionary ramifications for queers of color by Charles Fernández: "Undocumented Aliens in the Queer Nation."

4. A reference to an earlier discussion by Native American panelists at the "OutWrite '91" conference in San Francisco.

5. Similarly, Moraga's play *The Hungry Woman: A Mexican Medea* stages the death of "motherhood" in a retelling of the ancient story of the mother who kills her children.

6. The quote is from *Loving in the War Years*. For this notion of learning to love in the family, see also the 1986 interview with Moraga by Luz María Umpierre.

7. On this theme see the poem "La dulce culpa" [sweet guilt] in *Loving* (14–15), and Norma Alarcón's "What Kind of Lover Have You Made Me, Mother?"

8. "Latino and Chicano theaters have been notoriously sexist and homophobic and have not shown a great interest in doing women's work" (Andrea Lewis, Review of *Shadow of a Man*, 15). See Yolanda Broyles-González, "Women in El Teatro Campesino: '¿Apoco Estaba Molacha La Virgen de Guadalupe?'" and "Toward a Re-Vision of Chicano Theater History: The Women of El Teatro Campesino."

9. In the same interview with Roberto Lovato, Moraga remarks: "My concern as a writer is to explore those things that I need to understand, and that I feel as a people we need to understand" ("Yo Existo," 24).

10. Mexican soap opera.

11. "'Compadre' refers to the relation of a godfather to the parents of the godchild. In Mexican culture, it is a very special bond, akin to that of blood ties, sometimes stronger" (Moraga, "Note on Language," *Shadow of a Man* program, Eureka/Brava Production, San Francisco, November 1990).

12. Katia Noyes misses the culturally specific meaning of this gesture, interpreting Rigo's refusal to embrace Manuel "as a way of showing manliness" ("Disintegration," 27). Rigo's words to Manuel, as reported by Hortensia—"No, Dad, I'm a man, now. We shake hands"—cancel out Manuel's Mexican/Chicano definition of manhood with a European-American one (46).

13. The interpolation of the one Spanish phrase in this monologue, "lo que sabía mi compadre" (what my compadre knew), is indicative of the text's bilingual expressivity. The information contained in that phrase is too intimate and too revealing to be expressed in English, even to himself.

14. You're not a baby anymore.

15. You know, . . . with more shame.

16. With the boys.

17. A jewel.

18. In a misreading of this scene, Scott Rosenberg describes its thematic focus as "ruminations on time" (B-1).

19. Gringo-lover.

20. I am a man!

21. The little hairs.

22. Now, I have my house, my garden.

23. I exist. I exist.

24. Better than you. Do you know you have.

25. And a birthmark there . . . and another here?

26. Look at me, you bastard! . . . Look at me!

27. You know?

28. "Here comes the radical." Later, when Hortensia tells Leticia how handsome Rigo looked in his uniform, Leticia groans: "The entire Raza's on the streets protesting the war and my brother's got to be strutting around in a uniform" (*Shadow*, 60).

29. Sonia Saldívar-Hull explains in "Feminism on the Border": "Because the history of the Chicana experience in the United States defines our particular *mestizaje* of feminism, our theory cannot be a replicate of white feminism nor can it be only an academic abstraction" (220).

30. And we know when they turn into masks.

31. Or his mother or his.

32. Are you sleeping, my little girl? . . . right my little one?

33. You're my favorite, you know?

34. Moraga spoke of this secret interior life in her University of Washington lecture, "Shadow of a Man" (1990).

35. In the "Interview with Cherríe Moraga and María Irene Fornés" on *Open Window*, Moraga speaks of this need "to be relieved of oneself, to be loved." Moraga's third play, *Heroes and Saints*, explores variations on this need for communion.

Chapter Four

1. *Heroes* followed quickly on the grape boycott, the initiative of the UFW against pesticides, brought to a national public by their film *The Wrath of Grapes*, César Chávez' fasting and subsequent death, and the police attack on Dolores Huerta during a demonstration. In making theater that dramatizes the issues of the UFW, Moraga is working within a long tradition of Chicana/o writers and artists, from Luis Valdez' founding of El Teatro Campesino in 1965 to Barbara Carrasco's fifteen-year artistic association with the UFW from 1974 to 1989.

2. See Robert D. Bullard, *Unequal Protection: Environmental Justice and Communities of Color*; Barbara Deutsch Lynch, "The Garden and the Sea: U.S. Environ-

mental Discourses and Mainstream Environmentalism," *Social Problems* 40, no. 1 (February 1993); and the special issue "Latinos and the Environment" of *Race, Poverty and the Environment.*

3. In her depiction of "the People," Moraga seeks to link the struggle in the fields to the anti-authoritarian movements in El Salvador, Guatemala, and Nicaragua. Her representation of women's political leadership also recalls the mothers' movements of Chile and Argentina protesting the state's predatory violence. The images of death in the fields—indicated by machine-gun fire and helicopters offstage—construct a metanarrative of struggle in which parallels are drawn between the brutal regimes of Latin America and the poisoning of California's Central Valley by agribusiness. "The People" can thus be read as Moraga's construction of a broader community forged in relation to a single, unseen agent of force.

4. As Gilroy suggests in "It's a Family Affair," imaginings of the family may also include how it reproduces "the cultural dysfunction that disables the race as a whole" (312).

5. Like a woman.

6. You need a family, son.

7. Outside of marriage.

8. You are a man.

9. You're the only male.

10. You're an innocent.

11. It is also suggested that the cutting edge of Dolores' poisonous tongue and rigid ideas about the performance of gender roles contributed to the father's abandonment of the family: "¿Ves? [You see?] Half a father make half a baby" (103).

12. Like something dirty.

13. It repulsed me.

14. See also the end of act 1, scene 8 (114).

15. You disgust me.

16. Similarly, Cere explicitly defines a "real" man in terms of familial and collective political responsibility:

If I had your arms and legs, if I had your dick for chrissake, you know what I'd do? I'd burn this motherless town down and all the poisoned fields around it. I'd give healthy babies to each and every childless woman who wanted one and I'd even stick around to watch those babies grow up! (144)

17. Mario's AIDS coexists in the play with his recognition of the importance of safer sexual practices:

YOLANDA: (*running a slab of facial down his cheek, softly*): Better stay away from the jotos [queers], you don't wanna catch nothing.
MARIO: (*"slabbing" it back, teasing*): I got it covered, hermana [sister]. (97)

18. However, the equation of various struggles in Mario's comment points to a central problem in the play, that the fight in the fields loses specificity as the play conflates "Raza" and "the People" with the marginal and embattled people of Central and South America. Moraga must turn to myth at the end to sustain the dramatic tension created by the range of references the conflict takes on in act 2.

19. Do you speak Spanish? / I'm Mexican. / Really?

20. Later Dolores tells the priest "You still have the eyes of a man" (100), recognizing that in spite of the priesthood, he has desires.

21. Without any clothes on.

22. The assumption is that they are killed. *Watsonville* completes the action of *Heroes* intertextually. We learn from *Watsonville* that Cere dies and Father Juan survives, maimed but fully transformed into a liberation theologist.

23. See Anzaldúa's discussion of the "Shadow-Beast" for a similar conceptualization (*Borderlands*, 20).

24. Another metatheatrical device in *Heroes* stages the protest demonstration's display of photographs and public naming of the children who have died and the cancers that killed them (act 2, scene 3).

25. Ride; refers to a vehicle, in this case, Cere's wheelchair.

26. "No Voy a Sacarme Corazón': Reform and Resistance Among Chicana Catholics in East San Jose" (Ph.D. Diss., in progress, Stanford University).

27. One piece in López' "Guadalupe Series," done shortly after the U.S. invasion of Panama, consists of a retouched photograph of a black servant waiting on the Panamanian president, with the Virgin of Guadalupe presiding over the scene above the president's left shoulder. For an analysis of López' and Ester Hernández' reworkings of the historical icon of the Virgin of Guadalupe, see Angie Chabram-Dernersesian, "'I Throw Punches for My Race *But* I Don't Want to Be a Man,'" and "And Yes . . . The Earth Did Part: On the Splitting of Chicana/o Subjectivity."

28. Unlike that of other Chicana artists and writers, the scripting of Moraga's spirituality does not prominently feature the Virgin of Guadalupe. Her recent essay "Waiting in the Wings" records numerous acts of prayer, especially in the context of her premature son's struggle for survival, yet the Virgin of Guadalupe is described twice as "impassive." Moraga presents herself to the priest she persuades to baptize her son as "pagan and queer," and as a woman "who calls the Virgin Mary by her Indian name and, on occasion, can be caught worshipping the moon" (81). She identifies more with Coatlicue's daughter Coyolxauhqui, the healer of her "orphanhood," as Coyolxauhqui herself is a daughter in a "long line of vendidas" (see chapter 7). She tends to employ religious metaphors and imagery in the service of the representation of sexuality and political activism.

29. Rudy Busto, class lecture, Stanford University, November 30, 1995.

30. For an innovative reading of Chicano and black social protest theater of the 1960s and 1970s as ritual, see Harry Justin Elam, *Taking It to the Streets: The Social Protest Theater of Luis Valdez and Amiri Baraka.*

31. See Norma Alarcón's insightful essay, "Traddutora, Traditora," on translation as a historical metaphor of betrayal.

32. See María Moreno, "I'm Talking for Justice."

33. This image also connotes the sexual practice of "fisting" (discussed in chapter 1), lending it a specifically lesbian eroticism which disrupts the normative heterosexual construction of "the People."

34. The first part of the title of Gallardo's dissertation, "No Voy a Sacarme Corazón," is taken from an oral history and refers to Chicanas' rejection of Catholic gender ideologies that construct women in the perpetual sacrifice of self for others.

35. Compare Anzaldúa's "Not me sold out my people but they me" (*Borderlands*, 21).

36. "It is still a mythic construction; and our love of it must be recognized as the fantasy that it is—which is not to say that we must now fall out of love" (Dent, 18).

Chapter Five

1. In "F2M: The Making of Female Masculinity," Judith Halberstam puts "what we have known as 'lesbian sex' (sex between two genetic females being women)" into question (108). For Ann Cvetkovich, the "focus is ultimately on sexual acts, not sexual identities, but I am interested in how the sexual act[s] of 'being fucked' are represented by lesbians, whose experiences suggest possibilities that need not be exclusive to either self-identified lesbians or women fucking other women." See "Recasting Receptivity: Femme Sexualities," p. 125.

2. See Cvetkovich, p. 143, note 5, for useful bibliography on the sexuality debates of the 1980s. See also Lillian Faderman, *Odd Girls and Twilight Lovers: A History of Lesbian Life in Twentieth-Century America*, and Vera Whisman, "Identity Crises," for different takes on this history.

3. Radicalesbians, 1970 (quoted in Whisman, 51).

4. For Solomon, while the policing impulse survives, perhaps masking a persistent fear of diversity ("Dykotomies: Scents and Sensibility," 218), it may also be true that "the sex radicals won the sex wars" (Sarah Schulman, quoted in Solomon, 213). On Minneapolis and the Barnard College conference, see Faderman, p. 250–251.

5. See Lawrence Rinder, "Introduction," *In a Different Light*, p. 7–8, and Nayland Blake, "Curating 'In a Different Light,'" p. 26–27, for examples of generational differences in the visual arts.

6. Yes. Women are my religion.

7. In "Recasting Receptivity," Ann Cvetkovich confronts the limitations of language and the weight of negative connotations in seeking understanding of lesbian representations of sexual experience:

What is the experience of "being fucked" for lesbians? . . . My ability to name my topic is hampered by problems of vocabulary; even when used more literally to mean, for example, "being penetrated," "being fucked" has come to signify being dominated, being made weak, or being passive, giving rise to the rich range of figurative uses that seem inseparable from the more specifically sexual acts signified by the "passive" form of the verb "to fuck." The term sometimes seems so thoroughly associated with degradation as to be irredeemable, making it impossible to describe being fucked as a pleasurable experience without renaming it. I will sometimes focus on sexual "receptivity," in order to investigate lesbian representations of getting fucked or receiving sexual attention that give the experience a better name. (125)

8. The absence and presence of black women in Moraga's writing is a rich vein for future investigations. See, for example, the story "Pesadilla" in *Loving* (36–43), and the Pacific Ocean Park passage in *TLG* (117–118).

9. Belly.

10. Navel like honey.

11. Dense. Concealed like a hidden nest. A distant home, waiting for me.

12. I would like to stress that this particular construction of Tiny as stone butch forms part of this text's unique meanings and is not to be taken as a characterization of stone butches in general.

13. Dyke / queer / bad / flower; a word play on "mal flor," a derogatory word for dyke.

14. Yearning valley, . . . plain of desire.

15. Where is she who gave me my body as an offering to myself?

16. She / Distant. / Once, mine. / . . . Disappeared.

17. Punishment.

18. Compare Dorothy Allison, *Two or Three Things I Know for Sure*: "Of course it's never the same things, and I'm never as sure as I'd like to be" (5).

19. Since the preparation of this manuscript, Judith Halberstam's *Female Masculinity* has appeared (1998), providing an exhaustive analysis of alternatives to male masculinity posed by female masculinity. See also José Limón, "Mexican Speech Play: History and the Psychological Discourses of Power," for a critique of Paz and the discourse on Mexican masculinity.

Chapter Six

1. In his 1988 article "White," p. 44–64, Richard Dyer addresses the difficulty of "grasping whiteness as a culturally constructed category" (44) due in part to the ways "white power secures its dominance by seeming not to be anything in particular . . . to be everything and nothing" (45). For Dyer, the source of the representational power of whiteness lies in this property of simultaneous omnipresence and invisibility, as its invisibility not only "colonise[s] the definition of normal" (45), including class, gender, sexuality, and nationality as well as racial categories, but also masks "whiteness itself as a category" (46).

2. Thanks to Sharon Holland (personal communication 1995) for the term "directly mixed," indicating a person with parents of different "races," in contrast to the "ancestrally mixed" person or community. The lack of a satisfactory vocabulary for talking about racially diverse identities is exemplary of the vexed status of the contemporary debate. See Moraga (*TLG*) on the terms "biracial" and "half-breed," discussed below, and Frankenberg.

3. The treatment of whiteness is only one of a plethora of rich themes in *TLG*; for example, the vision of a pan-American identity in the essay "América con Acento." See José David Saldívar, *Dialectics of Our America: Genealogy, Cultural Critique, and Literary History*.

4. Examples of this larger project are Toni Morrison's analysis of the dependence of whiteness in early American literature on the African American presence, *Playing in the Dark: Whiteness and the Literary Imagination*; bell hooks' "Representations of Whiteness in the Black Imagination"; Richard Dyer's study of mainstream film, "White"; and Ruth Frankenberg's interrogation of the notion of white identity, *White Women, Race Matters*.

5. See Sharon Holland, "Humanity Is Not a Luxury: Some Thoughts on a Recent Passing," for an insightful reading of Lorde's thought.

6. See Herrera-Sobek's study of rape in Chicana literature, "The Politics of Rape: Sexual Transgression in Chicana Fiction."

7. Chicana lesbians betray the men of the race by sleeping with women; this betrayal is compounded if the women lovers are white (*Loving*, 119).

8. See duCille, "The Occult of True Black Womanhood," for a discussion of how racial difference conceived of as "authenticating stamp" augments women of color's experience of both "hypervisibility" and "superisolation by virtue of their racial and gender difference" (33).

9. There are moments in *TLG* that reformulate *mestizaje* to include whiteness; for example, "I, thoroughly hybrid / mongrel / mexicanyaqui / oakie girl. / "Yaquioakie" holds all the world / I knew" (99).

10. Kathy Russell, Midge Wilson, and Ronald Hall arrive at a similar conclusion in *The Color Complex: The Politics of Skin Color Among African Americans*.

11. I would add that the "bi" of biracial also implies the racial "purity" of the race of the parents. Lise Funderburg's *Black, White, Other* offers a full spectrum of personal histories by people who identify themselves as biracial, including liberal discourses of "enjoying the best of both worlds."

12. Compare:

It got her over
[. . .]
when hunger forced them
off the highway and into the grills

called "Red's" and "Friendly's"
coffee shops packed suburban
white on white, eyes shifting
to them   and away
to them   and away
and back again
then shifted into safety
lock inside their heads. (*Loving,* 70)

13. To clarify, in *Bridge* the authors and editors do not identify with their whiteness in the sense of affirmation as they do with other aspects of their identity. The point I am trying to make here is that the two texts—*Bridge* and *TLG*—represent opposite stances vis-à-vis the multiple aspects of identity: the refusal to choose among them versus the choice to refuse one of them.

14. See Mercer, "Black Hair/Style Politics," in *Welcome to the Jungle,* for a fine analysis of the interculturation process between Anglo and African American cultures that does not erase the relations of power presiding over the appropriation and commodification of black culture.

15. "What I know for sure is that class, gender, sexual preference, and racial prejudice form an intricate lattice that both restricts and shapes our lives, and that resistance to that hatred is not a simple act. Claiming your identity in the caldron of hatred and resistance to hatred is more than complicated; it is almost unexplainable" (Allison, "A Question of Class," 143).

16. When Moraga's "thoroughbred" male cousin appears in the dream, she envies him: "He is brown and beautiful, indifferent to the world of women around him. He does not have to choose. He remains aloof and elegant in his Mexican masculinity" (*TLG,* 124).

17. See Lora Romero's article "'When Something Goes Queer': Familiarity, Formalism, and Minority Intellectuals in the 1980s," on the father's "queerness" in *Loving.*

18. See Richard Fung's analysis of the representation of Asian men in gay male porn, "Looking for My Penis."

19. In *My History, Not Yours: The Formation of Mexican American Autobiography,* Genaro M. Padilla discusses recent Chicana/o autobiographers, who, "although recognizing themselves as occupying a social space of multiple identities, speak another (contradictory?) desire for a unitary and collective cultural economy imagined in the past, or on the other side of the border. Behind such a reaffirmation of multiple presence is the uneasy memory of an imaginary unity elsewhere" (238).

20. *TLG,* in other words, does not embody the liberal project of "embracing whiteness."

21. *When You Think of Mexico* (1986).

22. See Carol Camper, ed., *Miscegenation Blues: Voices of Mixed Race Women,*

for a critique of the idea that directly mixed (as opposed to ancestrally mixed) people are the hope of the future, implying the elimination of present-day racial/cultural groups.

Chapter Seven

1. I wrote this chapter in 1995, before the revision and publication of Moraga's essay in 1997 with the subtitle "Portrait of a Queer Motherhood." The original subtitle, "Reflections on a Radical Motherhood," echoed an anthology on radical motherhood for which Moraga composed the essay. An excerpt of Moraga's essay was also published in *Living Chicana Theory* as "Free at Last." While my reading is of the 1994 draft version, I indicate some differences found in the 1997 published essay, with the idea that insights into the process of revision might shed light on the meaning of the piece. I also observe the change in the published version of her lover's real name to "Ella," in line with Moraga's use of the pseudonym "Pablo" for the biological father. "Ella" can be read as either the name Ella or the Spanish pronoun "she." This last is open to several interpretations: the lover is reduced to a gendered but anonymous identity with resonances of the archetypal female counterpart. In her vacillation between "Ella" and "she," the lover mirrors some of the writer's ambivalence about her lover's ethnic identity ("not-Mexican").

2. I use the term "identity politics" in its retooled 1990s version, cognizant that the unity of the group is never absolute and that the awareness of differences within the group makes room for other kinds of alliances and coalitions. As Lisa K. C. Hall writes in "Bitches in Solitude: Identity Politics and Lesbian Community,"

> I've been a big fan of identity politics since the first time I realized the realities of my daily life were neither trivial nor irrelevant to what I wanted to do as an activist and to how I wanted to do it. For me, identity politics is about making connections between personal histories and a larger political and social context. Basic, but far from simple. Identity politics is important because it shatters the alienating split that we're taught exists between the realities of our personal lives and a public "political" reality. It's important because paradoxically, not recognizing and acknowledging where we're coming from makes it even harder to get beyond the limitations of our experiences. Both things are true: we are the world; we're just not all of it. (218)

3. See Carl Gutiérrez-Jones, *Rethinking the Borderlands: Between Chicano Culture and Legal Discourse*, for an analysis of how Pedro González was persecuted in the late twenties and early thirties for the "crime" of transgressing public space with his Spanish-language radio show, which gave a public voice to a *mexicana/o* population eager for greater enfranchisement (50–52).

4. Published as "Looking for the Insatiable Woman" in the expanded edition of *Loving*. Moraga addresses this public experience of vulnerability and rejection: "La boca

spreads its legs open to talk, open to attack. 'I am a lesbian. And I am a Chicana,' I say to the men and women at the conference. I watch their faces twist up on me. 'These are two inseparable facts of my life. I can't talk or write about one without the other'" (142). The public/private nexus of the conference provides the framework for the central image in my discussion of the (de)construction of the lesbian body in chapter 1 ("The Mouth is like a cunt [. . . .] My mouth cannot be controlled. It will flap in the wind like legs in sex, not driven by the mind. It's as if la boca were centered on el centro del corazón, not in the head at all. The same place where the cunt beats. *And there is a woman coming out of her mouth*" (*Loving*, 142). While my analysis of this textual maneuver elsewhere focuses on the construction of "cunt" as "mouth" (see also chapter 5), the public exposure entailed in Moraga's commitment to speaking/writing her sexuality (a writing which is presented as inexorable) makes the "mouth" itself over into "cunt" in the naming of lesbian sexuality and identity. The "attack" in "La boca spreads its legs open to talk, open to attack" is ambivalent: Moraga opens her mouth to "attack" the audience's resistance to Chicana lesbians, but the writer herself is thereby left "open to attack."

5. For example, a family sexual secret drives the dramatic action of *Shadow* and shapes the subjectivity of its youngest character, Lupe. In *Heroes*, when Dolores senses that Yolanda and Mario's conversation has touched on the topic of his homosexuality, she warns that "secrets kill sometimes" (97). Later, when Dolores tells Mario he is "leaving with a secret" (123), he objects to this enforced closeting of his experience ("It's no secret, 'amá. You're the only one that doesn't want to see it"). Her response ("I'm not talking about that. I know already for a long time") relates the (open) secret to a kind of hiding from the family and the self (123). In the dream of her white aunt and her Mexican aunts discussed in chapter 6, the dark, witch-like women huddle together "whispering secrets" (*TLG*, 123), suggesting an important connection between this image in Moraga's writing and her conflicted relationship to her Mexican mother, who represents an emotional complexity that both enthralls and stifles. On the sexual level, the "secret" is the "harbored, vulnerable place," site of "demons and old hurts," that opens, only with a sense of risk, to another woman (Moraga and Hollibaugh, 403).

6. Journal entries are italicized.

7. See chapter 6 of Tey Diana Rebolledo's *Women Singing in the Snow: A Cultural Analysis of Chicana Literature* for a discussion of how other Chicanas construct identities as writers; for example, as "testigos [witnesses]/historians/ethnographers, as translators of foreign mail, as cooks" (117).

8. In her efforts to get back into writing, Moraga uses fetal-related imagery to describe the centering process: "*I feel empty of stories, empty of ideas, words, images, impulses. But the creative juices used to fuel this baby's development make my hunger for writing stronger; I shape these letters onto the page as a dance circling circling circling until I arrive at the heartbeat, a pulse, a place from which the writing stirs new life*" (30–31).

9. Between your legs.
10. They are your children.
11. How can a woman feel.
12. "Wings" enumerates the alternatives open to the lesbian couple:

Lesbians don't make babies with our lovers. We make babies with strangers in one-night stands or on the doctor's insemination table, with friends in a friendly fuck or loveless mason jar, with enemies who at the time were husbands or boyfriends, or ex-husbands and boyfriends whom our children call "papi" and we may still consider family. We cannot make babies with one another. (22)

13. In Lesléa Newman's *The Femme Mystique*, Leslie J. Henson writes of the

pain of having had no authentic images of myself as a child learning a sexual identity, no mirrors in which to learn to move through the world as a femme lesbian. Instead, where my femme lesbian body should have been, there was a tear in the fabric of language and being. Without language, I have been a stranger to my own desire. (295)

Wendy Frost playfully explores one such model in the parallel between femmes and drag queens, both "deliberately costum[ing themselves] in femininity": "In the books I read . . . homosexuality was explained as the result of overindulgent mothers who had let their sons dress up in Mummy's clothes when they were little. . . . They forgot to warn parents of girls: Mothers, don't let your daughters dress up in your clothes; they might grow up to be femmes" (305–306).

14. For Becky Birtha,

femme is much more than a role; it's an identity that reaches beyond appearances, beyond interactions with other lesbians. It runs deeper than my longing for a lover who is comfortable calling herself butch, deeper than the desire for a woman to sometimes make love *to* me, rather than *with* me. I'm learning that femme is an attribute I can take pride in, take joy in, embrace, and respect. It's who I feel I am at heart, a quality something like race, something like gender, something like sexual orientation. Whether it is lived out in my relationships or is never even discussed doesn't change it. It's with me to stay. (289)

Birtha's incorporation of her racial identity as an African American woman into her discussion of femme is an exception to the rule in a debate in which race remains largely unexamined. As in the sex radicals' neglect of the historical ramifications of the sexualized representations of women of color (see chapter 5), butch-femme self-stylings at times fail to interrogate the racist construction of black maleness as hypersexuality in their construction of a female masculinity, for example when Amiee Joy Ross, a self-described "bulldaggerous Yid," refers to her dildo as her "big, black dick" ("Sincerely,

Poppa Butch," 159). For discussions of butch-femme, see JoAnn Loulan; Joan Nestle; and Lesléa Newman.

15. Tracy Morgan, "Butch-Femme and the Politics of Identity," puts a different spin on femme invisibility: "[according to nineteenth-century sexology] If . . . 'mannish' girls could be identified and 'cured' at a young age, the problem of the mannish woman would be no more. The womanly woman, like a good infiltrator, remained perpetually elusive and uncategorizable" (38).

16. I am trembling.

17. But, for nothing . . .

18. How many times you give him your breast, your husband is not your son.

19. In one of her poetic monologues, Marisa reveals

I blame women for everything,
for my mistakes
missed opportunities
for my grief.

I usually leave just before I wanna lay a woman flat.
When I feel that rise up in me,
that vengeance
that getting-backness,
I run muddy river.
I book.
Hop a train.
Split.
Desert. (*Ghost*, 19–20)

20. Fire, that flame, that richness . . . beauty, struggle, culture.

21. The discussion of the baptism is reduced to the following paragraph in the published version (1997) representing the baptism more emphatically as a betrayal. It is set between a reflection on alternative spiritualities (107) and the recounting of the dream in which she abandons Ella to save her son:

One year ago, I relinquished Rafaelito to his godparents at the baptismal fount of a humble East Los Angeles church. It is the church of the poor, and the presiding priest, a pastor of the poor. Still, when they return Rafaelito's new christened self back into my arms, I feel I have betrayed him. I hold him tight against the breast of an unanswered prayer. I want to protect my son from deceit, from the failure of male gods and god-fearing males. (108)

22. People in the Mexican Catholic tradition.

23. See chapter 4, in which I discuss this issue in terms of Dolores' sense of being defrauded by Mario's homosexuality of the power a son confers on the mother.

24.

My lover and I are in a prison camp together.
We are in love in wartime.

A young soldier working as a guard has befriended us.
We ask him honestly—the truth—are we going to die?

He answers, yes, it's almost certain. *I contemplate escaping. Ask him to help us. He blanches.*
That is impossible, he says. *I regret asking him, fearing recriminations.*

   I see the forest through the fence on my right. I think, the place between the trees—I
could burrow through there—toward freedom? Two of us would surely be spotted. One of us has
a slim chance. I think of leaving my lover, imprisoned. But immediately I understand that we
must, at all costs, remain with each other. Even unto death. That it is our being together that
makes the pain, even our dying, human.

Loving in the war years. (i)

   For a nuanced reading of this dream in *Loving*, see Ramón Saldívar, *Chicano Narrative: The Dialectics of Difference*, p. 187–189.
   25. In *Ghost*, Marisa declares, "My mother was a heterosexual / I couldn't save her. / My failures followed thereafter" (14). See also the poem "La dulce culpa" in *Loving*, and Norma Alarcón, "What Kind of Lover Have You Made Me, Mother?"
   26. When are you going to get married, child? You need a family.
   27. In search of the moon.
   28. The text describes the mothers in *Schindler's List* "*separated from their children, clawing like wounded lionesses*" (76). Another site in "Wings" with similar intertextual ramifications is the image of the "monster," discussed in chapter 1 as a battlefield of lesbian (self) representation. Moraga describes her son, after his operation, in the discourse of monstrosity: "*He has dehydrated, is unable to urinate. And my baby has bloated up to twice his size. His face is a monster's—his eyes, black seeds buried into a mass of fluid. When I put my hand to his cheek to caress him, the imprint remains, deforming him*" (59). As was the case with the "wound," the more the infant resembles Moraga's "female deformation" in his embattled flesh, the more she identifies with him and the more she is able to expand her writing project to include mother/son.
   29. A judge.
   30. If it is your will.
   31. Less wise, less like an old man.
   32. The description of how the milk returns to her breasts through textualizing her experience as mother occurs earlier in the published version (99). The published epilogue presents an image of Moraga, Ella, and Rafael in bed. Even as the writer affirms

that in constructing family, "blood matters," "it just does not matter more than love" (125), the book ends with the acknowledgement of impermanence (127).

33. The messianic presentation of the infant simultaneously inscribes Moraga as the Virgin Mary, a role rejected in *TLG*'s text on the dream of the "new breed" but assumed by Cere at the end of *Heroes* in a sacrifice, primarily for the children, that is for a better world. See chapters 4 and 6.

Works Cited

Alarcón, Norma. "Chicana Feminism: In the Tracks of 'the' Native Woman." In "Chicano/a Cultural Representations: Reframing Alternative Critical Discourses." Eds. Rosa Linda Fregoso and Angie Chabram. Special issue of *Cultural Studies* 4, no. 3 (October 1990): 248–256.

———. "Chicana's Feminist Literature: A Re-vision through Malintzin/or Malintzin: Putting Flesh Back on the Object." In *This Bridge Called My Back: Writings by Radical Women of Color.* Eds. Cherríe Moraga and Gloria Anzaldúa. Watertown, Mass.: Persephone Press, 1981. Reprint. New York: Kitchen Table, Women of Color Press, 1983. 182–190.

———. "The Theoretical Subject(s) of *This Bridge Called My Back* and Anglo-American Feminism." In *Making Face, Making Soul: Haciendo Caras.* Ed. Gloria Anzaldúa. San Francisco: Aunt Lute, 1990. 356–369.

———. "Traddutora, Traditora: A Paradigmatic Figure of Chicana Feminism." *Cultural Critique* 13 (1990): 57–87.

———. "Tropology of Hunger: The 'Miseducation' of Richard Rodriguez." In *The Ethnic Canon: Histories, Institutions, and Interventions.* Ed. David Palumbo-Liu. Minneapolis: University of Minnesota Press, 1995. 140–152.

———. "What Kind of Lover Have You Made Me, Mother?" In *Women of Color: Perspectives on Feminism and Identity.* Ed. Audrey T. McCluskey. Bloomington: Women's Studies Program. Indiana University, 1985. 85–110.

Alarcón, Norma, Ana Castillo, and Cherríe Moraga, eds. *The Sexuality of Latinas.* Berkeley: Third Woman Press, 1993.

Alarcón, Norma, et al., eds. *Chicana Critical Issues.* Berkeley: Third Woman Press, 1993.

Allison, Dorothy. "A Question of Class." In *Sisters, Sexperts, Queers: Beyond the Lesbian Nation.* Ed. Arlene Stein. New York: Plume, 1993. 133–155.

———. *Two or Three Things I Know for Sure.* New York: Dutton, 1995.

Anzaldúa, Gloria. *Borderlands/La Frontera: The New Mestiza.* San Francisco: Spinsters/Aunt Lute, 1987.

———, ed. *Making Face, Making Soul/Haciendo Caras: Creative and Critical Perspectives by Women of Color.* San Francisco: Aunt Lute, 1990.

Avila, Magdalena. Keynote address. National Association for Chicano Studies. San Antonio, 1993.

Barber, Matthew. Review of *Shadow of a Man. San Francisco Independent* 35, no. 82 (November 1990): 1.

Beam, Joseph. "Brother to Brother: Words from the Heart." In *In the Life: A Black Gay Anthology.* Ed. Joseph Beam. Boston: Alyson Publications, 1986. 230–242.

Bergmann, Emilie L., and Paul Julian Smith. *¿Entiendes?: Queer Readings, Hispanic Writings.* Durham, N.C.: Duke University Press, 1995.

Bersani, Leo. "Is the Rectum a Grave?" In *AIDS: Cultural Analysis, Cultural Activism.* Ed. Douglas Crimp. Cambridge, Mass.: MIT Press, 1989. 208–209.

Bhabha, Homi. "DissemiNation: Time, Narrative, and the Margins of the Modern Nation." In *Nation and Narration.* Ed. Homi Bhabha. London and New York: Routledge, 1990. 291–322.

Birtha, Becky. "Femme at Heart." In *The Femme Mystique.* Ed. Lesléa Newman. Boston: Alyson Publications, 1995. 285–289.

Blake, Nayland. "Curating 'In a Different Light.'" In *In a Different Light.* Eds. Nayland Blake, Lawrence Rinder, and Amy Scholder. San Francisco: City Lights Books, 1995. 9–43.

Broyles-González, Yolanda. *El Teatro Campesino: Theater in the Chicano Movement.* Austin: University of Texas Press, 1994.

———. "Toward a Re-Vision of Chicano Theater History: The Women of El Teatro Campesino." In *Making a Spectacle: Feminist Essays on Contemporary Women's Theatre.* Ed. Lynda Hart. Ann Arbor: University of Michigan Press, 1989. 209–238.

———. "Women in El Teatro Campesino: '¿Apoco Estaba Molacha La Virgen de Guadalupe?'" In *Chicana Voices: Intersections of Class, Race, and Gender.* Ed. Teresa Córdova et al. Austin: Center for Mexican American Studies, University of Texas, 1986. 162–187.

Bullard, Robert D., ed. *Unequal Protection: Environmental Justice and Communities of Color.* San Francisco: Sierra Club Books, 1994.

Busto, Rudy. Class lecture. Stanford University. November 30, 1995.

Camper, Carol, ed. *Miscegenation Blues: Voices of Mixed Race Women.* Toronto: Sister-Vision, 1994.

Case, Sue-Ellen, Philip Brett, and Susan Leigh Foster, eds. *Cruising the Performative: Interventions into the Representation of Ethnicity, Nationality, and Sexuality.* Bloomington: Indiana University Press, 1995.

Cassidy, Christine. "Dear Billie." In *The Persistent Desire: A Femme-Butch Reader*. Ed. Joan Nestle. Boston: Alyson Publications, 1992.

Castañeda, Carlos. *The Teachings of Don Juan: A Yaqui Way of Knowledge*. New York: Ballantine Books, 1970.

Chabram-Dernersesian, Angie. "And Yes . . . The Earth Did Part: On the Splitting of Chicana/o Subjectivity." In *Building with Our Hands: New Directions in Chicana Studies*. Eds. Adela de la Torre and Beatriz M. Pesquera. Berkeley: University of California Press, 1993. 34–56.

———. "'I Throw Punches for My Race *But* I Don't Want to Be a Man': Writing Us: Chica-nos (Girl/Us)/Chicanas into the Movement Script." In *Cultural Studies*. Eds. Lawrence Grossberg, Cary Nelson, and Paula Treichler. New York and London: Routledge, 1992. 81–95.

Chee, Alexander S., et al. "Queer/Nation." *Out/Look* 11 (Winter 1991): 12–23.

Córdova, Teresa, et al., eds. *Chicana Voices: Intersections of Class, Race, and Gender*. Austin: Center for Mexican American Studies, University of Texas, 1986.

Cvetkovich, Ann. "Recasting Receptivity: Femme Sexualities." In *Lesbian Erotics*. Ed. Karla Jay. New York: New York University Press, 1995. 125–146.

Cypess, Sandra Messinger. *La Malinche in Mexican Literature from History to Myth*. Austin: University of Texas Press, 1991

Davis, Angela. "Black Nationalism: The Sixties and the Nineties." In *Black Popular Culture*. Ed. Gina Dent. Seattle: Bay Press, 1992. 317–324.

de la Torre, Adela, and Beatriz M. Pesquera, eds. *Building with Our Hands: New Directions in Chicana Studies*. Berkeley: University of California Press, 1993.

De Lauretis, Teresa. *Alice Doesn't: Feminism, Semiotics, Cinema*. Bloomington: Indiana University Press, 1984.

———. "Oedipus Interruptus." *Wide Angle* 7 (1985): 34–40.

Del Castillo, Adelaida R. "Malintzin Tenepal: A Preliminary Look into a New Perspective." In *Essays on La Mujer*. Eds. Rosaura Sánchez and Rosa Martínez Cruz. Los Angeles: Chicano Studies Center, 1977. 124–149.

Dent, Gina. "Black Pleasure, Black Joy: An Introduction." In *Black Popular Culture*. Ed. Gina Dent. Seattle: Bay Press, 1992. 1–20.

Diamond, Elin. "Refusing the Romanticization of Identity: Narrative Interventions in Churchill, Benmussa, Duras." *Theatre Journal* 37, no. 3 (1985): 273–286.

Dolan, Jill. "Gender Impersonation Onstage: Destroying or Maintaining the Mirror of Gender Roles." *Women & Performance: A Journal of Feminist Theory* 2, no. 2 (1985): 5–11.

duCille, Ann. "The Occult of True Black Womanhood: Critical Demeanor and Black Feminist Studies." In *Female Subjects in Black and White: Race, Psychoanalysis, Feminism*. Eds. Elizabeth Abel, Barbara Christian, and Helene Moglen. Berkeley: University of California Press, 1997. 21–56.

Dyer, Richard. "White." *Screen* 29, no. 4 (Autumn 1988): 44–64.

Elam, Harry Justin. *Taking It to the Streets: The Social Protest Theater of Luis Valdez and Amiri Baraka.* Ann Arbor: University of Michigan Press, 1997.

Elam, Keir. *The Semiotics of Theatre and Drama.* London and New York: Methuen, 1980.

Faderman, Lillian. *Odd Girls and Twilight Lovers: A History of Lesbian Life in Twentieth-Century America.* New York: Penguin, 1992.

Fernández, Charles. "Undocumented Aliens in the Queer Nation." *Out/Look* 12 (Spring 1991): 20–23.

Feyder, Linda, ed. *Shattering the Myth: Plays by Hispanic Women.* Selected by Denise Chávez. Houston: Arte Público, 1992.

Frankenberg, Ruth. *White Women, Race Matters: The Social Construction of Whiteness.* Minneapolis: University of Minnesota Press, 1993.

Fregoso, Rosa Linda, and Angie Chabram. "Chicano/a Cultural Representations: Reframing Alternative Critical Discourses." Special issue of *Cultural Studies* 4, no. 3 (October 1990). 203–212.

Frost, Wendy. "Queen Femme." In *The Femme Mystique.* Ed. Lesléa Newman. Boston: Alyson Publications, 1995. 303–306.

Funderburg, Lise. *Black, White, Other: Biracial Americans Talk about Race and Identity.* New York: William Morrow, 1994.

Fung, Richard. "Looking For My Penis: The Eroticized Asian in Gay Video Porn." In *How Do I Look? Queer Film and Video.* Ed. Bad Object-Choices. Seattle: Bay Press, 1991. 145–168.

Gallardo, Susana. "'No voy a sacarme corazón': Reform and Resistance Among Chicana Catholics in East San Jose." Stanford University Dissertation. In progress.

García, Ignacio. "Chicano Organizational Politics and Strategies in the Era of Retrenchment." In *Chicanas/Chicanos at the Crossroads: Social, Economic, and Political Change.* Eds. David R. Maciel and Isidro D. Ortiz. Tucson: University of Arizona Press, 1996.

Gavin, Ellen. Review of *Shadow of a Man. El Tecolote* (November 1990).

Gilroy, Paul. "It's a Family Affair." In *Black Popular Culture.* Ed. Gina Dent. Seattle: Bay Press, 1992. 303–316.

———. *"There Ain't No Black in the Union Jack": The Cultural Politics of Race and Nation.* London and Melbourne: Hutchinson, 1987.

Gómez, Alma, Cherríe Moraga, and Mariana Romo-Carmona, eds. *Cuentos: Stories by Latinas.* New York: Kitchen Table, Women of Color Press, 1983.

Grant, Jaime M. "Born Femme." In *The Femme Mystique.* Ed. Lesléa Newman. Boston: Alyson Publications, 1995. 95–98.

Gutiérrez-Jones, Carl. *Rethinking the Borderlands: Between Chicano Culture and Legal Discourse.* Berkeley: University of California Press, 1995.

Halberstam, Judith. "F2M: The Making of Female Masculinity." In *Lesbian Words: State of the Art.* Ed. Randy Turoff. New York: Richard Kasak, 1995. 91–112.

———. *Female Masculinity.* Durham, N.C.: Duke University Press, 1998.

Hall, Lisa Kahaleole Chang. "Bitches in Solitude: Identity Politics and Lesbian Community." In *Sisters, Sexperts, Queers: Beyond the Lesbian Nation*. Ed. Arlene Stein. New York: Plume, 1993. 218–229.

Hall, Stuart. "Minimal Selves." *ICA Documents* 6 (1990): 44–46.

———. "New Ethnicities." In *Critical Dialogues in Cultural Studies*. Eds. David Morley and Kuan-Hsing Chen. London: Routledge, 1996. 441–449.

———. "What Is This 'Black' in Black Popular Culture?" In *Black Popular Culture*. Ed. Gina Dent. Seattle: Bay Press, 1992. 21–36.

Harding, Sandra. "The Instability of the Analytical Categories of Feminist Theory." *Signs* 11, no. 4 (1986): 645–664.

Hart, Lynda. Introduction. In *Acting Out: Feminist Performances*. Eds. Lynda Hart and Peggy Phelan. Ann Arbor: University of Michigan Press, 1993. 1–12.

Henson, Leslie J. "My Sister, My Blood, My Femme Lesbian Body." In *The Femme Mystique*. Ed. Lesléa Newman. Boston: Alyson Publications, 1995. 295–299.

Herrera-Sobek, María. "The Politics of Rape: Sexual Transgression in Chicana Fiction." In *Chicana Creativity and Criticism: Charting New Frontiers in American Literature*. Eds. María Herrera-Sobek and Helena María Viramontes. Houston: Arte Público, 1988. 171–181.

Herrera-Sobek, María, and Helena María Viramontes, eds. *Chicana Creativity and Criticism: Charting New Frontiers in American Literature*. Houston: Arte Público, 1988.

Holland, Sharon P. "Humanity Is Not a Luxury: Some Thoughts on a Recent Passing." In *Tilting the Tower*. Ed. Linda Garber. London: Routledge, 1994. 168–176.

hooks, bell. *Ain't I a Woman: Black Women and Feminism*. Boston: South End Press, 1981.

———. *Feminist Theory: From Margin to Center*. Boston: South End Press, 1984.

———. "Representations of Whiteness in the Black Imagination." In *Black Looks: Race and Representation*. Boston: South End Press, 1992. 165–178.

Irigaray, Luce. *This Sex Which Is Not One*. Trans. by Catherine Porter. Ithaca: Cornell University Press, 1985.

Jamison, Laura. "Fighter on the Fringe." *San Francisco Weekly* 11, no. 5 (April 1, 1992).

Jay, Karla, ed. *Dyke Life: From Growing Up to Growing Old: A Celebration of the Lesbian Experience*. New York: Harper Collins, 1995.

Joseph, Gloria, and Jill Lewis. *Common Differences: Conflicts in Black and White Feminist Perspectives*. New York: Anchor Press/Doubleday, 1981.

Julien, Isaac. "'Black Is, Black Ain't': Notes on De-Essentializing Black Identities." In *Black Popular Culture*. Ed. Gina Dent. Seattle: Bay Press, 1992. 255–263.

King, Katie. "The Situation of Lesbianism as Feminism's Magical Sign: Contests for Meaning and the U.S. Women's Movement, 1968–1972." *Communication* 9 (1986): 65–91.

Kuhn, Annette. "Women's Genres." *Screen* (January–February 1984): 18–28.

"Latinos and the Environment." Special issue of *Race, Poverty and the Environment: A Newsletter for Social and Environmental Justice* 4, no. 3 (Fall 1993).

Lewis, Andrea. Review of *Shadow of a Man. Mother Jones* (January–February 1991): 15.

Limón, José E. "Mexican Speech Play: History and the Psychological Discourses of Power." Austin: Texas Papers on Latin America Series, Institute of Latin American Studies, University of Texas, 1987.

López, Yolanda. *When You Think of Mexico: Commercial Images of Mexicans in the Mass Media.* Produced and directed by Carl Heyward. Oakland, Calif.: Piñata Publications, 1986. (Film.)

Lorde, Audre. *Sister Outsider.* Trumansberg, N.Y.: Crossing Press, 1984.

Loulan, JoAnn. "Butch Mothers, Femme Bull Dykes: Dismantling Our Own Stereotypes." In *Dyke Life: From Growing Up to Growing Old: A Celebration of the Lesbian Experience.* Ed. Karla Jay. New York: Harper Collins, 1995. 247–256.

———. *The Lesbian Erotic Dance: Butch, Femme, Androgyny, and Other Rhythms.* San Francisco: Spinsters Books, 1990.

Lovato, Roberto. "'Yo existo': The Woman of Color Breaks the Silence." *The City* [San Francisco](November 1990): 23–24.

Lugones, María C., and Elizabeth V. Spelman. "Have We Got a Theory for You! Feminist Theory, Cultural Imperialism and the Demand for 'the Woman's Voice.'" *Women's Studies International Forum* 6, no. 6 (1983): 573–581.

Lynch, Barbara Deutsch. "The Garden and the Sea: U.S. Environmental Discourses and Mainstream Environmentalism." *Social Problems* 40, no. 1 (February 1993): 108–125.

Mercer, Kobena. "Welcome to the Jungle: Identity and Diversity in Postmodern Politics." In *Welcome to the Jungle. New Positions in Black Cultural Studies.* New York: Routledge, 1994. 259–285.

Mesa-Bains, Amalia. "El Mundo Femenino: Chicana Artists of the Movement: A Commentary on Development and Production." In *Chicano Art: Resistance and Affirmation.* Eds. Richard Griswold del Castillo, Teresa McKenna, and Yvonne Yarbro-Bejarano. Los Angeles: Wright Art Gallery, UCLA, 1991. 131–140.

Miriam, Kathy. "Queer Theory: What's the Big Deal?" Paper presented at the Readers and Writers Conference, A Different Light Bookstore, San Francisco, May 21, 1994.

Moraga, Cherríe. *A Circle in the Dirt: El Pueblo de East Palo Alto.* Albuquerque: West End Press, 2001.

———. "Coatlicue's Call/El llamado de Coatlicue." Unpublished play, 1990.

———. "Free at Last." In *Chicana Lesbians: The Girls Our Mothers Warned Us About.* Ed. Carla Trujillo. Berkeley: Third Woman Press, 1991. 166–188.

———. *Giving Up the Ghost.* Los Angeles: West End Press, 1986.

———. "Heart of the Earth: A Popol Vuh Story." In *Puro Teatro: A Latina Anthology.* Eds. Alberto Sandoval-Sánchez and Nancy Saporta Sternbach. Tucson: University of Arizona Press, 2000. 46–88.

———. *Heroes and Saints and Other Plays (Giving Up the Ghost, Shadow of a Man, Heroes and Saints)*. Albuquerque: West End Press, 1994.

———. *The Hungry Woman: A Mexican Medea*. In *Out of the Fringe: Contemporary Latina/Latino Theatre and Performance*. Eds. Caridad Svich and María Teresa Marrero. New York: Theatre Communications Group, 2000. 289–363.

———. *The Last Generation*. Boston: South End Press, 1993.

———. "Looking for the Insatiable Woman." In *Loving in the War Years: Lo que nunca pasó por sus labios*. Expanded edition. Cambridge, Mass.: South End Press, 2000. 142–150.

———. *Loving in the War Years: Lo que nunca pasó por sus labios*. Boston: South End Press, 1983.

———. *Loving in the War Years: Lo que nunca pasó por sus labios*. Expanded edition. Cambridge, Mass.: South End Press, 2000.

———. "Notes from the Playwright," "Note on Language," and "Who's Who." *Shadow of a Man* program, Eureka/Brava Production, San Francisco (November 1990).

———. "Shadow of a Man." Guest lecture. University of Washington, 1990.

———. "Waiting in the Wings: Reflections on a Radical Motherhood." Unpublished manuscript. 1994.

———. *Waiting in the Wings: Portrait of a Queer Motherhood*. Ithaca: Firebrand Press, 1997.

———. *Watsonville: Some Place Not Here*. In *Latino Plays from South Coast Hispanic Playwrights Project*. Eds. Juliette Carrillo and José Cruz Gonzales. New York: Broadway Play Publishing, 2000.

Moraga, Cherríe, and Gloria Anzaldúa, eds. *This Bridge Called My Back: Writings by Radical Women of Color*. Watertown, Mass.: Persephone Press, 1981. Reprint. New York: Kitchen Table, Women of Color Press, 1983.

Moraga, Cherríe, and Amber Hollibaugh. "What We're Rollin Around in Bed With: Sexual Silences in Feminism." In *Powers of Desire: The Politics of Sexuality*. Eds. Ann Snitow, Christine Stansell, and Sharon Thompson. New York: Monthly Review Press, 1983. 394–405.

Moreno, María. "I'm Talking for Justice." In *Mexican Women in the United States: Struggles Past and Present*. Eds. Adelaida del Castillo and Magdalena Mora. Los Angeles: Chicano Studies Research Center, UCLA, 1980. 181–182.

Morgan, Tracy. "Butch-Femme and the Politics of Identity." In *Sisters, Sexperts, Queers: Beyond the Lesbian Nation*. Ed. Arlene Stein. New York: Plume, 1993. 35–46.

Morrison, Toni. *Playing in the Dark: Whiteness and the Literary Imagination*. Cambridge, Mass.: Harvard University Press, 1992.

Mulvey, Laura. "Afterthoughts on 'Visual Pleasure and Narrative Cinema' Inspired by 'Duel in the Sun' (King Vidor, 1946)." *Framework* (Summer 1981): 12–15.

Nestle, Joan. "Butch-Femme Relationships: Sexual Courage in the 1950s." In *A Restricted Country*. Ithaca: Firebrand, 1987. 100–109.

———, ed. *The Persistent Desire: A Femme-Butch Reader.* Boston: Alyson Publications, 1992.

Newman, Lesléa, ed. *The Femme Mystique.* Boston: Alyson Publications, 1995.

Noyes, Katia. "The Dream Images of Cherríe Moraga." *San Francisco Sentinel* (November 8, 1990): 18.

———. "Disintegration of Machismo." *San Francisco Sentinel* (November 29, 1990): 27.

Padilla, Genaro M. *My History, Not Yours: The Formation of Mexican American Autobiography.* Madison: University of Wisconsin, 1993.

Paz, Octavio. *The Labyrinth of Solitude.* Trans. by Lysander Kemp. New York: Grove, 1961.

Pérez, Emma. "Sexuality and Discourse: Notes from a Chicana Survivor." In *Chicana Lesbians: The Girls Our Mothers Warned Us About.* Ed. Carla Trujillo. Berkeley: Third Woman Press, 1991. 159–184.

Perry, Mary Elizabeth. *Gender and Disorder in Early Modern Seville.* Princeton: Princeton University Press, 1990.

Quintanales, Mirtha N. "Loving in the War Years: An Interview with Cherríe Moraga." *Off Our Backs* (January 1985): 12–13.

Rebolledo, Tey Diana. "The Politics of Poetics: Or, What Am I, a Critic, Doing in This Text Anyhow?" In *Chicana Creativity and Criticism: Charting New Frontiers in American Literature.* Eds. María Herrera-Sobek and Helena María Viramontes. Houston: Arte Público, 1988. 129–138.

———. *Women Singing in the Snow: A Cultural Analysis of Chicana Literature.* Tucson: University of Arizona Press, 1995.

Riggs, Marlon T. *Tongues Untied.* San Francisco: Frameline, 1989. (Film.)

Rinder, Lawrence. Introduction. In *In a Different Light.* Eds. Nayland Blake, Lawrence Rinder, and Amy Scholder. San Francisco: City Lights Books, 1995. 1–8.

Rodriguez, Richard. *Days of Obligation: An Argument with My Mexican Father.* New York: Viking, 1992.

Romero, Lora. "'When Something Goes Queer': Familiarity, Formalism, and Minority Intellectuals in the 1980s." *The Yale Journal of Criticism* 6, no. 1 (1993): 121–141.

Rose, Mary Beth. "Gender, Genre, and History: Seventeenth-Century English Women and the Art of Autobiography." In *Women in the Middle Ages and the Renaissance.* Ed. Mary Beth Rose. Syracuse: Syracuse University Press, 1986.

Rosenberg, Scott. Review of *Shadow of a Man. San Francisco Examiner* (November 13, 1990): B-1, B-4.

Ross, Amiee Joy. "Sincerely, Poppa Butch." In *The Femme Mystique.* Ed. Lesléa Newman. Boston: Alyson Publications, 1995. 159.

Russell, Kathy, Midge Wilson, and Ronald Hall. *The Color Complex: The Politics of Skin Color Among African Americans.* New York: Harcourt Brace Jovanovich, 1992.

Saldívar, José David. *The Dialectics of Our America: Genealogy, Cultural Critique, and Literary History.* Durham, N.C.: Duke University Press, 1991.

Saldívar, Ramón. *Chicano Narrative: The Dialectics of Difference*. Madison: University of Wisconsin, 1990.

Saldívar-Hull, Sonia. "Feminism on the Border: From Gender Politics to Geopolitics." In *Criticism in the Borderlands: Studies in Chicano Literature, Culture, and Ideology*. Eds. Hector Calderón and José David Saldívar. Durham, N.C.: Duke University Press, 1991. 203–220.

Sandoval, Chela. "U.S. Third World Feminism: The Theory and Method of Oppositional Consciousness in the Postmodern World." *Genders* 10 (Spring 1991): 1–24.

Scott, Darieck. "Jungle Fever? Black Gay Identity Politics, White Dick, and the Utopian Bedroom." *GLQ: A Journal of Lesbian and Gay Studies* 1, no. 3 (1994): 299–321.

Smith, Anna Deavere. *Fires in the Mirror: Crown Heights, Brooklyn, and Other Identities*. New York: Anchor Books/Doubleday, 1993.

Solomon, Alisa. "Dykotomies: Scents and Sensibility." In *Sisters, Sexperts, Queers: Beyond the Lesbian Nation*. Ed. Arlene Stein. New York: Plume, 1993. 210–217.

Stein, Arlene, ed. *Sisters, Sexperts, Queers: Beyond the Lesbian Nation*. New York: Plume, 1993.

El Teatro de la Esperanza. *Los Hijos: Once a Family*. In *Necessary Theater: Six Plays about the Chicano Experience*. Ed. Jorge Huerta. Houston: Arte Público Press, 1989.

Traub, Valerie. "Desire and the Difference It Makes." In *The Matter of Difference: Materialist Feminist Criticism of Shakespeare*. Ed. Valerie Wayne. New York: Harvester Wheatsheaf, 1991. 81–114.

Trinh, Minh-ha. *Woman, Native, Other: Writing, Postcoloniality and Feminism*. Bloomington: Indiana University Press, 1989.

Trujillo, Carla, ed. *Chicana Lesbians: The Girls Our Mothers Warned Us About*. Berkeley: Third Woman Press, 1991.

———, ed. *Living Chicana Theory*. Berkeley: Third Woman Press, 1988.

Turoff, Randy, ed. *Lesbian Words: State of the Art*. New York: Richard Kasak, 1995.

Umpierre, Luz María. "With Cherríe Moraga." *Americas Review* 14, no. 2 (Summer 1986): 54–67.

Valdez, Luis. *The Shrunken Head of Pancho Villa*. In *Necessary Theatre: Six Plays about the Chicano Experience*. Ed. Jorge Huerta. Houston: Arte Público Press, 1989. 153–207.

Viramontes, Helena María. *Under the Feet of Jesus*. New York: Dutton, 1995.

Walker, Alice. *Possessing the Secret of Joy*. New York: Harcourt Brace Jovanovich, 1992.

West, Cornel. "Nihilism in Black America." In *Black Popular Culture*. Ed. Gina Dent. Seattle: Bay Press, 1992. 37–47.

Whisman, Vera. "Identity Crises: Who Is a Lesbian, Anyway?" In *Sisters, Sexperts, Queers: Beyond the Lesbian Nation*. Ed. Arlene Stein. New York: Plume, 1993. 49–60.

Winn, Steven. Review of *Shadow of a Man*. *San Francisco Chronicle* (November 11, 1990).

Wittig, Monique. "The Point of View: Universal or Particular?" *Feminist Issues* 3, no. 2 (1983).

The Wrath of Grapes. Keene, Calif: United Farm Workers of America, AFL-CIO, 1986. (Film.)

Wright, Sheila. Review of *Shadow of a Man*. *Daily Ledger-Post Dispatch* [Antioch, Calif.] (November 15, 1990).

Yarbro-Bejarano, Yvonne. "Cherríe Moraga." *Dictionary of Literary Biography* 82, Chicano Writers First Series. Eds. Francisco A. Lomelí and Carl R. Shirley. Detroit: Bruccoli Clark Layman, 1989. 165–177.

———. "The Female Subject in Chicano Theatre: Sexuality, 'Race,' and Class." *Theatre Journal* 38, no. 4 (December 1986): 389–407.

———. "Sexuality and Chicana/o Studies: Toward a Theoretical Paradigm for the Twenty-First Century." *Cultural Studies* 13, no. 2 (1999): 335–345.

———. "Teatropoesía." *Revista Chicano-Riqueña* 11, no. 1 (1983): 78–94.

Zeig, Sande. "The Actor as Activator: Deconstructing Gender through Gesture." *Women & Performance: A Journal of Feminist Theory* 2, no. 2 (1984): 12–17.

Zinn, Maxine Baca, Lynn Weber Cannon, Elizabeth Higginbotham, and Bonnie Thornton Dill. "The Costs of Exclusionary Practices in Women's Studies." *Signs* 11, no. 21 (1986): 290–303.

Index